For Be...

Cheerful Companion in Panama
Remembering USIS
Harry Kendall

A FARM BOY IN THE FOREIGN SERVICE

SERVICE

Telling America's Story to the World

By

Harry H. Kendall

This book is a work of non-fiction. Names, places, events, and
situations are true to the best of the author's knowledge.

ISBN: 1-4033-8161-5 (e-book)
ISBN: 1-4033-8162-3 (Paperback)
ISBN: 1-4033-8163-1 (Hardcover)

This book is printed on acid free paper.

1stBooks - rev. 08/21/03

For Margaret, Betsy, Nancy and Judy who were there.

A Farm Boy in the Foreign Service:
Telling America's Story to the World
CONTENTS

Preface

This narrative began as an oral history interview conducted by my good friend and fellow U.S. Information Agency (USIA) alumnus G. Lewis Schmidt. I have since revised and enlarged upon it for a more complete account of my diplomatic experience. In the process I have drawn upon the oral histories of several of my U.S. Information Service (USIS) colleagues to confirm and fill out my story of a farm boy's 29 years in the Foreign Service. Although some conditions governing Foreign Service life have changed dramatically in the intervening years since my retirement at the end of 1979, many aspects of representing the United States overseas remain basically the same. In each of the chapters that follow I have sought to portray the milieu in which USIS operated at the time and to relate some of my experiences in the conduct of my official duties as well as in travel and living abroad. Because families are so important to Foreign Service life I have also sought, as appropriate, to describe some aspects of my family life as a member of the American Foreign Service community. I have told the story chronologically because it seemed logical and I was more comfortable with it that way.

Some may ask why I, as one who did not achieve ambassadorial status, have bothered to publish my memoirs. It is a valid question. In fact, however, only a miniscule number of USIS officers have reached that status. This is not because they lack the competence but rather because the Department of State has favored and continues to favor political officers in making such appointments, even though top level USIS personnel have far more experience than most political officers in managing large programs. In this account I make no pretensions of having brought about dramatic changes in U.S. foreign policy; rather I seek to portray the life and times of a rank-and-file Foreign Service Officer confronting the day-to-day problems of telling America's story to the world. It was work in which I took great pride and thoroughly enjoyed as did virtually all of my USIS colleagues.

Mine was one of more than a hundred taped interviews conducted by Schmidt and several other USIA retirees to create a historical record of the U.S. Information Agency from the time it was established as a separate agency. These oral histories chronicle the personal experiences and appraisals of USIS efforts overseas by men and women who were directly involved in the United States Government's conduct of public information and cultural affairs abroad, i.e., public diplomacy. While many retired diplomats have published their memoirs, each account is different and makes its own contribution. But a world of unpublished information is also contained in oral histories recorded by Foreign Service Officers of both USIS and Department of State. These histories are maintained at the Association for Diplomatic Studies and Training (ADST) in Arlington, Virginia. Transcripts and/or CD-ROM discs are available for students of the U.S. record in foreign affairs.

My first thanks for making this account possible go to my wife Margaret who accompanied me to each of my posts abroad except Vietnam and was a part of the USIS team throughout and to our daughters Betsy, Nancy and Judy who brought fulfillment to our life as a family. I extend thanks also to Lew Schmidt, to his wife Kyoko and to Clifton Forster for their comments on the chapter about Takamatsu; to Allen Hansen for urging me onward; to the late Douglas Pike and Forrest Fischer for their help on the chapters about Vietnam; to Tom Tuch who critiqued the original version of the manuscript, to Professor Robert A. Scalapino who also read the original manuscript and was my mentor, traveling companion and employer during my second career at U.C. Berkeley, and to many other USIS alumni and friends who gave me encouragement in preparing these memoirs.

My warm thanks go also to my many Foreign Service colleagues, both American and overseas nationals, with whom I worked throughout the Cold War years to promote the best interests of the United States and to my co-workers at U.C. Berkeley's Institute of East Asian Studies. These good friends may or may not be mentioned except in passing, but they are all warmly remembered for making my life interesting and, I think, productive. I apologize in advance for any misquotes or lapsis memoria, but to the best of my memory, this is the way it was.

Harry Haven Kendall
Berkeley, California
Summer 2002

Introduction

Growing up on a farm near Lake Charles in southwestern Louisiana, it never crossed my mind that one day I would become a member of America's elite diplomatic corps. But Dame Fortune is unpredictable, and a twist of fate can make or break one's career. In my case Providence was kind. To paraphrase Robert Frost, the outcome may have resulted from the path not chosen. Who can tell where other paths may have taken me? The one I opted for led to an adventurous life of foreign travel, life and work in many cultures in the interest of peace and at the service of my country. I am happy with the path I chose, and this is my story of some of its highlights. First, a brief prologue.

My father died when I was but two, leaving my mother with seven children and another on the way. Her parents took us in to live on the dairy farm my grandfather established so we kids could help earn our keep. Even so, my mother had to make money to buy schoolbooks. Since she had been home schooled by her parents, both college graduates, she put her older children in charge of their siblings, obtained a teaching certificate at Louisiana State University, and got a job teaching the first through the sixth grades at a one-room country school. Most of her pupils came from French speaking Cajun families, and she had to teach them English before teaching them to read and write. At the age of five I joined my mother's first grade class. In my mind she always seemed stricter with me than with other pupils, but this helped instill me with personal discipline. When Louisiana consolidated its rural schools under Governor Huey P. Long and the state began providing textbooks my mother quit teaching to devote more time to her family. From then on through high school I attended LaGrange consolidated school, five miles from my grandfather's farm.

Farm chores left little time for normal childhood activities. Work was a part of my daily life. Like each of my brothers and sisters—we were four boys and four girls—throughout elementary and high school I had farm chores to perform before boarding the school bus in the morning and after returning home in the afternoon. Summers were equally busy. There were crops to be planted and harvested, pigs, chickens and other farm animals to be watered and fed, cows to milk and bottles of milk to be delivered to customers in town. That was one of my jobs, leaving full bottles and picking up empties as one of my older siblings drove our Model T delivery truck. It was hard but healthy work, though I must confess that as the youngest of four boys, my elder brothers bore the brunt of the hard work. After evening chores were finished I did my homework by the light of a kerosene lamp. Another of my duties was keeping the lamps filled and the globes clean. Electricity didn't reach our home until after World War II. There wasn't even a telephone to distract me. Television was unknown. Movies? Well, maybe three or four times a year. The most memorable—and most frightening—were *Birth of a Nation* (my first) and *King Kong*. It was the time of the Great Depression and there was scarcely enough money to buy the necessities of life, let alone movie tickets for eight kids. For most of my boyhood we relied on an outdoor toilet. Our toilet paper consisted of old newspapers and Sears Roebuck catalogs. If we had to get up at night for a pee, there were plenty of bushes around. Until I was about 12 our water source was a shallow well and a hand operated pump. We had running water all right, but I did the running. In the mid thirties we went modern. We dug a deep well and used a one-cylinder engine to pump water into a cistern perched atop a 20-foot-high derrick. Pipes from the cistern to the farmyard-watering trough and to the house reduced my running significantly. We also installed indoor plumbing, but the outhouse remained in use until after I left the farm.

I was never what one would call a brilliant student; but with my family's encouragement I was diligent about my studies and consistently made good grades. Like my mother I became an avid reader. I never thought of myself as an exceptional student; but my eagerness to learn showed, and my classmates dubbed me "Egghead." My fellow pupils were a blend of cultures drawn from the rice and cotton farm families in the surrounding countryside—Cajun, German, Anglo-Saxon and an occasional Latino. My three best friends were sons of German speaking immigrants, French speaking Cajuns and a Mexican family who spoke only Spanish at home. Thus, at an early age I learned to adapt myself to different cultures and found it natural to hear languages other than English. Even so, the big Latino migration to *El Norte* had not yet begun, and Orientals were still a rarity.

Huey Long was the dominant public figure of my childhood, passionately adored or hated by every Louisianan. His assassination during my senior year in high school contributed to the legend that grew up around him and continues to this day. On the national front Franklin D. Roosevelt captured and held my admiration as he brought the nation out of the Great Depression and to victory in World War II. As a farm family we were pretty much self sufficient and suffered little from the depression; but my eldest brother joined the CCC (Civilian Conservation Corps) and sent home his pay to help my mother clothe the rest of her brood. Our local newspaper published little or no international news, and my knowledge of foreign countries came primarily from magazines such as the *Saturday Evening Post* where I read Edgar Snow's serialized "Red Star over China" and books like Pearl Buck's *Good Earth* and Edgar Rice Burroughs' Tarzan novels as well as many others borrowed from the Lake Charles Carnegie Library. Except for historical circumstances I would have probably lived out my years in the community where I grew up.

By 1940 at age 20 I had been working two years at my first job in an auto parts house when my life took a dramatic change. With war clouds gathering over Europe and the Japanese running amuck in China my generation was destined to be swept up in the maelstrom of World War II. Congress, under pressure from President Roosevelt, was seriously debating the need for a military draft. I decided not to await a draft call and signed up for service in the Air Corps' Army Airways Communications System (AACS) that sent me to radio school at Scott Field, Illinois, for training in Morse code and air-ground communications. My first assignment was as a control tower operator at an Air Corps gunnery school in Eglin Field, Florida. There I found myself giving take off and landing instructions to cadet pilots in training preparatory to joining fighter squadrons that would later see combat in Europe, North Africa and the Pacific. The most interesting groups I encountered were an elite all-Negro squadron established at the behest of President Roosevelt and a B-25 squadron under the command of Colonel Jimmy Doolittle preparing for their famous aircraft carrier-based bombing raid on Tokyo. Of course I had no inkling of the Doolittle mission, but I recall him graciously declining my offer to join it. Eager to get into the fray myself, I applied and was accepted as an air cadet; but after sixty hours flight time I washed out and was sent back to AACS, probably the reason I am alive today. Many of my flight mates who won their wings did not survive the war.

My AACS duty eventually took me to Kunming, China, where I spent a year handling radio traffic for over-the-Hump (trans-Himalayan) Air Transport Command flights from India to China. A stroke of luck resulted in my being assigned to operate a radio-weather station in

Lanzhou in northwest China. My station and another at Urumchi on the Soviet border provided meteorological data used in weather forecasting for USAF bombing operations over Japan. Living and working among the Chinese in an immense multinational effort to defeat Japanese aggression opened my eyes to a much wider world than I had ever imagined. My China experience helped persuade me to become a part of that new universe.

At the War's end, in one of its most generous and socially significant acts, Congress passed the GI Bill that enabled thousands of World War II veterans, including myself, to obtain a university education. An avid interest in international affairs acquired during my military service led me to a BA in journalism at Louisiana State University where I studied Spanish and French, an MA in international relations at Yale and work toward a PhD in political science at the University of North Carolina in Chapel Hill. It was there that I met my future wife.

By 1950, having used up my four years' study authorized under the GI Bill, I was working as a feature writer for the *Charlotte Observer* when an opportunity arose to join the Foreign Service. Congress, this time responding to the challenge of Soviet communist anti-American propaganda, funded an overseas information and education program within the Department of State. Its assigned mission was to reveal the true nature of communism and give the world a realistic picture of the United States. Given the resources, State recruited several hundred journalists and other communications specialists, including myself, to work on the front lines of the Cold War. For me, that was the beginning of a fascinating Foreign Service career of "telling America's story to the world," now subsumed under the term "public diplomacy."

In 1953 President Eisenhower and Secretary of State John Foster Dulles decided that the U.S. Government's action-oriented propaganda operations did not belong in the State Department. So by executive order the President created an independent U.S. Information Agency, stipulating that USIA would receive policy guidance from the State Department but report direct to the President on the overseas impact of U.S. policies, actions and statements. The new agency was administratively independent in Washington, but the U.S. Information Service—USIS as it was called overseas—formed an integral part of every American Embassy establishment and was responsible to the ambassador. USIS establishments operated with their own budgets and communicated direct with their Washington headquarters on operational matters.

Because my Foreign Service career (1951-1979) covered the first three decades of the U.S. Information Agency, it also encompassed the flowering of public diplomacy as an essential element of American foreign policy that was unique in its strong emphasis on personal contact and American cultural values. During that period USIA developed an organizational structure that supported an overseas corps of highly skilled personnel adept at public diplomacy. At first, at the behest of Senator William Fulbright, the cultural support elements were retained in the more prestigious Department of State even though USIS personnel handled these activities overseas. Later these cultural responsibilities were transferred to USIA. It is important to note that coordinating and assisting private education and cultural international exchanges constituted one of a USIA's most important and successful activities.

In the pages that follow I have attempted to reveal some of the details of life and work in the Foreign Service as I experienced them through interaction with audiences in Latin America, Europe and the Asia-Pacific region. I also give a personal account of how USIA, working with NASA, kept an eager world public informed on the unfolding story of America's conquest of outer space and the manned flight to the moon.

The highly effective personal style of public diplomacy described in this autobiographical account is unlikely to return, but history must give due credit to the small band of public diplomats who manned the front lines of the Cold War around the world and helped achieve victory in that ideological struggle. I am proud to have been one of them and to have played a modest but important part during a significant chapter in the history of American foreign policy.

Following the end of the Cold War dwindling budgets forced USIA into increasing reliance on the evolving techniques of mass communications such as Internet and global television. In 1999, on the mistaken theory that USIA was a useless duplication of State Department functions, Congress dismantled the Agency and merged it into State where the concept of public diplomacy struggles for survival in a sluggish bureaucracy and in competition with State's traditional concept of diplomacy as government-to-government relations.

The horrendous events of September 11, 2001, and the vicious hate campaigns conducted against the United States by radical Islamic elements vividly demonstrated the shortsightedness of abolishing USIA. Aghast at this seemingly baseless propaganda, the White House and Congressional foreign policy leaders became convinced of the urgent necessity for resurrecting a U.S. Government institution capable of conducting the nation's public diplomacy activities overseas, particularly in sensitive mid-Eastern areas. As Congressman (R. Il.) Henry Hyde, Chairman of the House International Relations Committee, asked:

"How is it that the country that invented Hollywood and Madison Avenue has such trouble promoting a positive image of itself overseas? Over the years, the images of mindless hatred directed at us have become familiar fixtures on our television screens. All this time, we have heard calls that 'something must be done.' Clearly, whatever has been done has not been enough."[1]

As of this writing in mid-2002, Congress, the media and numerous publicly minded institutions are vigorously debating the shape and responsibilities of a renewed public diplomacy program as a crucial part of our foreign policy effort. We can only hope that the solution finally arrived at will serve the nation as effectively as USIA did during the decades of the Cold War.

---

[1]. "Speaking to our Silent Allies: the role of Public Diplomacy in U.S. Foreign Policy," Henry Hyde Member, U.S. House of Representatives (R-IL); Chairman, House International Relations Committee, at Council on Foreign Relations, June 17, 2002

I. In the Foreign Service

On January 22, 1951, I took the oath as a Foreign Service Staff Officer of the United States. I was now a member of the State Department, the official organization charged with carrying out U.S. foreign policy and representing the United States abroad.

Harry Truman was President of the United States. Dean Acheson was Secretary of State. The Korean War was at its apex. Chinese "volunteer" troops had overrun United Nations positions, and UN forces were struggling to throw them back. Western Europe and the United States were engaged in a Cold War with the Soviet Union. The Truman Doctrine had staved off a communist takeover in Greece and stymied similar offensives in Western Europe.

On the home front, anti-communism was growing in intensity, fueled by Congressional hearings on alleged communist influences in the U.S. Government. Senator Richard Nixon had singled out Alger Hiss, a top echelon State Department official, for attack. Senator Joseph McCarthy had launched his charges, mostly unfounded, against the Departments of the Army and State for alleged communist influences. Several veteran China specialists were about to be railroaded out of the Foreign Service, accused of having turned China over to the communists. One of them was Jack Service with whom I was destined to become good friends in my post-Foreign Service career in Berkeley.

On the diplomatic front, backed by America's predominant military and economic strength, we were using a "Campaign of Truth" to combat communist anti-American propaganda. In Latin America, where I was heading, virtually the whole continent was living under military dictatorships, anti-communist in name, but oppressive in character, creating fertile fields for communism.

A plaque on the USIA[2] headquarters building at 1776 Pennsylvania Avenue read "Telling America's Story to the World." Through my oath I had sworn to help tell that story. It was a heady thought. I had been a member of the U.S. military forces fighting fascist aggression during

---

[2]. USIA (United States Information Agency) is known overseas as USIS (U.S. Information Service). Until its separation from the Department of State in 1953 it was called USIE (U.S. Information and Education), but for the sake of consistency I will use the terms USIA and USIS throughout this narrative.

World War II. Now I was once more joining the fray, this time in the diplomatic service, America's first line of defense against communist aggression.

I found a room in a private home on Cathedral Avenue and immediately began orientation for my assignment as "Information Assistant" at the American Embassy in Caracas. There were a dozen new Foreign Service recruits in my group, including Stan Moss, my classmate and good friend at the University of North Carolina in Chapel Hill. Stan had specialized in Latin America at UNC but was being assigned to Cebu in the Philippines instead. I had served with the U.S. Air Force in China and had focused on East Asia at LSU but was going to Latin America.

"Just like the Army," Stan said.

Pressure was on State to fill openings abroad, and we were both being sent where we were needed without any country-specific training to equip us for the tasks ahead of us. Most of our three-week training period was directed at familiarizing us with State Department administrative procedures, cultural exchange programs, and Washington support services to field posts. These included press and motion pictures in Washington, and the Voice of America in New York. (VOA would move to the capital later.) Television was still in its infancy and USIA had not yet established a television branch.

One memorable training exercise focused on how to handle communist hecklers. The training officer played the role of a communist agent. Addressing himself to each of us individually, he fired vitriolic accusations against the United States charging Americans with supporting racist and colonial policies, a lack of any real culture, violence in their cities, and economic imperialism. Our task was to respond coolly and factually to each of these charges. My experience with communist activists at a student conference on international relations at the University of Oklahoma served me well, and I came out of the exercise sweating but with the feeling that I had met the challenge. But the real test would come in the field.

Later I would learn much more about the duties and responsibilities of life in the Foreign Service. At that time my colleagues and I looked forward to representing the United States to foreign publics, to serving on the frontline of America's engagement abroad. We hoped to have some impact on our audiences and play a part in making history, but this was still pretty much of a dream. Part of that dream was travel abroad, experiencing new cultures, learning new languages, seeing new sights and finding lifetime friends in foreign cultures. I already had a taste of this from my China experience and looked forward to great deal more. We understood from what we had read and from our short acquaintance with State Department officials that we would be working with highly talented individuals and that the challenges of our new jobs would never give us a moment to get bored. In recompense we would be provided housing and free medical care while living abroad. The salary I would be drawing at first was modest, but it was still considerably more than I was receiving as a journalist. Even so, what appealed to me most was the challenge of the job itself. I was excited and looked forward eagerly to this new phase of my life.

My orientation period was hectic, but I also had to equip myself with a diplomatic wardrobe for service in the tropics in mid-winter Washington. Stan was a big help. He had grown up in nearby Baltimore and knew his way around the capital. The month passed quickly. Before leaving Washington in mid-February, I wrote a protocol letter to my Ambassador-to-be in Caracas and advised him that I would arrive at the Maiquetia airport on February 22.

My travel orders gave me four days leave en route. I used them bid farewell to Margaret, my college sweetheart in Chapel Hill, and to say goodbye to my family in Lake Charles, Louisiana. My hometown paper published an item about my Foreign Service assignment accompanied by a photo of me boarding a plane for New Orleans and the overnight flight to Caracas.

II Caracas - Getting Started

It was a restless flight. Questions kept popping into my head. Would I be able to handle Spanish well enough to do my job? The State Department did not test my ability in the language; they just took my word that I knew it. Had my journalism training and newspaper experience prepared me adequately for this new responsibility? What would my new boss be like? Did I really want a Foreign Service career? Wouldn't I have been happier working as a newspaper correspondent? Why Caracas and not some place in Asia where I had served during the War? Would Margaret be willing to join me? In six months, a year, if ever?

It was George Washington's birthday, and the Embassy was closed. The Marine guard on duty directed me to the Potomac (pronounced po-tow-mac) Hotel on a palm tree-lined avenue three blocks from the American Embassy. Shortly after I checked in, a forty-fiveish, bespectacled man looking as though he had just stepped out of Grant Wood's "American Gothic" walked into the lobby accompanied by an attractive blonde woman about his own age. It was my new boss, John Turner Reid, and his wife Marian.

Amenities over, Reid explained the structure and functioning of USIS Caracas. We were an integral part of the Embassy establishment under Ambassador Norman Armour, a distinguished career diplomat. Armour had recently come out of retirement to render his services to President Truman at a time when the United States was confronted with one of the many crises of that era. I considered it a great honor to be able serve under him at my first post.

Then, following a short discussion about my own background and expectations of a Foreign Service career, the Reids left me to get settled into the hotel where I would live until I could find more permanent quarters. I reported for work the following morning.

USIS Caracas

The offices of USIS Caracas were located in a converted two-story residence adjacent to the American Embassy in the San Bernardino section of the old colonial town of Caracas. The Embassy itself occupied a six-story former apartment building. Neither building was outwardly impressive.

4

Reid introduced me to the American and Venezuelan members of the USIS staff. There were three American officers, including myself, plus an American secretary and ten locally employed Venezuelans. John Turner Reid was the Public Affairs Officer (PAO) and directly responsible to the Ambassador. As a scholar in American literature and music, Reid's concept of public affairs focused on promoting knowledge of American culture. He would retain responsibility for dealing with members of the press, although he did not really enjoy that aspect of the job. As Reid explained, his successor, due to arrive in about six months, was a newspaperman; and he preferred to leave any permanent arrangement with him.

Alice Stone, thirty-fiveish, was the Cultural Affairs Officer (CAO) and second in command. She handled cultural and educational exchanges between the United States and Venezuela.

Gloria Draper was our American secretary. She handled personnel matters and classified correspondence. She would become a lifetime friend.

Reid assigned me responsibility for managing the post's radio and motion picture activities. My official title, Information Assistant, would later be changed to Public Affairs Assistant. I was disappointed not to be given responsibility for working with the press since I felt that was the field in which I was most qualified. Motion pictures were not in my area of expertise; but someone had to handle them, and I was the junior officer.

As I was to learn, local employees or Foreign Service Nationals (FSNs) constitute the backbone of USIS operations overseas. They provide not only the language and cultural skills essential to communicating with the populace in the countries wherever we operate, but also the personal contacts needed to conduct those operations. American officers come and go, with changes occurring every two to four years. The local employees provide continuity and a memory bank that would otherwise be lost. They are paid on salary scales prevalent in the host country, often considerably below their value to the U.S. Government. Many spend their entire careers working with American embassies abroad.

I took an immediate liking to the senior local employee and press chief, Ricardo Andreotti, a crusty, 60-year-old Italian gifted with an ironic sense of humor. He edited and translated our Embassy press releases, wrote a daily column under a pseudonym, and maintained

5

contact with members of the news media. After he retired we replaced him with Aristides "Ary" Moleon, an intelligent, quick-thinking and dedicated young Argentine newsman formerly with United Press International. He became my right hand man and continued so under my successor. Later, for personal reasons, he transferred to the International News Service and eventually wound up in Washington as their Latin American specialist. Carmen Rivas, Alice Stone's cultural affairs assistant, would become my Spanish tutor and good friend. Other employees included a films librarian, a radio librarian and producer, a mobile films unit operator and a vivacious Venezuelan receptionist. Others would join the staff later, but except for Moleon, this was the core group on my arrival.

A Bachelor in Caracas

Hotel Potomac, where I lived for my first several weeks in Caracas, was a watering hole for the younger set of Embassy and petroleum company employees, later to be designated as "yuppies." It was an international group—American, Venezuelan, and a goodly number of post-World War II European immigrants, especially Italian. I found them compatible and soon formed a small circle of friends, both male and female, with which I met socially at the hotel during off-duty hours, even after I had moved into private quarters.

The Embassy provided me with a temporary living allowance that paid my hotel bill while I looked for more permanent quarters. I was urged, none too subtly, to find them as quickly as possible. I still had much of the student in me, both in terms of economical living and a desire to improve my Spanish. I soon found a *pension* (boarding house) run by a Spanish family within walking distance from the Embassy. No one there spoke English. If I wanted to get laundry done or otherwise communicate I was compelled to rely on my college Spanish. I was hesitant at first, but as my vocabulary grew so did my confidence. In a short time I found myself able to chat in simple phrases with other *pensionistas* and with the landlady's attractive young daughter. Nothing came of this acquaintance save a strong memory of delicious Spanish omelets the girl served me every morning for breakfast.

After I had been in the pension about three weeks I was offered a small but delightful penthouse vacation apartment. It had two balconies, one facing east, the other west so I could enjoy both the sunrise and the sunset. On each balcony the owner had installed a profusion of flowering tropical plants, making it seem like a sort of jungle in the heart of the city. The price was right and the location ideal, only two blocks from the Embassy. It was too good to resist and I didn't. A Venezuelan maid, Maria, came with the apartment at what seemed a minuscule salary. It was only after she had worked for me for a month that I learned she was supporting five children on what I was paying her. On my beginner's salary, I was not overly wealthy myself, but my soft heart led to a small raise for Maria. She stayed with me throughout my tour in Caracas. Although I lived in that small penthouse for only three months, for some reason, varying images of it have recurred in my dreams ever since. My next home was a roomy, fourth-floor walkup penthouse in Edificio Caura, a new apartment building adjacent to the Centro Medico in San Bernadino. It was bare bones empty, no stove, no refrigerator, not even an empty box to sit on. I acquired the essentials, a bed and a bar, and moved in. With the help of friends I added several items to make the place livable. What I liked most about the place was its large, 20 x 30 foot balcony where I could plant flowers, hold outdoor parties, and enjoy the spectacular sunsets.

I seldom had to spend an evening alone during my bachelor days in Caracas. My vanity would have it otherwise, but it was really because of the scarcity of young, eligible bachelors among the single employees of the Embassy and various American oil companies. John Reid and Alice Stone gave receptions to introduce me to our Venezuelan contacts. Other Embassy officers, including the Ambassador, included me in their guest lists to even out the sex ratio at private or official dinners. It was not long before I began seeing the same familiar faces over and over again. Without realizing what was happening, I had become a member of the "cocktail circuit."

My closest friend during my bachelor days in Caracas was Pepe Massa, an immigrant Italian construction engineer who drew me into his circle of lively Italian friends. Pepe drove a Lincoln Continental convertible, and on weekends we frequented Macuto Beach near LaGuaira. One Sunday, knowing I was going to the beach, John Reid asked me to meet Herbert Matthews, the New York Times' Latin American correspondent who was arriving that afternoon at Maiquetia Airport, and take him to the PAO residence for dinner. After a day at the beach Pepe and I picked up the elegant Mr. Matthews and drove up the winding Caracas-LaGuaira highway with the convertible's top down. By the time we reached Reid's house Mr. Matthews still looked elegant, but I looked like I was fresh off a windblown desert. Reid said nothing about my appearance, but his look shriveled me in my seat. During his brief stay in Caracas Matthews met with Embassy, oil company and Venezuelan officials. The following week the New York Times devoted a full column to his review of the Venezuelan political situation, filed from Panama.

Caudillos and Oil

Matthews described Venezuela as a military dictatorship that had been one for more than a century after Venezuela gained its independence from Spain in 1821. During this period, interrupted only for a brief democratic interlude from 1945 to 1948, military leaders from the Andean provinces dominated political life, tolerated no opposition and had only contempt for the ideals of democracy as practiced in North America. The most notorious was Juan Vicente Gomez who ran the country as his personal fiefdom from 1908 until his death in 1935. Even in 1951, as Matthews noted, Venezuela had not yet recovered from that dictatorship which left the people browbeaten, three-quarters illiterate and without a trained civil service. This made it possible for the small military clique to argue that the people were not capable of ruling themselves and that the country could only be ruled by force.

The discovery of oil on the shores of Lake Maracaibo in 1913 opened the door to an eventual democratic challenge to cacique rule. Within 15 years petroleum had transformed the Venezuelan economy from primarily rural to one dominated by the extraction of oil and made the country the world's second largest oil producer. In 1938 the Lopez Contreras government, successor to Juan Vicente Gomez, outlined a scheme for "sowing the petroleum," i.e., using oil revenues to provide for national development.[3] Over the next decade successor governments made valiant but ineffective attempts to carry out this policy.

In 1946 the Democratic Action Party (*Accion Democratica*, AD) won a constituent assembly election and drew up a new constitution that went into effect in July 1947. Subsequently, AD candidate Romulo Gallegos, a teacher and novelist, won the first free, universal and secret presidential election in the nation's history and took office in February 1948. The Gallego government, determined to industrialize the country and

---

[3]. H. I. Blutstein et al, Area Handbook for Venezuela, 3d ed., 1977.

improve the people's livelihood by "sowing the petroleum," introduced new reform laws that frightened conservative forces, including the army that had originally supported the AD. Gallego lasted less than a year before being overthrown by a three-man junta. Nevertheless, future governmental leaders enlarged upon the Gallego policies and sought an ever-increasing share of income from the country's most abundant natural resource. During my Caracas assignment in the early 1950s, Venezuela forced foreign oil companies, predominantly American, to accept a 50-50 policy. This would later become 75-25 in the government's favor and eventually a complete government takeover.

Marcos Perez Jimenez

In November 1948 a three-man junta consisting of Colonel Delgado Chalbaud, Lt. Col. Marcos Perez Jimenez, and a figurehead civilian president, German Suarez Flamerich, ousted the Gallegos government and took control. As minister of defense, Perez Jimenez—widely known as PJ—controlled the National Guard and the Army and was the real power behind the throne. In November 1950 Col. Chalbaud, a "voice of reason" within the junta, was mysteriously assassinated; and Perez Jimenez became the country's new strong man, suppressing sporadic anti-government activity with an iron fist. He ruled the country through the puppet junta, spending vast sums of money on massive public works designed to ingratiate himself with the populace. This program with its appearance of prosperity brought PJ an element of popular support, but in fact, he bought out his opposition and suppressed those he couldn't buy.

In late 1952, deceived by his own propaganda, Perez Jimenez sought to legitimize his position by holding a relatively free presidential election. As the returns came in Perez saw that he was losing badly and imposed tight controls on the electoral machinery, jailing hundreds of his political opponents. On December 2, 1952, he simply announced himself the winner.

Perez Jimenez remained in power for the remainder of my four-year stay in Venezuela. He made a few gestures of support for democratic thought and ideals, but they turned out to be meaningless. Even though Perez brought elements of the more conservative Christian Democrat (COPEI) party into his government, he ran it as a military dictatorship, pure and simple. This was the time of the Cold War. Venezuela was staunchly anti-communist and very much on the American side. Official

Washington liked it that way. American policy makers saw our national interest as maintaining access to Venezuelan petroleum and the newly discovered iron ore in eastern Venezuela. We did not upset the apple cart by promoting human rights.

Communism

Six months after my arrival in Caracas I wrote to Ed Hunter, my former managing editor at the *Charlotte Observer*: "Communism is giving us our troubles, but ignorance and a lack of real sense of moral responsibility on the part of the leading classes are more serious problems…In this country there is no such thing as a free and unfettered discussion of political issues. Venezuela has lived so long under military dictatorships that have tolerated no criticism that newspapermen and editors automatically steer clear of any controversial political issue. There is no prior censorship by the government, but too many newspapers have been suspended or closed down entirely for the editors not to know where to draw the line. Usually rather than take the chance of a run-in with the government, they just avoid issues completely."

The communist movement was underground, but some of its members either worked for the news media or were able to use it for their purposes as indicated by occasional press articles and radio programs. On one such occasion our press chief, infuriated by a pro-communist commentary he had heard on a popular radio station, sent an anonymous letter to its director refuting the communist arguments. I was secretly pleased when the director, whom I knew, told me of the letter and his concern over communist infiltration of his radio station. Unfortunately I never heard whether he had fired the culprit.

The Perez Jimenez government found Venezuela's small communist movement a convenient whipping boy, making it out to be much stronger than it was in reality in order to divert public attention from the social problems that continued to plague the oil-rich country.

Even so, governmental surveillance of the news focused primarily on information and commentary that might affect the Junta's exercise of control. Official policy encouraged Venezuelan news media to use the Washington produced anti-communist materials that we provided them at no charge. As a result USIS had full access to the news media that readily accepted our press materials and made extensive use of our international news items.

At the time the United States was deeply engaged in the Cold War. We not only tolerated Venezuelan and other Latin American dictatorships, turning a blind eye to their exploitation of their own people, we aided and abetted them in the interest of combating the communist threat to the Free World. As a member of the United States Foreign Service I became an instrument, albeit a willing one, of our foreign policy of the time, a soldier on the front lines fighting communism.

After I left Venezuela the government's abuses of power grew more and more outrageous. Unfortunately, the tardy action by the Department of State in distancing itself from the hated Perez Jimenez regime enabled the country's underground communist movement to promote anti-Americanism by exploiting PJ's connections with the United States.

USIS had a close working relationship with Venezuelan media personnel; and in the end it was they who took enormous personal risks to arouse the Venezuelan public into a revolt against the dictator and the outrages committed by his national security police, putting an end to the regime.

Bob Amerson, my successor, was witness to the events surrounding the dictator's downfall and was on duty when then Vice President Richard Nixon visited Caracas a short time later. The United States had given asylum to the dictator, and Venezuelan communists used public resentment against this act to mobilize huge anti-Nixon demonstrations. Angry mobs spat on the Vice President at the Maiquetia airport and stoned his official motorcade as it passed through Catia on the outskirts of Caracas. Nixon handled himself remarkably well during the death-threatening event. The resultant publicity made headlines around the world. Amerson describes these events eloquently in his book *How Democracy Triumphed over Dictatorship in Venezuela - Public Diplomacy in Venezuela* (American University Press, March 1995). It is a matter of Venezuelan national pride that since the overthrow of Perez Jimenez every president has been democratically elected and every transition of power has been peaceful.

Ambassador Warren

In November 1951 Fletcher Warren of Texas, a career diplomat, succeeded Norman Armour as U.S. Ambassador to Venezuela and remained there throughout my assignment. He was a genial, fatherly figure skilled in the arts of diplomacy; but as an old line Foreign Service Officer he focused his attention on government-to-government relations and left public affairs matters pretty much in the hands of USIS. While there was no question about his abilities as a professional diplomat, in his efforts to keep the Perez Jimenez government on the side of the United States, he may have overlooked the need to maintain the support of the Venezuelan public. His most significant failure was in going along, albeit reluctantly, with the State Department's 1954 decision to award the much-hated Perez Jimenez the "Legion of Honor" for his "spirit of friendship and cooperation." Warren made the presentation at a special ceremony in the Caracas Embassy. PJ, of course, made the most of the award to promote his own image among his countrymen; but it was destined to backfire against the United States in the anti-Nixon demonstrations described above.

Public Diplomacy

USIS was the public diplomacy (information and cultural) arm of the American Embassy. Our primary purpose was to support American foreign policy objectives in Venezuela. It was our responsibility to work with the local news media in an effort to keep the Venezuelan public informed about the rationale behind American actions in world affairs, particularly those influencing Venezuela. It was also our mission to explain the main aspects of American culture and to promote good cultural relations between our two countries.

In no way did USIS replace the various commercial news sources available to the Venezuelan media, but through our contacts and our daily output we insured their access to official American viewpoints that affected our bilateral relations. Likewise USIS was available to lend an official hand, if needed, to the many non-governmental organizations that conducted their own cultural activities in Venezuela.

We depended on the cooperation of Venezuelan news media to reach the Venezuelan public at large, and that required that we foster good interpersonal relations with news media personnel. Similarly, promoting good cultural relations required the cooperation of the Ministry of Education and the various cultural institutions, both public and private. Good relations with members of these institutions were essential to carrying out our cultural programs.

Motion Picture Programs

With my assigned responsibility as the USIS motion picture officer I needed to know what we were showing to the Venezuelan public, so I set about familiarizing myself with our documentary film holdings and learning how to operate a 16-mm projector.

Our motion picture section maintained a lending library of American 16mm films, produced or acquired and narrated in Spanish by USIA Washington for use in Latin America, plus some twenty RCA Victor projectors. We made these available on loan at no cost to Venezuelan schools and cultural organizations. In addition we operated two mobile units that roved the countryside giving outdoor showings of USIS documentaries in working class neighborhoods, schools and town plazas for audiences ranging into the hundreds, sometimes thousands. Since the rural Venezuelan literacy level hovered around 25 per cent, we chose film programs that included documentaries on non-controversial topics such as health and culture with only a minor emphasis on political topics. For example, a two-hour evening program usually included only a single twenty-minute political documentary; more than that would have lost half the audience. In effect, we sugar coated the political message. We had ample resources at the time, and we used them to help the national government carry out its educational function. In a sense, we were performing a task undertaken later under the aegis of the Alliance for Progress as set forth by Presidents Kennedy and Johnson.

On many occasions I accompanied our operators to these showings and circulated among audiences to monitor their reactions to our film programs. In retrospect, though effective in its way, this activity seems the ultimate luxury, but it was in keeping with our operating philosophy at the time. With the advent of television we discontinued the mobile unit program and loaned our films to the TV stations that reached much larger audiences. In the earlier stages of television Venezuelan stations lacked materials and took whatever we had to offer. As the stations built up their own entertainment film resources, however, they relied less and less on us, but we continued to reach our audiences through loans to educational institutions.

My experience traveling around the countryside and meeting with Venezuelans on every social stratum convinced me that they were strongly pro-American. This was in the early 1950s. The United States was very powerful worldwide. We had just recently come out of the Second World War as a very strong nation. Venezuela was benefiting

13

enormously from the American oil companies operating there. National income was on the rise and people were feeling good about their future.

Radio Programming

I found radio an exciting and effective means of getting our message across to the Venezuelan public. One of my first acts was to pay courtesy calls on the directors of the principal radio stations. During these and subsequent visits I became familiar with the radio stations' needs and tried to adapt our media services to meet them. These personal attentions put me on a first name basis with the station directors and many of the country's leading radio journalists. The Radio Broadcasters Association of Venezuela regularly invited me to their annual meetings, and I met frequently with individual station directors and their staff members on both official and social occasions.

With the exception of a half-dozen Caracas stations, Venezuelan radio broadcasters were unable to afford the services of international news agencies and were eager to receive any assistance they could get. Those unable to afford wire services simply read items from Caracas dailies for what passed as their news programs. Since capital city newspapers were usually a day late in arriving to cities in the interior, these stations welcomed my offer to relay the VOA's Spanish language broadcasts to Latin America. There was no cost to the stations. All they had to do was tune in VOA on their short wave receivers and flip a switch. We supplemented this with radio bulletins culled from USIA's "Wireless File" (see below) that they could use at their convenience. We also helped fill their need for dramatic programs with VOA Spanish language dramas recorded on 16-inch platters. At the time taped programs were still a technology of the future.

We found a ready market for these materials. Radio dramas, produced professionally by VOA's Spanish language service and carrying a built-in anti-communist message, were one of our most popular products. Their dramatic quality was several cuts above anything available in Venezuela. The radio stations liked them, partly because they were free and partly because their public called in and asked for more. Even so, some of the packaged, anti-communist materials were so hard-lining they sometimes made me gag. We tended to use most of them because the market was good. With 20/20 hindsight I can't really say we were as discreet as we might have been in utilizing these products because we, too, were imbued with Cold War mentality. One might even say we were victimized by it.

While a portion of our informational output emphasized anti-communism, it by no means dominated our activities. Most programs were devoted to promoting good U.S.-Venezuelan relations and the interests of the free world by demonstrating how America functioned as a democratic society in the family of nations.

The "Wireless File," mentioned above, was the principal source of our news output. It was produced by USIA Washington's press service, transmitted to field posts via Morse code and copied by a locally employed radio operator. It contained news, commentaries and statements by U.S. Government officials, particularly the President and Secretary of State. As such it was also valuable in keeping American officials abroad informed on policy matters. As communications technology improved, radio teletype supplanted Morse code; but the term "Wireless File" stuck until the mid 1990s when it was renamed "Washington File" and transmitted via Internet.

Revista Internacional

Not long after my arrival in Caracas it became obvious to me that we needed a locally produced radio program to carry "freight," i.e., materials designed to promote U.S. policy abroad. The nature of our audiences called for something other than straight news and commentary read over the air. In conversation with a Venezuelan colleague at Radio Caracas I hit upon a dramatic format in which professional actors would reenact (in Spanish) major events of the week. Best of all, Radio Caracas offered to provide studio time and broadcast the program free. We named it *Revista Internacional* (International News Magazine) and drew on the Wireless File as our prime news source. In looking for someone to write and direct the radio program, I chose Renny Ottolina, a young graduate from Venezuela's Central University who was just beginning a career as a radio and newsreel announcer. I was impressed by his quick intelligence, his authoritative voice and convincing radio style. Our program was an immediate hit and within a short time we were able to place it on nearly twenty stations. Partly through this program, but largely through Renny's own competence and ambition, he developed into Venezuela's premier radio and television personality and remained in that position for many years. Eventually he ran for president of the country. Unfortunately, during his campaign for the presidency, he was killed in an airplane accident. It was a great tragedy. He was a good friend of strong moral character and unusual ability.

The "Courier"

In March 1952 the "Courier" came to Venezuela. The Voice of America, seeking to improve its radio signals and expand its Latin American audience, had equipped a transport ship with rebroadcast facilities, renamed it "Courier" and sent it to LaGuaira, seaport to Caracas, where it was to serve as a relay station for the indefinite future. Joe McEvoy, who had succeeded John Reid as Public Affairs Officer, and I organized an inauguration extravaganza. Our program included a nationwide broadcast originating in VOA Washington's studios and rebroadcast from the "Courier" to a network of stations headed up by Radio Caracas. Because the mountains between La Guaira and Caracas tended to block the Courier's radio signals, the ship's engineers planned use a helium filled balloon to hoist a special antenna to relay VOA's signals to Radio Caracas. The broadcast was scheduled for 6:00 p.m. At 5:30 as the balloon was rising, it hit one of the ship's masts, tore a hole in its side, and collapsed onto the ship's deck. There was no time to replace it. Acting on advice from Amable Espina, director of Radio Caracas, Courier engineers decided to relay the broadcast over a telephone line that was being used for communicating with the studio. The line ran from the ship to a phone inside an adjacent warehouse. The signal would be lower quality but at least a signal. The phone line ran through a metal door. At 6:00 p.m., just as the program was about to begin, the warehouse employees finished work for the day, exited the metal door and slammed it shut cutting the telephone wire. (We learned of this only later.)

I was in the Radio Caracas broadcast studio. We were completely unaware of the foregoing events. Our communications with the ship had been cut off when the door slammed. When no signal came from the Courier either by radio or by phone there was momentary panic while we figured out what to do.

From the broadcast console the studio engineer turned to Program Director Jesus Maella and said, "I've got VOA on a direct broadcast. Why don't we use that?"

"Plug it in," said Maella.

16

The next day the Radio Caracas network stations reported that the VOA "Courier" rebroadcast had been a huge success. We accepted the praise with gratitude and kept our mouths shut.

The "Courier" remained in La Guaira for an extended period relaying VOA shortwave broadcasts to Latin America, but we never tried another nation-wide Venezuelan hookup.

Cultural Activities

Although my official functions were primarily in the information field, unofficially I was quite active in the cultural field. The locale for my extra-curricular activities was the Centro Venezolano-Americano, an English teaching institution operated privately with a bi-national board. There were similar centers in other countries, but they originated and were most prevalent in Latin America. USIA subsidized the centers by providing American directors plus library and cultural program support, thus enabling them to perform a significant cultural exchange function. Their main source of income, however, came from fees paid by students who wanted to learn English.[4]

The Centro was located in a traditional colonial style house in the heart of Caracas right off the Plaza Bolivar. Its large interior patio served as a stage for public programs, as well as a meeting place for the center's sizable clientele of young Venezuelans who came there to study English. Working with the director, I developed an inter-American folk dance program that drew on Latin American ethnic groups resident in Caracas. There were Argentines, Chileans, Brazilians, Peruvians, Mexicans, and even Spaniards from the Canary Islands. All seemed to have their own folk dance groups and all were happy for an opportunity to demonstrate their talents.

Renny Ottolina, who had a talent for animating audience participation, served as master of ceremonies. Initially we intended to entertain the Centro's student body with small programs, but they became so popular the Centro was unable to handle the crowds. We found ourselves renting the Teatro Nacional, the biggest theater in town,

---

4. For a discussion of the history and role of binational centers, see Allen C. Hansen, *Public Diplomacy in the Computer Age*, 2nd ed., Praeger, 1989, p.150-152. Hansen was a colleague of mine in Caracas and later in Madrid. The book, published after his retirement, is one of the more authoritative studies of the Agency

which filled to overflowing with enthusiastic audiences. For me, the experience was exhilarating. We had a marvelously good time and brought considerable credit and popularity to the binational center. I like to think that in the process we promoted good inter-American relations and generated a lot of good will. Fred Drew, the director, spoke of these programs as the Centro's best during his term as director.

VIP Visitors

One of the greatest personal rewards for a young USIS Foreign Service Officer is contact with the continuing parade of VIP (very important person) visitors ranging from chiefs of state, Congressmen and cabinet members to famed movie stars and other professional artists he or she encounters as part of his official duties. I met many during my four years in Caracas. The country was in the midst of an oil boom; and the free-spending government and oil companies lavished money on international conferences, bringing in big name personalities, both official and unofficial, from the United States. Our Embassy had responsibility for managing visits by U.S. Government officials, and USIS was charged with public information activities. We also coordinated numerous official and unofficial cultural visitors. Fortunately for me, all the official visits during my watch were peaceable.

Here are a few examples of "my" VIP visitors:

President Truman's Secretary of the Interior Oscar Chapman came to Caracas in September 1951 to address a National Petroleum Convention to which 27 countries had sent representatives. Chapman had been Truman's primary fundraiser during the historic 1948 election campaign, the one who "charmed money out of the pockets of bigwig Democrats"—to use his phrase. Now, he was a member of Truman's inner circle and was being warmly welcomed by the Venezuelan government at a huge reception in his honor. I was seated at a table with some friends when Mr. Chapman, trying to escape overly attentive Venezuelan officials, joined our small group and stayed with us for about half an hour before he was finally dragged away to his official table. It was my first experience with a member of the President's cabinet. From him I learned that the best way to impress people is to be natural, that affected charm works in the opposite direction.

In June 1953, Dr. Milton Eisenhower, the President's younger brother and himself president of the University of Pennsylvania, visited

18

Caracas on the first lap of a South American good will tour. We organized a press conference for him and I attended the Ambassador's reception for some 500 guests, including the President of Venezuela and all of his cabinet. The attendees represented about 75 per cent of the wealth of that wealthy country.

In March 1954, Secretary of State John Foster Dulles came to Caracas to attend an Inter-American Conference. The principle item on the agenda was Guatemala. That Central American country had recently elected a new president, Julio Arbenz, whom the United States (read United Fruit Co.) considered to be a communist. In reality Arbenz had been elected because he offered hope for cleaning up the abuses of the country's dictatorial regime. Under Eisenhower, John Foster Dulles ran U.S. foreign policy, and Dulles wanted Arbenz out. I was not privy to the negotiations that went on between Dulles and his Latin American counterparts; but since all of them wanted something from the United States, one can imagine there was much hard bargaining. Dulles drove through a vote condemning the Arbenz government as communist, essentially getting hemispheric approval for the United States to unseat him, and left immediately afterwards. A short time later the CIA engineered a coup. Arbenz was overthrown and a president more acceptable to Mr. Dulles was installed in his place. Unfortunately, the aftermath of this action was a long series of military dictators and forty years of bloody civil war that has only recently come to an end. The repercussions, however, are still being felt.

My most memorable experience with Dulles was helping VOA Correspondent John Hogan tape a statement on the conference proceedings for broadcast to Latin America. During a conference break Hogan set his microphone on a small glass top table, shaped like a champagne glass, in front of a sofa. Dulles found the sofa too low and asked to be seated on a straight chair nearby. I grabbed the mike in one hand and the table's single leg with the other intending to move both to the new position. Keeeerash! The glass top slid off the table and came crashing down at Dulles' feet. My face turned all shades of crimson. I was grateful that Dulles was discreet enough to say nothing.

The Columbia Broadcasting System sent Correspondent Daniel Schorr to Caracas cover Dulles' visit and the Inter-American conference. He was having problems obtaining the needed local radio and TV support so I introduced him to the appropriate people at Radio Caracas-TV, helping out with language as necessary. On returning to the United

States Schorr wrote USIA Director Theodore Streibert: a warm letter of "gratitude and praise" for my services: "I know your personnel have a lot of other things to do, and it is not their job to hold the faltering hand of U.S. network correspondents. But the extra-duty assistance I received in Caracas will be long remembered."As I write this more than 50 years later Dan Schorr is also long remembered and appreciated, especially during his Sunday commentaries on national and international affairs over the Public Broadcasting System.

In March 1955, Eisenhower's Secretary of Agriculture, Ezra Taft Benson, later head of the Mormon Church, came to Caracas to look at Venezuelan agriculture and animal husbandry. He particularly wanted to see how "Bramangus" (a cross between Brahman and Angus) beef cattle had adapted to Venezuela's tropical climate. "Doc" James Kempton, our Embassy's genial agricultural attaché, spent weeks arranging appointments for him. Since Venezuelans were inclined to go all out on hospitality for such high level visitors from the United States, Kempton was careful to point out that as a Mormon, Mr. Benson drank no alcoholic beverages, coffee or tea. Each time he went through this routine he drew the response, "Oh, yes, we know all about your Mormons. They don't drink coffee, tea, or liquor, but they sure do like their women." Mr. Benson's hosts served him lemonade. I accompanied the secretary to handle relations with the news media and provide coverage of the visit for the Voice of America. With my dairy farm background I enjoyed this assignment and was able to empathize with our Venezuelan counterparts. The secretary sweated profusely under the tropical sun, but he comported himself superbly well and left a fine impression everywhere he went. Oh yes, he was also pleased with the cattle he saw and VOA was happy with my coverage.

Marian Anderson, America's foremost contralto of the period, came to Caracas for a concert. The Centro Venezolano-Americano offered a reception in her honor, and we spent an hour together on the roof garden discussing the state of the arts in America. Ms. Anderson was very much aware of racial problems in the United States but insisted that although she was Negro (the term then in use) she was primarily an artist and declined to get into a discussion of the topic of race. Her warm personality left a lifelong impression on me.

Early in 1955 William Faulkner was transiting Maiquetia Airport en route from a USIS-sponsored lecture tour in Brazil to the wedding of his daughter in Memphis. He agreed to meet Venezuelan press representatives during a brief airport layover. After the press conference we learned that his plane had been delayed for four hours. Faulkner and I spent the time together as two Southerners, enjoying Cerveza Polar (a Venezuelan beer), while conversing about growing up in Louisiana and Mississippi, the backdrop for his writings. Later that year USIA sent Mr. Faulkner to Japan on another lecture tour. I had just arrived on a new assignment and attended an official reception USIS gave in his honor. As I approached to greet Mr. Faulkner he said, "God, it's good to see you. I don't know a soul in this crowd." He asked me to handle his relations with the Japanese press, but I was too much of a novice in Japan to undertake such a task. In any case USIS Tokyo had the matter well in hand.

Colonia Tovar

It was Gloria Draper, our USIS American secretary, who introduced me to the gregarious younger set of American women working for the American Embassy and the oil companies. They loved to party, whatever the occasion. Being single, I felt like a marriage candidate up for grabs; but I certainly wasn't ready to go into complete seclusion. I drew a protective screen around myself with stories of my fiancée back in Chapel Hill and avoided dating any one of them, preferring group activities.

Gloria's group also loved to explore unusual places around Venezuela. One weekend they proposed a hike to Colonia Tovar, a German village some 25 miles west of Caracas at about 6,500 feet altitude in the coastal Andes Mountains. The village had been settled by German immigrants in 1842 and for more than 100 years was completely isolated from Venezuela's predominantly Hispanic population. The colony's inhabitants lived much as their rural ancestors had and still spoke mostly German. Rumors said excessive intermarriage had produced children with six toes on each foot or six fingers on each hand, and similar unfortunate results. Eight of us—four men and four women—from the Embassy and Creole Petroleum Company decided to see the place for ourselves.

The only access to Colonia Tovar was by a 22-mile footpath through the jungle. We set out one Saturday intending to remain overnight and hike back on Sunday. On the way our Indian guide deserted us, we took a wrong path and spent the night in the jungle huddled around a campfire we kept burning to ward off snakes and the mountain chill.

21

Dawn revealed a bedraggled group of office workers, stiff from the previous day's hike and from sleeping on the cold ground on a high ridge overlooking a valley. At a peasant's hut down the slope a quarter of a mile below, we learned of a dam construction project a short distance away. An engineer who wanted to go to Caracas anyway found us a good excuse. The eight of us piled aboard his four-passenger jeep and were back home in Caracas in time for lunch.

A month later several members of our group repeated the excursion to Colonia Tovar and found a delightful, self contained village, every house surrounded by a profusion of flowers and no one with six fingers on each hand. In 1994 I returned to Caracas to find that a busy highway had replaced the jungle path, and Colonia Tovar had become a tourist mecca.

Married

During my first year in Caracas my official and social life as a bachelor continued unabated; but when I returned home in the evening I found my apartment lonely, definitely needing a feminine presence. Margaret and I had kept up a steady stream of correspondence from the time I arrived in February, writing to each other two or three times a week. Each of us derived much satisfaction from the letters, but they were no substitute for being together. In November, ten months into my assignment, I wrote her a long letter and asked, "Will you marry me?" She cabled, "Yes." I phoned[5] and we set the date for Thursday, December 27, 1951.

The wedding was a small family affair at the Munch residence in Chapel Hill with a few close friends invited. We honeymooned in Haiti, a poor but more peaceable land than at present. On our first New Year's Eve together we were guests at a party USIS Haiti Public Affairs Officer Homer Gayne and his wife gave for their many Haitian friends. This occasion introduced me to the common bond that knits USIS officers' lives together as they travel abroad in the service of the U.S. Government. It was a bond that would I would increasingly appreciate during the remainder of my career and beyond.

---

[5]. In those pre-satellite days international phone calls, carried by short wave radio, were expensive, unreliable and used only on very important occasions.

We arrived back in Caracas on Margaret's birthday, January 2, 1952. I presented her with an apartment, our new home together, and took another week's vacation from my official duties to show her around Caracas and get us settled. We needed virtually everything.

Going back to work I resumed my travel to the interior, visiting radio stations and local authorities. The difference was that this time Margaret went along. Where my Venezuelan contacts had been courteous before, they now bent over backwards with generous hospitality. Margaret had become a definite asset to the United States Government.

Our first child, Elizabeth Anne, whom we nicknamed Betsy, was born in February 1953 while Margaret and I were on home leave following my first two-year tour in Caracas.

Home Leave and Return

Home leave included five days consultation in USIA headquarters and a week in New York for training in television. I visited the major TV networks—NBC, CBS and some smaller stations—and picked up pointers for programming in Caracas.

In Washington the federal bureaucracy was in turmoil. The new Republican Administration under President Eisenhower and Secretary John Foster Dulles were carrying out their long promised changes. Cold War rhetoric in Congress and the media had produced an anti-communist mania that permeated every element of American society. Senator Joe McCarthy continued his vicious witch-hunt against the State Department personnel, leaving nobody knowing who would be his next victim. McCarthy's aides Roy Cohn and David Schine ran rampant through USIS libraries abroad pulling from their shelves books supposedly influenced by communists. People who had devoted their whole careers to the Foreign Service were being labeled as traitors. Loyal public servants were dismayed when neither President Eisenhower nor Secretary Dulles made any apparent efforts to refute the charges. Morale was restored only after Edward R. Murrow, in his historic television documentary, revealed the truth behind McCarthy's tactics and the unfounded charges he had foisted upon the American public; and the Senate finally put a stop to the nonsense with a vote of censure. McCarthy faded from the national picture, but the bitterness he had spread and the very name McCarthyism became a depressing part of American history.

23

A mountain of work awaited me on our return to Caracas. While we were still in the United States, Joe McEvoy, had written me ("Querido Papacito," he wrote) to say I should plan to attend the annual meeting of the Venezuelan Chamber of Radio Broadcasting (Camara Venezolana de Radiodifusion) in Valencia. It was a week-long affair that offered ample opportunity for networking with the station directors and resulted in the Embassy getting more free radio time than ever before for our VOA programs.

The political contention on the home front notwithstanding, our work in Caracas continued unabated. I was deeply involved with radio and television activities. Since most of our programs were broadcast in the evenings, at home after work I would find myself monitoring them on the local stations. At times Margaret wondered whether I was married to her or to my job.

My second tour in Caracas slipped by much faster than the first. As the veteran USIS official in Caracas, I bore the brunt of the transitions, carrying duties considerably beyond my rank as my superiors departed Caracas and I broke in the newcomers.

But it was not all work. Weekends we found time to enjoy the new Hotel Tamanaco's large swimming pool, where I taught Betsy to swim. She took to water like a duck and developed a lifelong fondness for swimming. The Caracas-LaGuaira Autopista (freeway) completed in 1953, changed an hour-long tortuous mountain trip into easy 20-minute drive, and we went there frequently to "escape the altitude" as we told ourselves. Actually we enjoyed LaGuaira's sultry warmth, and it gave us a change from the almost too perfect weather of Caracas.

Undertow Scare

It was at the Macuto beach, just east of LaGuaira, that I had the most frightening experience of my life. Margaret and I had gone there one Saturday morning with Rosa Cappachione, our USIS secretary (who had replaced Gloria Draper) and her Marine guard friend, leaving Betsy with our maid. After relaxing on the beach for a while, Margaret and I decided to go in for a short swim. Rosa and her boyfriend declined. They had not brought swimsuits.

I had been in the water for only a few minutes when an undertow grabbed me, carrying me more than a hundred yards out to sea. In the struggle to escape the undertow I swallowed a lot of seawater. I am a fairly good swimmer and somehow managed to stay afloat on my back.

Rosa and her friend, seeing what had happened, ran to a nearby dock and asked two men to go out in a boat to rescue me. When the men finally pulled me into their boat I had been in the water about an hour, trying to work my way towards the shore. All this time I had been under the impression that Margaret, too, had been caught in the undertow and was worrying about our poor orphan baby back in Caracas.

"Mi mujer, mi mujer, por favor, busquela" (my wife, my wife, look for her), I gasped at them.

The two men took turns diving but found no trace of Margaret. When they took me to shore, there, to my immense relief, stood Margaret with Rosa and the Marine guard. She had been only a few feet from me in the water but miraculously had not been caught in the undertow. Doctors at the LaGuaira hospital removed about a gallon (or so it seemed) of salt water from my stomach.

My rescuers were two Canary Island sailors. I rewarded each of them with a quart of Scotch whiskey, but I was unable to give them what they really wanted—a job aboard a ship.

It was only after my experience that the Macuto city authorities decided to put up a "DANGER" sign warning against the undertow.

Career Choice: State or USIA

I entered the Foreign Service as an information specialist classified as a Foreign Service Staff Officer (FSSO), as distinct from a career Foreign Service Officer (FSO). There were definite class distinctions and pay differentials. FSOs had to pass rigorous written and oral entrance examinations; but once appointed and through the initial probation period they were given tenure and, if they maintained basic standards, they could progress through the ranks to ambassador. Staff officers were hired on the basis of their particular skills but without tenure. They could gain promotions within their category but rarely if ever reached the ambassadorial level. FSOs took great pride in their exalted status, arguing that they achieved it the hard way and that more was expected of them than of staff officers. This is a valid argument except that in the field every officer is rated on his abilities and is subject to the Foreign Service up or out policy.

To become a career FSO I would have to follow the established procedure. In 1952 I took the Foreign Service written exam, passed it, and was scheduled for the orals. However, after Eisenhower and the Republicans took over in 1953, Secretary John Foster Dulles engineered the separation of USIA from the Department of State. He wanted State to focus on policy issues without being distracted by responsibilities for an activist information program. Interestingly, he did this after first circularizing field posts and getting a negative reaction to the proposal. Since I saw my career interests as being more oriented toward USIA's information activities than the Department of State's political, economic or consular work, I set aside my opportunity to become a State FSO and stayed with USIA. Subsequent legislation created a corps of Foreign Service Information Officers (FSIOs) based on their passing the required entrance exam. I took it again and passed. I never regretted my original choice. Ironically, in 1999 with the Cold War over, Congress forced the President and State Department to re-amalgamate State and USIA. By that time USIA had taken advantage of its independent status to develop a corps of skilled public diplomacy specialists with a high esprit de corps who had to be dragged kicking and screaming into the folds of the parent foreign service agency.

One of the great rewards of working in the Foreign Service is the uniformly high caliber of your colleagues. Of course, there can always be personality clashes, but they are relatively rare. In difficult situations one can always take solace in the knowledge that a transfer for one or the other is not far in the offing.

Mobile Colleagues

In Caracas I became keenly aware of Foreign Service mobility. During my four years there I worked under two ambassadors, Norman Armour and Fletcher Warren, and three different USIS directors. The three USIS directors were John Turner Reid, Joseph F. McEvoy and George Butler, in that order. I also worked with three different cultural affairs officers—Alice Stone, Harvard educated Dr. Albert Harkness and Andy Wilkison, a professional Latin Americanist with a passion for tennis. With the exception of the two ambassadors and my first cultural affairs officer who left the service after Caracas, I would encounter all of them again at different posts during the course of my career.

McEvoy was my favorite boss. He was a former Associated Press correspondent with many years experience in Latin America and came to Caracas on his first diplomatic assignment. He was a bit nervous at his first meeting with the press a day or two after his arrival, but he spoke fluent Spanish—with a distinct Irish-American accent—and was quick on the repartee. He understood the Latinos and, as a professional newsman, he quickly won them over and enjoyed their deep respect. McEvoy had a delightful sense of humor, as did his wife Ann. A couple of instances:

Joe and I occupied adjacent offices and used the same phone number. Once Joe picked up on a call for me from Jesus (pronounced hey-sus) Maella, the program director of Radio Caracas. Maella asked for me and Joe called out, "Hey, Harry, Jesus is calling you." On another occasion I showed up at the office proudly wearing a shiny new rayon suit. Joe took one look at me and asked, "Say, Harry, where do you get your suits simonized?"

George Butler transferred from the International Cooperation Agency (forerunner of US Agency for International Development), and Caracas was also his first USIS assignment. He was a good administrator and a whiz with electronic devices but a novice in the information field. He relied almost entirely on me for handling that end of our operation. After I left he turned his technical abilities to television and—with Bob Amerson, my replacement—converted our *Revista Internacional* radio program into a successful television series.

Other Caracas colleagues were Allen Hansen (see footnote 2), a junior officer trainee, with whom I later served in Spain and developed an enduring friendship; and John Crowley who left USIA for State and eventually returned to Caracas as Deputy Chief of Mission. He wound up his career as American Ambassador to Guyana.

Transfer

As the end of my second tour of duty in Caracas approached I wrote USIA and requested that my next assignment be in the Far East, preferably Japan. Much to my surprise it came through. I was appointed provincial public affairs officer and director of a Japan-America Cultural Center in the city of Takamatsu. I had never heard of the place. Scurrying to an atlas I located it on Shikoku, the smallest of Japan's four major islands. I was authorized two months home leave, consultation in Washington, D.C., and surface travel all the way.

Margaret, Betsy and I departed Caracas May 25, 1955, aboard the Alcoa ship Cavalier bound for Mobile, Alabama. After visiting relatives and friends in Louisiana and North Carolina and a brief orientation period for my new post in Japan we took a leisurely 18-day drive across the northern part of the United States. On August 2 we boarded the President Grover Cleveland and watched with awe as our passenger liner sailed majestically beneath the Golden Gate Bridge. This was to be the first and last time we were to enjoy the luxury of traveling between two overseas posts entirely by surface.

During the author's tenure in Caracas the U.S. Information Service was housed in this converted residence adjacent to the American Embassy, left, both considerably more modest than today's official establishments.

The author, left, and writer/producer Renny Ottolina, discuss Revista Internacional, a USIS Caracas radio news program. At right, recording a program.

Newsman Daniel Schorr, facing camera, in Caracas to cover the 1954 Interamerican Conference for CBS, enjoys a relaxing moment with the author, center, who assisted him in contacts with Venezuelan radio personnel and facilities.

III Takamatsu – The Daimyo of Shikoku

Tokyo Briefing

Japan at last. On August 16, 1955, two weeks after leaving San Francisco, we docked in Yokohama and set foot in Japan for the first time. We were beginning a new and exciting phase of our life in the Foreign Service.

An American Embassy general services officer met us dockside and saw our luggage through the customs. The trip from Yokohama to Tokyo was almost like a dream. We rode with a retired FSO and his Japanese wife who were returning to Japan to live. "You'll love it," he said as our chauffeur bumped us over a rough road, blowing his horn constantly.

"That's what everybody told us," I replied as we stared out at the dingy factories and shanties that lined the highway. It had been ten years and two days since President Truman had announced the unconditional surrender of Japan, thus ending the terrible destruction of World War II. During that war American B-29s had laid flat the Yokohama-Tokyo industrial district. Under the benign U.S. Occupation the area had recuperated rapidly, but aesthetics got shoved aside in the boomtown-like growth.

The driver deposited us at the Tokyo Grand Hotel, two blocks from the Embassy, and drove off as we were bowed graciously into the lobby. Our room was big and air conditioned, but it was too cold for Betsy so we had the conditioning turned off. When the toilet began to smell we decided to move to the Sanno Hotel ("officer category") run by the U.S. Armed Forces. As a hotel the Sanno was unexceptional, but we were grateful for the English speaking staff and the playground equipment on the front lawn.

USIS Tokyo was between directors. Joseph Evans and Arthur Hummel had been named PAO and Deputy PAO, respectively, but neither had yet arrived. Executive Officer G. Lewis Schmidt was in charge. Summer transfers and vacations had further decimated the American staff and all remaining personnel were overworked. Yet somehow things seemed to get done. William Faulkner[6] had just arrived

---

[6] For two close-up accounts of Faulkner's visit see oral history interviews with Leon Picon and with Jack Shellenberger, ASDT Collection, Arlington, VA. Picon was his

to take part in the Nagano Seminar, a seminal USIS program on American literature; John Steichen was arranging to bring his *Family of Man* exhibit to Japan under joint sponsorship of USIS and the *Asahi Shimbun*, a major newspaper; USIS and the *Yomiuri Shimbun*[7] were teaming up to bring in the biggest Atoms for Peace exhibit ever shown, and I was arriving to go to Takamatsu.

Paul Bethel, the acting field supervisor, took responsibility for me while I was waiting for an opportunity to see Acting PAO Schmidt. Since there was no specific task for me I focused on getting acquainted with various aspects of the USIS organization. At that time there were 60 American officers and over 300 Japanese employees in USIS Tokyo and in the 14 American Cultural Centers (ACC) located in major Japanese cities, literally dwarfing the small operation I had grown accustomed to in Caracas. I was interested to learn that Japanese local employees carried out the vast majority of routine operations, thus enabling American officers to concern themselves with overall policy direction.

It was the better part of a week before the PAO's secretary called me for my appointment with Schmidt. He apologized for having been so inaccessible. The Ambassador, John Allison, had needed him to help handle a series of Congressional visitors. As we exchanged amenities a Japanese secretary entered silently and served us steaming hot barley tea, a delightful practice I would become accustomed to in Takamatsu. I told Schmidt how impressed I was with the magnitude of the USIS Japan operation. Schmidt filled me in on some of the background.

When the U.S. Army had ended its occupation of Japan on April 29, 1952, USIS assumed responsibility for almost all of its information and cultural operations designed to institutionalize American style democracy among the Japanese people. On their side, the Japanese were hungry for knowledge about the United States, and there was a ready market for USIS informational output. At that time there were 24

USIS escort officer; Shellenberger produced a USIS film on the visit entitled *Impressions of Japan*.

[7]. Conversation with Lew Schmidt: Shoriki, the founder and publisher of *Yomiuri*, funded much of the cost of the Atoms for Peace exhibit. He hoped to become Japan's first director of atomic energy and was successful in doing so, thanks to his sponsorship of the exhibit. USIS officers Tom Tuch and the late Frances Blakemore deserve major credit for getting the atoms for peace exhibits launched in Japan and elsewhere.

libraries run by CIE/SCAP (Civil Information and Education/Supreme Command Allied Powers). The expense of running all of them was too much for the USIS budget, so ten were turned over to local city or prefecture governments. The remaining fourteen were converted into American Cultural Centers, keeping the Japanese staffs and putting USIS officers in charge. The libraries turned over to the Japanese were transformed into Japan-America Cultural Centers (JACC) or integrated into local library systems without American participation. The Japanese officials were not overly happy about this process, but all except one accepted it as inevitable.

The exception was Kagawa Prefecture's Governor Masanori Kaneko, a man with a strong and determined personality. He wanted very much to have an American director of the JACC to insure continued communication with American cultural institutions and help the people of his prefecture overcome their traditional backwardness. He made several trips to Tokyo to see the ambassador and to talk with Schmidt and other Embassy officers and even latched onto a U.S. congressman who was in Japan looking into USIS activities to invoke support for his cause. The congressman asked USIA to see what could be done. Jerry Novick, regional public affairs officer (RPAO) in Kobe, looked into the matter and reported back that the prefecture was very cooperative. They had offered to staff the Center with prefecture employees and cover administrative expenses if USIS would provide an American director and pay the rent on the Center's building. However, Novick said, for the arrangement to be successful the new director would have to be a man of exceptional capabilities. It was on that basis that USIS agreed to go ahead with the project on an experimental basis. "We asked USIA Washington to find us a qualified person," Schmidt concluded, "and that's where you came in."

I told Schmidt I had grown up on a farm and that I was excited about going to work in rural Japan but was curious to know what Takamatsu and the island of Shikoku were like.

Schmidt explained that Takamatsu was a city of 140,000 with an agriculture-based economy, much like the other four prefecture capitals on the island. Shikoku was basically rural and conservative, like early 20th century Japan, and a good deal of the island's unique charm came from its isolation. He thought I would find much to admire and enjoy in the island's culture. I would be responsible for USIS activities in Kagawa and Tokushima while the director of the Matsuyama Center, at the opposite end of Shikoku, would handle Ehime and Kochi prefectures. What I could achieve would depend on me personally and my ability to enlist the cooperation of my prefecture employee staff (as opposed to a staff of U.S. Government employees). This was not the preferred arrangement for USIS, but given budgetary considerations and the governor's exceptional interest it appeared to be worth the experiment. Schmidt said he frankly did not know whether such an arrangement could succeed but he wanted me to do my "damndest" to make it work.

The prefecture had identified a house for me, and USIS was in the process of negotiating a U.S. government contract. Schmidt offered me the option of waiting in Tokyo or going on to Takamatsu and finding temporary quarters until the contract was completed.

I responded that I was not needed in Tokyo. I would much prefer go on and take my chances and do my "damndest" to make his Takamatsu experiment work.

Kobe

The next day we shipped our car to Takamatsu and took the train to Kobe. Japanese railroads were excellent, but the highways were still almost non-existent. We rode first class in the observation car and felt like presidential candidates. It rained all the way to Kyoto, but we could enjoy the countryside as we whizzed by. Tokyo and Yokohama with their mushrooming, post-war construction had given us a false impression. Growing rice in myriads of half-acre and quarter-acre fields had turned the countryside into a luxuriant green landscape, dotted here and there by small agricultural villages. This was the Old Japan we had read about in our elementary and high school geography texts.

Passing through Kyoto we were able to discern that the ancient city had been left untouched by the war's massive bombing. This, we learned, was due to the influence of President Franklin D. Roosevelt's Secretary of War, Henry L. Stimson. He had studied there as a young man and learned to appreciate the cultural treasures of the city that had been Japan's imperial capital for 800 years. He convinced FDR that Kyoto's irreplaceable cultural and artistic treasures should be preserved.[8]

---

[8] The only factory in Kyoto, a Mitsubishi engine plant, was outside the main city to the west. The only bombing the city experienced was a bomb dropped by a damaged plane returning from a raid on Tokyo-Yokohoma. The pilot, needing to jettison weight, saw what he thought was a military barracks. Unfortunately it was a school. Several dozen school children were killed, Kyoto's only casualties of World War II.

As we entered Osaka, Japan's big industrial city and the backbone of Japan's economy, we noted that it duplicated the sight that had first greeted us in Yokohama and Tokyo. We wondered how Japan would tackle the problems confronting its lack of land to grow food, lack of markets for its industrial produce, and lack of dollars.

Jerry Novick met us in Osaka. Based in nearby Kobe, Novick had responsibility for USIS operations in the Kansai and Shikoku regions, including the five American Cultural Centers located in Kobe, Osaka, Kyoto, Hiroshima, Matsuyama and my Japan-America Cultural Center (JACC) in Takamatsu. An American director, called Provincial Public Affairs Officer (PPAO), headed each of the centers. With their staffs of local employees and designated areas of responsibility the centers resembled miniature USIS country operations. The Center directors came under the RPAO who was responsible to the USIS Tokyo field director, at that time Walter Nichols. The field director reported to the Deputy PAO, Arthur Hummel[9], who ran the whole USIS Japan operation for the Country PAO, who was in turn responsible to the ambassador and USIA Washington. I felt myself at the tail end of a long line of command.

Crossing the Inland Sea

On the morning of September 1, 1955, Margaret, Betsy, and I went to the Kobe pier to await a Kansai Kisen ferry that would take us to the island of Shikoku. Jerry and Mary Novick, their two small boys and Jerry's interpreter, Kumagai and his wife, joined us. Jerry would host an official reception for us in Takamatsu to introduce us to Governor Kaneko, the JACC staff and the center's clientele. We were grateful to have his support and the company of his family.

It was a gorgeous day. The temperature was in the low seventies, and we were all looking forward to the six-hour boat ride through the scenic Inland Sea. Precisely at the appointed hour of 10:00 a.m. the ferry, an old fashioned steamship, chugged in from Osaka, a number of Japanese

---

9. Hummel was born in China where his father, Arthur Hummel, Sr., was a teacher, missionary and a distinguished China scholar. Subsequent to Tokyo Art had a distinguished Foreign Service career culminating in his appointment as first U.S. Ambassador to China following renewal of diplomatic relations. See "Ambassador Arthur W. Hummel, Jr., Oral History Interview, conducted by Dorthy Robins-Mowry." ADST Collection, Arlington, VA.

passengers already aboard. After Kobe the boat would stop first in Takamatsu, then head on for Matsuyama and its final destination of Beppu on the island of Kyushu. There was no commercial air service to Shikoku, and the ferry was the sole means of getting there and back.

We boarded the ferry in a jolly mood. This would be the last leg of our long trip from Caracas to Takamatsu. Our party was assigned to two of the half dozen first class suites on the upper deck. Japanese tea and cakes appeared like magic; but we were more interested in sightseeing and lined the ship's rail to observe the busy port activities as we pulled away from the pier and headed for the open sea.

The *Seto Nai Kai* (Seto Inland Sea) is located entirely within Japan's borders and serves as the principal waterway for the western half of the archipelago. It is 270 miles long and 38 miles across at its widest. The *Seto* runs in an east-west direction separating Shikoku from the main island of Honshu. The Bungo Straits to the southwest of Shikoku and the Kii Straits to the northeast are the two major passages to the Pacific Ocean. Shipping primarily uses the Kii channel for entry into the major port cities of Osaka and Kobe.

Having just crossed the Pacific where sighting another ship was a rarity, we were amazed at the amount of traffic of all kinds on the Inland Sea. However, as we got further and further from the Kobe-Osaka area, freighters grew fewer and fishing vessels increased. In the early afternoon we began seeing small islands in the distance. A light haze had settled over the horizon, giving the whole seascape the appearance of a classical Oriental painting. It was at once an eerie and reassuring sight. I decided right then and there that no matter what my official work might bring, I was going to enjoy living in this area.

I wrote to my former colleagues in Caracas:

"It was a story-book journey, the kind you only read about or see in color film travelogues. There was a crisp coolness in the air. The sun picked out the dark green mountains and made them even greener. Here and there a village nestled in an inlet where people draw their livelihood from the bountiful sea[10]."

---

[10] Until overfishing reduced stocks to a bare minimum in the latter half of the twentieth century the Inland Sea did indeed constitute a principal resource for Japanese fisheries.

Takamatsu

At 4:00 p.m., six hours out of Kobe, we pulled into the Takamatsu harbor. Jerry spotted several prefecture dignitaries on the dock waiting to receive us, including the wife of Kagawa Vice-Governor Michijiro Ida[11] representing her husband who was ill. Among them was Kaoru Nishimura who had been acting director of the Japan American Cultural Center and who was to serve as my interpreter and guide to this entirely new life. Also there was Helen Kimura, an American born Japanese, who was to be my secretary and Margaret's interpreter.

Our official greeters welcomed us ashore with a profusion of low bows and warm greetings and escorted us to the Kawaroku (six rivers) Hotel in the center of town. This was to be our home for the next several weeks until we found something more permanent. Once we were checked in they left us with a promise from Mr. Nishimura to return the next morning to take us to our Center for the official welcoming ceremony. He said Governor Kaneko had been looking forward eagerly to our arrival and would be there along with many others from the local community. Helen Kimura stayed with us to make sure we were properly established.

The Kawaroku's owners, Mr. & Mrs. Nishiyama who operated the hotel as a family enterprise, showered us with attention worthy of high-level diplomats. They took special notice of Betsy, admiring her red hair, and introduced their six-year old daughter, Yoko-chan[12], to her as a playmate.

The hotel offered both Western and Japanese style rooms. We chose the Japanese. If we were going to live among the Japanese it seemed appropriate to start off by adapting ourselves to their life style. Mr. Nishiyama accompanied us to our room and gestured us into a small antesala where we exchanged our shoes for slippers. Stepping through sliding doors we encountered a large room in soft beige colors with

---

11. Together with Governor Kaneko, Ida had been instrumental in bringing us to Takamatsu. He died of cancer shortly after our arrival.

12. Chan is the diminutive for "san," meaning Mr. or Ms. Children were usually addressed by their given names plus "chan"; adults by their family names except by immediate family members or by intimate friends, eg. even after more than 40 years I still address Mr. Nishimura as "Nishimura-san."

tatami (woven rice straw) mat floors and ample closets. The only visible furniture was a handsome black lacquer table, 18 inches high, a single floor lamp of similar dimensions, and two legless chairs that served as back-supports for sitting at table on the tatami floor. Seeing the quizzical look on my face Mr. Nishiyama slid open one of the closet doors and pointed to folded up bedding (futons), including a small one for Betsy. In the evening, he said, the room maid would prepare the beds for us. On one side of the room was a half-bath with a washbasin and a toilet but no tub or shower. Again our host read my expression and motioned us down the hall where he opened the door to a large communal bathroom equipped with showers and a steaming tub of water about 12 feet square. It was a Japanese *ofuro*. He took care to instruct us to take a shower first and then get in the hot tub.

Back at the room a maid appeared, dressed in a summer kimono (*yukata*), bringing cool towels to refresh our faces. As we did so she set out tea and cakes, saying *"Dozo"* (please help yourselves).

The effusive display of hospitality we had experienced since our arrival made us feel very welcome, but there was more, much more to come.

We were too excited to remain long in our room. Unpacking could come later. We joined the Novicks and went out to investigate the city that was to be our home for the next two years. As we strolled along Marugame *Machi* (street), a pedestrian-only arcaded shopping mall, we noted that although unpaved it was clean. Shopkeepers regularly sprinkled the area in front of their shops to keep down the dust. Dozens of small, family operated stores offered a myriad of products—dry goods, home necessities and handicrafts, particularly ceramics, and delicate lacquer wares that caught the eye of our two ladies. Margaret was evidently pleased at what she saw.

As the Novicks and we ambled along, our children in tow, numerous Japanese passersby—many dressed in kimonos and wooden *geta* (sandals)—paused to stare at this Western invasion. I kept hearing the word *"gaijin"* over and over. Jerry explained the word meant "foreigner." We were curiosities because so few foreigners came to Takamatsu. I remarked that it was nice to be noticed and was glad they were friendly, but I hoped they would still be that way after we had been there a year or so.

Back at the hotel, after a Japanese dinner served in our room, we kept hearing a klack-klack, klack-klack sound coming from the street.

Mystified, I looked out our second story window to see several men, dressed in summer kimonos out for a walk, their wooden *geta* (sandals) klack-klacking on the street. As I learned, in towns like Takamatsu it was the custom for men to soak themselves in the hot public baths each evening and then cool off with a stroll before bedtime.

The next morning as Nishimura-san and I walked to the Center, only ten-minutes away, he gave me his version of what I had heard from Lew Schmidt in Tokyo. He explained that the JACC building had once housed a department store. In 1948 CIE/SCAP had taken it over for a library and operated it under the direction of an American librarian until the end of the Occupation in 1952. During those four years the library had served as a link with the United States and had become a very popular institution. When the U.S. Army left USIS took over operational responsibility for the library but withdrew in a 1953 budget cutting exercise. The library and its staff were turned over to the prefecture government to be run by the department of education as a Japan-America Cultural Center. The prefecture had reduced the staff drastically and cut the salaries of those remaining by more than half. At present the staff consisted of six people, including Nishimura-san and one unpaid volunteer. As acting director he reported to the prefecture's director of libraries who knew no English and had little understanding of a library with a primarily English language collection. This, he said, was one of the reasons they were so happy to have another American director for their library.

I told Nishimura that if the governor was looking for a librarian he would be disappointed in me, but I would do my best to make the JACC a successful cultural center.

The Center staff met us at the entrance, bowing in unison and welcoming me to the Takamatsu *Nichi-Bei Bunka Kaikan* (Japan-America Cultural Center).

After introductions Nishimura-san and Helen escorted me to my office and showed me the seat of honor, an army swivel chair with arm rests. As I sat down the swivel creaked from lack of oil. Looking about the room, I saw the pictures of two former CI&E directors hanging on the wall: Elaine Boylan, who founded the center in 1948 and was now living in Caracas, and Margaret Lawson, her successor in 1951. The center, I was to learn, was steeped in their memory. Many of the programs they initiated, long outmoded, were still being carried on.

I reflected on the parting advice of Dora Dean, the USIS Tokyo librarian, who had told me to take it easy and remember that I was going to the most conservative part of Japan and "those people don't change easily."

There was a package in my "In" basket. It contained office supplies Melita Schmidt, Jerry's secretary, had prepared for me before I left Kobe. Inside was a small box of aspirin.

Any lingering doubts I may have held about my being welcome were dispelled at the afternoon reception. Governor Kaneko, Takamatsu's Mayor Kunito, the president of Kagawa University, their wives and numerous subordinates turned out to welcome us. None greeted me more warmly than the Governor himself who told me he had waited a long time for this moment.

I thanked the governor, telling him I would do my best, but would need all the help I could get from him and everyone in the prefecture to make the experiment successful. He assured me that I could count on it.

Tokushima

The next morning Jerry and I, each with our families, and Kumagai-san as interpreter took a two-hour train ride to Tokushima, the other prefecture for which I was responsible. It was a protocol visit, designed to introduce me to the officials and local dignitaries with whom I would be dealing.

The mayor of Tokushima greeted us at the station and escorted us to an all-Japanese hotel whose most memorable feature was an aquarium in the toilet.

Jerry and I and Kumagai-san left immediately for lunch with the mayor and Prefecture Governor Kikutaro Hara, leaving our families in the care of one of the mayor's assistants—who took them to a children's park. Hara was a delightful personality, a big man—for a Japanese—in his sixties with a shaven head and a twinkle in his eye. Though he had never traveled abroad he spoke some English, had a keen interest in international business affairs and liked to read *Fortune* and The *New York Times Review of the Week*. He preferred riding his bicycle to work rather than using his official car, telling people he was out "checking the roads."

In the evening the mayor took Jerry, Kumagai and me to a "men only" geisha party where our hosts inveigled us into singing American folk songs. Since I had just come from Venezuela I was easily persuaded into demonstrating Latin American culture in the form of a mambo dance with an accomplished hostess. The audience, judging from their reaction, was not disappointed.

The next day we all returned to Takamatsu, the Novicks and Kumagais went back to Kobe, and I was on my own in Shikoku.

Getting Settled

Getting my family settled in our own home was my first concern. The Kawaroku was enjoyable, but too expensive and unsuited for conducting my official representation duties. Eventually we would move into the house that the prefecture government had identified for me, but not until the U.S. Government lease had been approved and it had been remodeled to suit our western needs.

We had been in Takamatsu two weeks when out of the blue came an invitation from an obstetrician and his wife, Dr. and Mrs. Toshio Ishihara who were friends of the JACC, to stay in their guest house. Their children had flown the nest, they said, and we could stay with them until we found something more permanent. We accepted gratefully. It was a Japanese style house with a garden that Margaret and Betsy enjoyed immensely. The Ishiharas were gracious hosts, and we became close friends. At the end of September we moved into a large western style house loaned to us by an American Baptist missionary family who were going to Hokkaido for two months.

By this time we had acquired a Japanese housekeeper, Eiko-san. She had formerly worked for my predecessor, Elaine Boylan, and would cook and also serve as amah for Betsy. Eiko-san spoke English and soon became virtually a member of our family. Margaret was utterly dependent on her for managing our household and helping with our official entertainment responsibilities.

Having our own house, albeit temporary, and a domestic employee, Margaret and I decided to host a reception for our new Japanese friends and their wives, including Governor and Mrs. Kaneko. Nishimura-san drew up a list of about 25 recommended guests, but we were taken aback when he said we should invite them for 4:00 to 6:00 in the afternoon. In Caracas, 8:00 p.m. was the usual hour to invite guests. Even so, people would sometimes arrive at nine or even ten o'clock for dinner and stay until after midnight.

Although we found four o'clock a bit strange for our official reception, we determined to make it American style.

Margaret and Eiko-san set about preparing an assortment of cakes, cookies, and other typical American goodies to serve with tea and coffee. These they spread out on tables, buffet style, so our guests could help themselves. All was ready at the appointed hour, and precisely at four came a knock on the door. I opened it, expecting to welcome our first guest, only to encounter every single person we had invited, many carrying *omiage* (hostess gifts) wrapped in colorful *furoshiki* (large kerchiefs commonly used to carry small items).

The sight of the tables laden with delicacies brought oohs, and aahs from our women guests. At first they were hesitant to help themselves, but with Margaret's and Eiko-san's urging—*"dozo, dozo"*—they moved in, and we soon noticed cookies and slices of cake disappearing into *furoshiki* and handbags. Well before six o'clock every table had been swept clean, hardly a crumb remaining. Then exactly at six, Governor Kaneko thanked us saying they had enjoyed our party. With that our guests departed en masse.

Our first reception had proved enormously successful. Margaret had achieved local fame as a hostess, and we had been launched into the Takamatsu social whirl, such as it was.

On November 15 we moved into our new house on Sakuramachi (cherry blossom street) located opposite the gymnasium of Takamatsu's leading high school and a ten-minute walk from Ritsurin *Koen*[13] (garden), renowned as one of the finest in Japan.

A local banker had built the house for his newly married son, and the newlyweds had lived there less than a year before being transferred to Kochi. It was a lovely place of classical Japanese architecture with both Japanese and Western style gardens. It resembled a Japanese house we had seen on display at the Museum of Modern Art in New York before we left for Japan. The house gave us a unique experience in Japanese living, and our memories of life there remain strong to this day.

Learning Japanese

I had come to Japan without any knowledge of the language,[14] so one of my first moves was to look for a Japanese tutor. Dr. Leighton

---

[13].Ritsurin *Koen* was originally the villa of Lord Matsudaira of Kagawa prefecture. A walk through the carefully manicured classical Japanese garden was a "must" for every tourist visiting Takamatsu. Annual visitors were numbered in the hundreds of thousands. It is still considered one of Japan's best public gardens.

[14] Subsequently, knowledge of Japanese was made a mandatory requirement for all

Brown, a Fulbright professor of American literature at Kagawa University who attended my welcoming reception, recommended one of his students. Shortly thereafter Yoshinori Yokoi, an economics major, appeared at my office. He was modest and unassuming, communicated easily in English, and struck me as being bright and intelligent. I hired him on the spot.[15] From then on, every morning, five days a week for the duration of our stay in Takamatsu, Yokoi-san and I met for an hour's lesson. To call Japanese a difficult language is an understatement. It uses Chinese pictographs, called kanji, which must be memorized, plus two kinds of Japanese phonetics: hiragana for Japanese words for which there are no kanji, and katakana for words of foreign origin. Many foreign words, especially English, have been adapted into the Japanese language and are rendered in katakana, but the Japanese pronunciation of them is frequently unrecognizable to the native English speaker. For me the most difficult aspects of Japanese was learning to speak in phrases as the Japanese do, trying to master the many tenses and the word order, with long sentences ending up in verbs. Because of the latter simultaneous interpreters must invariably remain a sentence or two behind the speaker for whom he/she is translating. By comparison, Chinese word order is quite similar to English; Japanese word order more closely resembles German. Thus, even though Chinese is tonal and Japanese is not, I found Chinese easier to learn than Japanese.

While it is possible to learn the Japanese based on the Roman alphabet (romaji), to become literate one must learn kanji, hiragana, and katakana. The State Department assigns its Japanese language officers to a two-year training period to bring them from zero to an S-3 R-3 rating (S-5 R-5 being bilingual). Upon completion they should be able to read the daily newspapers (that use a high school level Japanese) and conduct routine work activities in the language. Even so Japanese contains so many innuendos that Embassy language officers engaged in delicate negotiations still rely on interpreters. Because my time for study was limited I focused on the study of romaji. I cannot claim to have become proficient, but just before leaving Takamatsu I was interviewed in

---

Center directors.

[15]. Yokoi later obtained a PhD in economics at the University of Chicago and became a distinguished professor of economics at Kagawa University.

Japanese by a local radio station and gave a speech in Japanese at a farewell party.

At Work

My job was to run a cultural center. There was some similarity to what I had been doing in Caracas but not much. In Caracas I had been an information officer, dealing primarily with news media. Here I was to be a cultural affairs officer with few media responsibilities. As I understood it, my job was to help bring American culture to the Japanese hinterland. I encountered an eager audience.

Takamatsu City had been about 90 per cent destroyed during one massive U.S. Air Force firebombing raid on July 4, 1945. Much of the city had been rebuilt but many of the inhabitants, who had lost everything during the war, remained poverty stricken. It was, in fact, a Third-World situation.

With my family settled I focused on developing cultural programs for the Takamatsu Center. People wanted to know what Americans were thinking, why Americans acted as they did, and how they, as Japanese, could get to know the United States and its people better. Much has been written about the psychological aspects of post-war Japanese attitudes toward the United States, but for me in Japan at that time it meant finding a means to convey American culture and a sense of American democracy to people who had accepted the need to align themselves with the nation that had resoundly defeated them in war. Throughout the country the vanquished Japanese were earnestly seeking more information about their American conquerors. My job was to provide it for those in Shikoku as best I could with the resources available.

Besides a library of American books and journals, Kagawa Prefecture had inherited a CIE/USIS documentary film collection and some 20 projectors that were loaned to schools for educational purposes. The books and journals were a prime source for university students researching American economic and cultural subjects. Films on Americana themes produced by USIS Tokyo were used extensively by high schools around the prefecture.

As the American director I was considered the representative and bearer of American culture. Governor Kaneko looked upon me as a means for getting more U.S. oriented materials into that library—more books, more films as well as more visiting artists and speakers on American themes.

My staff of prefecture employees, though very helpful were poorly paid. In fact it was a real hand-to-mouth existence for them. But they were loyal, they worked hard, they accepted my direction, and at the same time they took me in hand and led me through the intricacies of Japanese culture. I was a willing student, and undoubtedly learned more from them than they did from me.

As a Provincial Public Affairs Officer I reported directly to the RPAO in Kobe—first Jerry Novick and later, beginning in 1956, Clifton Forster. The regional office channeled what support it could to provincial posts in its jurisdiction, but it was our job to work up our own programs.

The program support—visiting lecturers and artists—we received from Kobe and Tokyo was important and constituted the more prestigious aspect of our cultural activities. Nevertheless, I found it insufficient to satisfy the demand for contacts with Americans. Therefore, I made a point of associating the Center and myself with community service organizations such as the Rotary Club where I learned to sing the Rotary anthem, "Oh Rotarian," and responding to frequent requests for talks about the United States. In these activities Nishimura-san and I constituted ourselves into a team, frequently supported by Margaret and Helen Kimura.

Here I should make a point about cross-cultural communications with Japanese audiences. They know their language is difficult, and they do not expect foreigners to be able to speak or understand it. In fact, they are often surprised if a foreigner speaks to them in Japanese. Thus, it seemed quite natural for me to speak through an interpreter, Nishimura-san not only rendered my words into Japanese, but also did it in a context they understood and were comfortable with. The same held true for Margaret speaking through Helen Kimura. We were keenly aware that the vast majority of our audiences were unable to understand our words, only those of our interpreters; therefore we paid close attention to our body language, making every effort to insure that it conveyed the desired meaning.

Many requests came from schools to lend an American presence. Sometimes it was to give a talk on American life or judge a fashion show. More often, though, it was to judge an English speaking contest between schools where students recited passages they had memorized.

At first I was surprised, but later only amused to find, on congratulating the winners, that no matter how good their presentations they could not understand spoken English.

Kagawa schools were never heated and always seemed cold, even in the summer. In winter they were freezing. Custom forbade wearing shoes on their bare wooden floors. Schoolchildren wore straw sandals; but we visitors were given slippers, always too small for my feet but useful for jokes about big footed Americans.

Not having an official car at the time, we got around in my personal car. It had reached Takamatsu shortly after our arrival. Negotiating Shikoku's one-lane dirt roads built for the three-wheeled Japanese motorcycle truck (called bata-bata for the noise it made) was a trial in itself. When I bought that oversized Pontiac station wagon in New Orleans I had no idea that Shikoku roads would be so narrow. Somehow we managed, but it was not unusual, as I rounded a tight corner, for the rear wheel to slip off into a ditch. We got the wheel out by jacking up the rear end of the car and shoving it off the jack toward the center of the road.

My teammate, Nishimura-san, was slightly over five feet tall, a waif of a man with a good Japanese education, an excellent command of English, and a bountiful supply of common sense. Even though he had served with the Japanese army in Manchuria during the war, he was a very unmilitary man. He was an economist by training but also had an abiding interest in many fields. He was widely read in American and English literature and highly literate in Japanese contemporary and classical works. He served as my teacher in things Japanese, my interpreter and cultural bridge to the people of Shikoku. He was even able to interpret my rather poor jokes and make people laugh.[16] As head of the JACC prefecture staff Nishimura-san enjoyed the confidence of the governor and good rapport with members of the Kagawa government bureaucracy. English teachers, in particular, greatly admired him and frequently came to him for advice and assistance in their profession.

---

[16] A recurring story about a visiting American fireman has him telling a long, complicated joke. His interpreter, rather than try to repeat it, simply told the audience he had told a joke and asked them to laugh. They did so heartily, much to the visitor's delight. I am blissfully unaware whether this ever happened to me.

Emiko (Helen) Kimura—everybody called her Helen—was an American-born Japanese whose parents had lived Conway, Washington, but had returned to Japan when she was fifteen years old, shortly before World War II. She had been the chief librarian under the CIE/SCAP program, spoke colloquial American English and was gifted with boundless energy and a heart as good as gold. Her American background led the Japanese, especially women, to look upon her as a go-between with Americans in the community. The Americans (a very small group of missionaries), likewise, relied heavily on her for guidance in dealing with their Japanese counterparts. Helen was instrumental in forming the Takamatsu International Women's Club, to which Margaret belonged, and was the pivotal person in JACC contacts with Japanese women.

The other members of my initial staff were Akira Yamada who handled our administrative and financial matters and lived with his wife and son in the back of the building; and three librarians: Fukuzo (Peter) Hosokawa, a gentle caring person whose special talent was bookbinding; Yoshio Kawaguchi, music and book librarian; Sumie Torii, our unpaid volunteer whom I was later able to hire; and Choichi Oki, half-time janitor. Eventually USIS gave me a jeep and money to hire a driver, Shozo Aoki, who doubled as a film projectionist and worked primarily in Takamatsu City.

Cultural Programs

At first USIS Kobe and USIS Tokyo sent few programs my way. Later, Cliff Forster worked out an arrangement for sending distinguished Japanese scholars around the region to lecture on Japanese-American relations. The speakers he chose, already well known from their published writings, seldom got to out-of-the-way Shikoku. They drew important audiences to our center and added to our prestige.

Visiting artists from the United States were a rarity. Those who did come were given a warm welcome. One of the more memorable was Tom Two Arrows, a Native American who performed Indian folk dances, a real novelty for our Shikoku audience who knew about American Indians only through Hollywood's cowboy and Indian movies. Another was John Sebastian, a harmonica player. He made an impact for a very special reason. In the immediate post-war era the prefecture was trying to re-establish music education in its schools, but they had few musical instruments to work with. Governor Kaneko persuaded the school board to equip the schools with inexpensive harmonicas so that each school was able to form its own children's harmonica orchestra. When John Sebastian came to town playing both classical music and well-known Stephen Foster folk songs on the harmonica, teachers and children alike met him with an outpouring of enthusiasm. The schools brought out all their students to hear him and then reciprocated with a children's harmonica concert. Sebastian was touched and so was I.

Glen Shaw

One person who came to Takamatsu on several occasions was Glen Shaw, the American Embassy's cultural attaché and, incidentally, a relative of Margaret's by marriage. Glen was a cultural treasure for the United States as well as for Japan. His mastery of the Japanese culture had earned him the title of "Living Cultural Treasure" of Japan. Glen had first gone to East Asia in 1913 on a trip to China, Korea and Japan, paying his way by teaching English in each country. He liked Japan best and taught in Osaka for a year. In 1916 he went back to his native Colorado, married Reba Hood and returned with her to teach in Yamaguchi prefecture on the western end of Honshu. There he immersed himself thoroughly in Japanese language, literature and culture. Within a few years he had mastered them sufficiently to translate Japanese literary works into English and to serve as a columnist for the *Asahi Shimbun*, one of Japan's leading newspapers.

Glen left Japan in 1940 when it became obvious that short of a miracle, war was inevitable. Returning to Colorado, he taught Japanese at the U.S. Navy language school at the University of Colorado in Boulder using the same techniques he had employed to teach himself the language. Many of his students, including Robert A. Scalapino with whom I was later to work at UC Berkeley's Institute of East Asian Studies, would become distinguished Japan scholars. The University of Colorado awarded Shaw a doctorate in literature. Nine years after leaving Japan he returned to work with the Department of State, first with a historical project microfilming documents, then as cultural attaché of the American Embassy, his position when we arrived in 1955.[17]

---

[17]. *Asahi Evening News*, May 18, 21, 1957, "Dr. Shaw Returning to U.S. after 47 Years in the East," a biographical account of Shaw's Japan experience based on an interview by Alfred Smoular; *English Mainichi*, June 17, 1957, "Little Portrait of Big Man" by Burton E. Martin.

Glen was a tall, gangling six-feet-six, fully a foot taller than even a relatively tall Japanese of his era. His legendary sense of humor, often turned on himself, captivated individuals and audiences alike and helped bridge the communications gap with the Japanese. His first visit to Takamatsu during our stay was to help inaugurate a statue of the writer Kikuchi Kan, a native son of Takamatsu and one of Japan's leading novelists of the 1930s whose plays and poems Glen had translated into English.

After the statue ceremony in the center of Takamatsu, Governor Kaneko took Glen and Reba and Margaret and me on a trip around Kagawa prefecture, stopping at sites of particular interest—a fish farm, a pearl growing industry, temples, and spots of scenic beauty. The Japanese like to have their guests sign visitors' registers and Glen would compose a haiku (a 17 syllable Japanese poem, usually on nature) for each occasion. At one spot, the Kotohiki Park overlooking the Inland Sea, he wrote, in Japanese:

"I throw away my pen and leave it to the wind in the pines."

He signed the haiku with a brush profile of himself.

When Glen boarded the overnight ferry for Kobe, Governor Kaneko asked, "Dr. Shaw, how are you going to fit your lanky self into that small sleeping compartment?"

"Well," Glen replied, "I'm just going to curl up like a snake and sleep all the way to Kobe."

Glen returned later for a series of lectures on American literature and culture that packed our JACC auditorium with capacity audiences.

English Teaching Programs

English teachers in rural Shikoku rarely had opportunities to talk with native speakers of English, and it showed. Many came to visit me at the JACC just to have a chance to practice. Some of them spoke so poorly I could hardly understand them, and they had equal or greater difficulty understanding me. I pitied their students. Unfortunately, Japanese universities had long emphasized the study of written English using classical texts such as Shakespeare, rather than teaching modern spoken English. The system propagated itself so that the Japanese gained the unenviable reputation of being the world's worst speakers of English.[18] Margaret and I enjoyed working with the teachers as a group

---

18. In recent years the Japanese government has conducted an energetic campaign to

and taking part in their social occasions where everyone was obliged to speak in English. In the process I even learned to cook sukiyaki.

The JACC enjoyed a close rapport with the English Teachers Association of Shikoku. Besides providing them up-to-date teaching materials, we brought in Fulbright teachers of English to conduct seminars and give teaching demonstrations at the JACC and in their individual schools.

Our first Fulbright English teacher, Fae Morris, was the most memorable. She had come down from Tokyo and I met her at the pier.

"Got any horse thieves in your family?" she asked with a strong Texas accent.

"None that I like to talk about," I replied, wondering what she was getting at.

"Well, I just wanted to know before I claimed kin to you. My maiden name was Kendall, and I come from Kendall County, Texas."

We didn't find any close family connections, but I had studied about her grandfather, George Kendall, when I was an undergraduate journalism student at LSU. He was the founder of the New Orleans Picayune and had been a war correspondent during the War with Mexico before settling in Texas where the county was named after him. Fae conducted several well-attended seminars for the Kagawa prefecture teachers of English. She was received with such enthusiasm that the Fulbright Commission in Tokyo sent a team of five teachers to Takamatsu to conduct a three-day series of lecture-demonstrations.

Japan-America Forums

One winter day in 1955, Nishimura-san and I were driving back to Takamatsu following an official visit to Tokushima. It was cold, the roads were rough, and we were both badly in need of something to warm us up. We stopped for coffee at the only cafe in Anabuki, a mountain village at the prefecture border. The coffee was terrible, but it was hot. We had hardly finished our first grimace when the cafe owner

---

improve English ability in its schools by employing young American university graduates as high school teachers of English. Recruitment is handled through Japanese diplomatic establishments in the United States. Many young people specializing in Japanese studies have taken advantage these teaching jobs to strengthen their Japanese language capabilities.

asked if I was an American, a rarity in those parts. With my affirmative nod he began a bombardment of questions on everything from American attitudes toward the Korean conflict to sex and marriage in the American society. A man with a vision larger than his business indicated, he complained that the people of his town—the mayor, the school teachers, and many others—were eager for contact with Americans from whom they could learn more about the United States. His questions matched those I had encountered in earlier discussions with my Japanese contacts, and I found that I could handle them just as well as any lecturer who might be riding the USIS circuit.

Continuing our journey to Takamatsu, Nishimura-san and I hit upon the idea of holding a series of Japan-America Forums with community leaders around Shikoku in which I could respond to whatever questions they might have about the American people and U.S. policies in Japan. The forums would need no outside resources that were not very abundant anyway. Margaret and I would be the principals with Nishimura-san serving as interpreter and interlocutor. We wouldn't even need approval from Kobe or Tokyo since we would be operating in my territory of Kagawa and Tokushima prefectures. By the time we got home we had worked out a program of action.

Over the next year and a half we held many of these forums in my two prefectures as well as in Ehime and Kochi. Working with prefecture and town officials Nishimura-san organized the meetings, each lasting about two hours, with local intelligencia—usually high school teachers, principals, or professionals. On trips around Shikoku lasting two or three days each we met twice daily with groups in schools or town halls over tea and cakes and talked about things American and Japanese. At each session I made a few introductory remarks and then we opened ourselves to questions on whatever might be on their minds. The groups were almost unanimously friendly. Most wanted to know about American customs. The women invariably asked Margaret questions about American family life. One even asked: "How is it possible for you to get away from your family to come on this trip with your husband?"

Margaret's reply pleased them. "I have a very reliable Japanese housekeeper. I would trust my daughter with her any time and any place."

More significantly they touched on such topics as American education, local government financing, social security for the elderly, and the conduct of American soldiers in Japan. They also wanted to know about attitudes toward marriage and the family (One asked, "Is chastity important in American marriage?") birth control, youth and community organizations, among many others. None of the questions were particularly hard to handle, but they showed a keen interest in and curiosity about the nation that had conquered them. The forums took us all over Shikoku during varying seasons of the year. One memorable spot was the town of Hiwasa, surely at the end of the earth, where we were assailed by a swarm of gigantic insects and forced to take refuge behind mosquito nets.

On only one occasion did we encounter hostile questions. It happened in Tokushima prefecture where a communist youth organization had made racism in the United States a public issue. We were going through our usual routine, answering questions about education and schooling, and after each exchange one or more of a group of young men would say, "Well, what about the people in Alabama? What about Selma? What about discrimination against the Negro?"

This was during the period of the civil rights struggle in the South. Martin Luther King's civil rights demonstrations and sit-ins were being fiercely repulsed, and the news media gave the communists more than ample ammunition to challenge American style democracy. Since we could not ignore the questions I tried to respond to them as factually as possible.

After some time I said, "Well, you know, we are not alone. Racism is not confined to any one country. You have problems with it right here in this country with the Eta.[19] They do not enjoy the rights of other Japanese citizens."

I thought I had scored with that remark; but later Nishimura-san said to me, "You know, I didn't translate that bit about the Eta. It wouldn't have done any good and may even have antagonized the audience. They've got an Eta village right in this town."

Nevertheless, despite this rare, negative heckling, our Japan-America forums proved to be one of our most valuable and memorable experiences in Shikoku. Our conviction of their value was confirmed by the women's editor of the *Birmingham News*, Miriam G. Hill, who was studying the role of women in Japan on a Niemann Fellowship. Shikoku

---

[19]. Also known as *burakumin*—people who work with leather and dead animals.

was on her itinerary so we invited her to take part in one of the forums. She made the event the subject of a lengthy article in her newspaper, writing of how well she had been impressed by questions that village young people asked her. Later, on our return to the United States, the Birmingham News gave a dinner in our honor.

Governor Kaneko Visits the United States

My most important long-term achievement in Takamatsu was the awarding of a USIS "leader grant" to Governor Kaneko. Under that program, now called "international visitors," USIS invited promising local and national leaders to visit the United States for a first-hand view of American society and to gain a better understanding of how the country functions. Invitees generally took the opportunity to look for solutions to problems in their own communities. Until that time it had been against USIS Japan policy to award leader grants to Japanese government officials. But because Kaneko was such an unusual person our Embassy agreed to make an exception in his case. The Governor's staff gave him a long list of items to study on his trip.

Kaneko toured the United States for three months and then went to Brazil for another two weeks to visit Kagawans who had migrated there in the immediate postwar years. He described his travels and observations in frequent cards and letters published in the Kagawa Shimbun, the local newspaper. An example:

"While I was in New York I visited the villa of President Theodore Roosevelt at Oyster Bay, Long Island, in the suburbs of New York. He was the mediator at the Portsmouth Treaty ending the Russo-Japanese War, and the Japanese people cannot forget his contribution toward better relations between Japan and America. The neighboring coast reminded me of the scenery of the Seto Inland Sea."

In helping Kaneko plan the trip, I recommended that he visit the University of North Carolina at Chapel Hill and gave him names of several professors he would find it useful to talk with, especially Gordon Blackwell who specialized in sociology of the community. I also hinted that while in Chapel Hill he might pay a call on Margaret's mother. A consummate politician, Kaneko seized on the opportunity to personalize the occasion and visited Mrs. Munch and Margaret's sister who was at home on vacation. They were delighted. The Governor wrote Margaret and me from Chapel Hill's Carolina Inn and enclosed "a lily of the valley petal that I picked from beside your mother's home."

Kaneko returned to Takamatsu brimming over with new ideas for improving the quality of life in his prefecture. Most significant was his conviction that Shikoku could end its history of isolation from the Japanese mainland by building a bridge across the Inland Sea.

In recounting the occasion he told me that ever since he was a boy he had a vision of a bridge across the Seto Nai Kai. But he had never imagined that Japan would be able to build such a structure until he saw those magnificent bridges over the Golden Gate, the Oakland-San Francisco Bay and New York's Verrazano Narrows. As he stood there looking at the Golden Gate Bridge he said to himself, if the Americans can do it, we can too.

Shortly after returning from his visit to the United States Kaneko began a campaign to get his dream bridge built. Eventually his idea was picked up on a national level and developed into three bridges connecting Shikoku with the Japanese mainland. Insofar as Kaneko was concerned, the most important was the one linking Okayama on Honshu to Kagawa Prefecture near Takamatsu.

Margaret and I were pleased to attend the inauguration of the Seto Ohashi (Great Seto Bridge) on April 8, 1988. Unfortunately, Kaneko was in the hospital at the time and could not attend the ceremonies, but he still reveled in the glory of the occasion. While the bridge is undoubtedly ending Shikoku's isolation it will probably change the rural nature of Shikoku forever. Nevertheless, Kaneko felt his dream had finally been accomplished and he gave me full credit for helping him to realize it.

Kaneko's visit to the United States also inspired him to other achievements. One of the more interesting grew out of his visit to a Frank Lloyd Wright museum in Wisconsin. It resulted in a Kagawa art museum based on Wright's concept of designing architecture to meld in with the landscape.

In New York, Governor Kaneko met Isamo Noguchi, the Japanese-American sculptor, since deceased. On seeing some of Noguchi's stone sculptures Kaneko told him that Kagawa had some very fine stonecutters, but said all they were doing was making gravestones. He invited Noguchi to Takamatsu, and today there is a very fine studio a few miles from that city producing artistic sculptures along the lines taught them by Noguchi. One of these presides at the entrance to the Bank of America headquarters in San Francisco. With these lasting intercultural exchanges in mind, I hope I can be forgiven for the sense of pride I feel about my work in Shikoku.

Governor Kaneko died in 1996. On hearing of his passing I wrote his widow. The governor's son, responding to my letter on behalf of his mother, said he still had fond remembrances of attending a Christmas party at our home when he was ten years old.

The Matsuyama ACC

For about six months, besides running the Takamatsu Center, I also served as interim director of the American Cultural Center in Matsuyama pending the arrival of a new director to replace one who had been transferred. The Center had a competent Japanese staff, but U.S. government regulations required that a USIS officer approve all program expenditures—including local salaries. This meant that twice a month I spent several days in Matsuyama supervising that operation.

The Takamatsu-Matsuyama trip took four hours by train, pulled by a coal burning locomotive that spread its dust indiscriminately over the passengers. On arrival I always needed a bath to wash off the coal dust. The Center's studio apartment where I stayed had no bath so as soon as I had checked in I headed for the Dogo Hot Springs for a good soak in the mineral waters, always a pleasant experience. The hot springs, operated by the city of Matsuyama, have been in existence since the early 1300s and are among the oldest in Japan. Once in the countryside, the facility is now completely surrounded by the city and stands on a busy urban intersection. On occasions when I had to escort American visitors on USIS programs I stayed with them in a Japanese ryokan in the Dogo area, an expense I could afford in the days when the exchange was 360 yen to the dollar. In the evening a maid would come to your room to take your order for breakfast the next morning. It didn't matter what you ordered, their concept of an American breakfast was always ham and eggs and that's what you got. One night, returning from an evening on the town with a visitor, we stuck our heads in the kitchen and spotted our breakfast ham and eggs all cooked and ready to be served the next morning. My visitor's comment: "Very efficient, these Japanese." My commutes ended when Bernard Dekle arrived to take charge of the Matsuyama ACC. The fact that Bernie and I had both worked as reporters for the *Charlotte Observer* gave us a common bond that served us well for the remainder of my Shikoku assignment.

Helping Out

Since I was the only American public official in Takamatsu Japanese private citizens and public functionaries who needed help from the United States Government would come to me as their first point of contact. I do not believe it immodest to relate several ways I lent my Japanese hosts a helping hand that proved quite useful in promoting their economic interests in tourism, trade and agriculture.

Kagawa Prefecture has many attractions, both natural and man-made. To anyone approaching Takamatsu by ferry, the Tamamo castle on the city's shore suggests antiquity mingled with modernity. The city itself, rebuilt entirely after the war, is laid out in an inviting, people-friendly fashion. Yashima, a flat-topped mountain a few miles from Takamatsu, offers a scenic overview of the Inland Sea's many small islands that play an important role of Japan's folklore. A stroll along Yashima's pathways helps to visualize the historic 13th century battle between the Genji and Heike clans that put the winning Genji in control of the region for several centuries to come. Ritsurin Koen, mentioned earlier, is unsurpassed among Japan's world famous gardens. Shodo Island with its spectacular Inland Sea scenery, its olive groves and Mediterranean atmosphere would delight any visitor.

Thus, boosting tourism became one of the prefecture government's major economic goals. Kagawa was doing well with the Japanese tourism but had little or no means for appealing to foreign tourists. Their solution was to publish an English language tourist brochure. A Japanese English teacher translated their standard tourist handout, and the director of tourism asked me to "brush up the English." A quick perusal proved the "Japenglish" to be almost unintelligible. I rewrote the text from scratch and in the process learned a great deal about Kagawa.

On another occasion Masatoyo Irimajiri, the Kagawa prefecture chief of agriculture, appealed to me for help in getting access to American sugar beet technology to expand local sugar beet production. What he needed was an assortment of seeds that he could use in finding a variety suited to local soil and climate conditions. He had neither contact with the American sugar beet industry nor dollars to purchase the seeds because of the finance ministry's tight controls. Could I, he asked, help out? This activity was not exactly part of my job description, but with the assistance of the Embassy's agricultural attaché in Tokyo, I obtained a list of American seed houses, wrote directly to them, sent them my personal check, and got him his beet seeds. Of course he reimbursed me in yen, but he used the seed very diligently and was able to improve the prefecture's beet production. On various occasions he invited me to his agricultural experiment station to demonstrate his progress. Naturally, I was pleased and felt rewarded for my efforts. We have heard from Mr. and Mrs. Irimajiri at Christmas every year since then, more than 40 years.

Not long after the sugar beet exercise Governor Kikutaro Hara of Tokushima sent two of his forestry specialists to seek my assistance in expanding that prefecture's lumber production through the introduction of new varieties of pine. I repeated the process I had followed with the sugar beet seeds and got the Tokushima foresters the seeds they needed. When I was preparing to leave Takamatsu in 1957, the governor sent his representatives over to Takamatsu with a replica of the typical Tokushima dance—the Awa Odori—done with bamboo figurines encased in a glass box, a fine souvenir that Margaret and still I treasure.

During my second year in Shikoku our Embassy informed me that they were sending a commercial trade mission to Shikoku to meet with Japanese businessmen and government trade officials. They asked me to organize discussion meetings in Ehime and Kagawa prefectures. I enlisted the assistance of the two prefecture governors who responded enthusiastically and engaged their most important local business leaders in the two sessions with the U.S. mission members. The purpose, almost laughable today, was to teach the Japanese how to export to the United States. One might say we were talking when we should have been listening, but the mission was designed to fulfill the American policy of helping the Japanese get back on their economic feet. They learned their lesson well, perhaps too well.

In the years since we left Shikoku the island has changed from being an area of poverty stricken, backwater prefectures to a very prosperous island. When Margaret and I return to Takamatsu—and we have done so several times—we find that our friends, the people we worked with so many years ago still remember us. I like to think it is because we were able to contribute something when they needed it most.

Community Relations

Margaret and I lived a high profile existence in Takamatsu. As director of the Japan-American Cultural Center, the local media and community organizations looked to me for answers to their legitimate questions about the United States as well as to satisfy their curiosity about how Americans lived and their attitudes toward Japan. Their curiosity was insatiable but not intrusive. We looked upon it as a means to promote the cultural center and to further good Japanese-American relations.

A year after our arrival the Shikoku Shimbun asked me to pen a few thoughts about our life in Takamatsu. In the article I sketched out some aspects of life in Takamatsu that we enjoyed. They included "the magnolias of Ritsurin Park glistening with the pearls of a spring rain; the manicured Japanese countryside, spring, summer, fall and winter," and concluded with this thought.

"Most of all we like to feel that we have become members of this community since our arrival here a year ago. We have perhaps received more than our share of hospitality, but we like to think it is directed not only to us, but to all Americans."

We played a vigorous role in the community life of Takamatsu, both with the activities described above as well as the many others we initiated or were invited to take part in. Somehow many of these events made their way into the local newspaper. Some examples: A Christmas party for the children of our JACC staff with the local Mainichi Shimbun correspondent playing Santa Claus; Betsy's presentation (with paternal urging) of flowers to Governor Kaneko on his departure for the United States, and even her attendance at a Japanese kindergarten; visiting a Japanese shrine as a family, all three of us dressed in kimonos; accompanying Governor Kaneko to greet prefecture employees on New Year's day; dancing the Awa Odori in the streets of Tokushima during the August harvest festival; weekly English conversation classes for university students at our home; Margaret's classes for Kawaroku Hotel employees on how to set a table and make a bed western style, and her participation in a fashion show dressed in maternity clothes.

One event was particularly touching. In the summer of 1956 Ambassador John Allison received a letter from Chigusa Ishikawa, a 13-year old girl in Kochi saying that her father, a village chief, was dying of cancer. She implored the Ambassador to send some American medicine to save her father's life. Rather than trying to explain by letter that no such medicine existed, the Ambassador asked me to go to Kochi and extend his sympathies to the girl and her family, which I did. Chigusa's father was on his deathbed and succumbed shortly thereafter. On hearing from Chigusa of his death, I sent her a round trip rail ticket and invited her to come to Takamatsu and spend ten days with my family as

59

Betsy's guest. The Mainichi Shimbun carried a photo of Chigusa, Betsy and me together with an account of what had happened.

Nancy

Unquestionably our most important family event during our stay in Takamatsu was the arrival of our second child on November 24, 1956. Cliff Forster, our Regional Public Affairs Officer in Kobe, and his wife graciously invited Margaret to stay at their home until the baby arrived so she could be under the care of an English speaking (Canadian) obstetrician at the Yodogawa Christian Hospital in nearby Osaka. Nancy, whom we named after Mrs. Forster, was an immediate hit with Eiko-san, our housekeeper, who took charge of caring for her on the many occasions when Margaret was involved in the Center's activities. After we left Japan Eiko-san married and named her own daughter Nancy.

Sayonara

Takamatsu was a two-year post. In September 1957 my tour would be up. At mid-year word came that USIS was undergoing another budget reduction and would have to close one of its centers. Despite USIS Tokyo's expressed satisfaction with my work and an earlier commitment to continue its support of the JACC, the Takamatsu center was going to get the axe.

The budget cut came about at the hands of Lyndon B. Johnson, then Senate Majority Leader, as a reaction to some rather indiscreet remarks about the Democrats made by Arthur Larson. In late 1956 in a speech to the Young Republicans Club in Honolulu shortly before President Eisenhower appointed him Director of USIA, Mr. Larson remarked that during the 20-year Democratic regime the United States government had been under an alien influence. He asserted that the new Eisenhower administration would correct that situation. Senate Majority Leader Lyndon Johnson, who was also nominal chairman of the committee that controlled State and USIA appropriations, took Larson to great task the first time he appeared before that committee[20]. USIA suffered a budget cut of more than 25 percent.

---

[20]. Larson had not yet been confirmed when he made the Honolulu speech, but his nomination was public knowledge. Though Lyndon Johnson seldom attended hearings, he made a point of being on hand for Larson's meeting with the Senate

The fact that I was due for home leave in September made it administratively easier for USIA and USIS Tokyo to close out my post. They could simply give me home leave and transfer, a standard Foreign Service procedure. But explaining the closure of the post was a bit more difficult. To make it easier for me, I was instructed to say nothing about closing the post, only that I was being transferred. After my departure Cliff Forster visited Takamatsu and informed Governor Kaneko that the Center was being closed.

The closure of my center hurt to the quick. I felt I had held up my end of the bargain with USIA by doing my "damndest" to make the Takamatsu experiment work; but I had been let down, even if unintentionally, by my superiors in Tokyo and in Washington. Nevertheless, I was compensated by my new assignment to Madrid. Joe McEvoy, my former PAO in Caracas, then USIS director in Madrid, had heard that I would be available for reassignment and asked USIA that I be sent to fill a position open on his staff. So the Agency, in effect, made me an offer I could not refuse.

At the end of two years in Takamatsu I could look back and say with confidence that I had made a difference. The programs I had been able to bring to Shikoku, the resonations from Governor Kaneko's visit to the United States, plus my own personal grass roots efforts had made a useful contribution to the total United States endeavor.

The day after we left Takamatsu the English language Mainichi, published in Osaka, carried a column entitled "Creator of Friends." The writer said: "The one-million people of Kagawa Prefecture, Shikoku have lost—at least physically—one of their most beloved American friends, Harry H. Kendall and his family. Kendall (who) won the hearts of the people of Kagawa and its neighbor Tokushima through his devotion to duty for the past two years, his far-reaching cultural promotion projects and his pleasing personality as well, yesterday left Takamatsu for good (for assignment) in Madrid, Spain."

Governor Kaneko gave us a farewell party, attended by some 150 people, and presented me with an album of photographs of our many activities in Kagawa Prefecture. Inside the front cover, face-to-face, were photos of the Governor and myself. I made a farewell speech in

---

appropriations committee. His greeting to Larson: "Mr. Larson, we have been waiting a L O N G time for your appearance."

Japanese, trying to be as lighthearted as possible. I had written it in English; Nishimura-san translated it into Romaji and helped me practice. I was pleased that my audience understood what I had to say.

A huge crowd of people came to the Takamatsu pier to see us off. I can still visualize the mass of colorful streamers between the pier and the ferry as we pulled away to the tune of "Auld Lang Syne."

It was a tearful time. Our beloved Eiko-san accompanied us to Tokyo and looked after our two children while Margaret and I enjoyed some of the sights there before abandoning Japan for Spain. When we checked in at Haneda Airport for our departure we were surprised and delighted to encounter Governor Kaneko, there to say one last goodbye.

Later that year, in our annual Christmas letter, we wrote: "The people of Takamatsu gave us a heart filling sayonara when we left on September 2, two years after we had arrived. In their wonderful Japanese fashion they had made us feel as though our work there had been really and truly appreciated. We deeply regretted that there was no one coming to replace us. Our Japanese friends gave us many omiage (souvenirs) to help us remember Japan, but the one we shall always treasure is the memory of their warm and unrestrained friendship, particularly that of Governor and Mrs. Kaneko and the JACC staff."

On to Madrid

We made the return trip across the Pacific in a lumbering Boeing Stratocruiser from Tokyo to Wake Island, to Honolulu and then to San Francisco. It was a marvelous airplane with a bar in its belly. It took 17 hours to make the trip that today's jets make in eight or nine, but we enjoyed every minute of it. From Oakland we took a train across country, stopping in St. Louis and Indianapolis to visit Margaret's brothers Ralph and John. In Indianapolis we bought a 1957 Ford Fairlane to replace the Pontiac station wagon we had sold in Takamatsu, then drove on to Washington for consultation and thence to North Carolina and Louisiana to visit our respective families before leaving for our new assignment in Spain.

On New Year's Day 1957 the author, Mrs. Kendall and their daughter Betsy donned traditional Japanese dress to visit Takamatsu's Hachiman Shrine.

The author's official residence in Takamatsu. (Block print by Margaret Kendall.)

Kagawa Prefecture Governor Masanori Kaneko, the author and Mrs. Kendall commemorate Arbor Day by planting a tree.

Japan-America Forum: The author, Mrs. Kendall and Kaoru Nishimura of the Japan America Cultural Center discussed issues of common interest with community leaders at meetings such as this throughout Shikoku.

A Takamatsu radio reporter, left, interviews Mrs. Kendall on her life in Japan. Helen Kimura of the Takamatsu Japan America Cultural Center serves as interpreter.

Kagawa Governor Kaneko, leaving for a visit to the United States on a State Department Leader Grant, gets a bon voyage bouquet from the author's daughter Betsy.

Creator Of Friends

THE 1-million people of Kagawa Prefecture, Shikoku, this week have lost—at least, physically—one of their most beloved American friends, Dr. Harry H. Kendall and his family.

Kendall, Provincial Public Affairs Officer, who has won the hearts of the people of Kagawa and of its neighbor Tokushima through his devotion to duty for the past two years, his far-reaching cultural promotion projects and his pleasing personality as well, yesterday left Takamatsu for good.

As the author departs Japan for a new assignment The English Mainichi calls him a "Creator of Friends."

IV MADRID - Harry's Traveling Circus

"De Madrid al Cielo"[21]

(Popular Spanish saying)

Five days after we arrived in Spain I already felt myself a *Madrileno*. In a letter home I wrote:

"The air is clear and pure, the sun warm and friendly. The city is clean and attractive, big city sounds muted. Light traffic moves smoothly along wide boulevards. Paseos and sidewalk cafes invite an evening stroll. The language is musical and comprehensible to my ears. People seem pleased to hear this blue eyed foreigner speak an acceptable Spanish."

Jack Higgins and his wife Tui met us at the Madrid airport and escorted us to our temporary quarters at the Commodore hotel on Plaza Argentina, a short distance from the American Embassy. This would be our home until our effects arrived from Japan and we could move into something more permanent. Tui warned Margaret that Madrid social life would be demanding and that she should get someone to help look after the children. We were fortunate. With the help of the Embassy we found an excellent maid almost immediately. Twelve days after we arrived Sabina Chicharro helped us celebrate Nancy's first birthday and remained with us throughout our stay in Spain.

Jack, a gruff former UPI newsman, was USIS Madrid's Information Officer and my immediate supervisor. The morning after our arrival he came by and took me to the Embassy. The weather was brisk and sunny. As we walked along the Paseo de la Castellana (then called Avenida Jose Antonio after a founder of Franco's Falangist Party), Jack filled me in on several aspects of a Madrid assignment to which we would have to adjust. Embassy office hours conformed to the Spanish practice in order to facilitate working with our counterparts. These were 9:00 to 2:00 p.m. with a mid morning break, a two-hour lunch period—usually at home with siesta—followed by an afternoon shift from 4 to 7 p.m. Dinner was

---

21. From Madrid to Heaven

usually at 9 or 10 p.m., but frequent social obligations meant an evening out at official dinners or receptions. Contacts on those occasions, he said, could be even more important than the ones made during the day. It was quite a change from our tranquil evenings at home in Takamatsu.

USIS was located in an annex of the American Embassy, a seven-story rectangular building of stressed concrete built in the early 1950s following post-war normalization of Spanish American relations. Though efficient and attractive from American standards, the building did not blend well into the ornate Spanish architecture of the surrounding neighborhood. Spaniards disdainfully referred to it as "the matchbox," which indeed it did resemble. The official chancery entrance was through the Embassy parking lot at 75 Serrano, a block off the Paseo de la Castellana. Ironically, the USIS entrance, on the opposite side, was through a spacious garden fronting the Paseo itself. Jack explained that the State Department's Foreign Buildings Office had designed and built the Embassy as a combined chancery and ambassador's residence. But when the ambassador arrived to take up residence, his wife refused to live in her "husband's office." Faced with a woman's wrath, the Embassy succumbed and found a new home for its ambassador. State offered the residence to USIS, which gladly accepted and named it the Casa Americana.

USIS Madrid

Joe McEvoy, the USIS director, was expecting me and gave me a strong *abrazo*, Latin America style. At that moment John Turner Reid, the cultural affairs officer, walked in and gave me a similar welcome. It felt like old home week. I had worked under both men in Caracas, first with Reid and then with McEvoy, his successor. Joe came to Madrid as press attaché, but when the former chief of USIS Madrid was transferred to Paris, Ambassador John Davis Lodge asked USIA to appoint Joe as his successor. The Agency had another person in line for the job but acquiesced in the Ambassador's request.

Greetings over, Joe filled me in on the background of current Spanish-American relations and the role USIS played in furthering U.S. policy in the country. I have elaborated somewhat on his briefing in the following paragraphs.

At that time Generalissimo Francisco Franco ruled Spain with an iron hand. He had only contempt for democratic forms of government and made no pretenses about Spain being a democracy. He and his Falangist Party had taken power in 1939 after a bloody three-year civil war that cost a million lives and had been in firm control ever since. Although officially neutral during World War II, Franco's sympathies were with Germany and Italy because the Nazis and the Fascists helped him win the civil war. The fact that the United States maintained diplomatic relations with Spain meant simply that we were dealing with reality as it existed, not that we approved of its government. Many Spaniards intensely disliked Franco and the Falangistas but were very friendly to the United States. It was important that USIS, as the public information arm of the Embassy, respond to the Spanish people's desire for closer relations. As representatives of the United States we were duty bound to portray the positive aspects of American democracy and explain the negative.

The United States Government's primary concern—and hence, the Embassy's—was insuring Spanish collaboration in the operation and maintenance of the U.S. air and naval bases on the Iberian Peninsula as an integral part of the American defense system against Soviet expansionism.

The U.S.-Spain Bases Agreement of 1953 provided for the stationing of our military forces on the Iberian Peninsula. Since Spain was not yet a member of NATO (North American Treaty Organization), the United States had negotiated a separate agreement to extend the European and North American defense perimeter. Under that agreement the United States had established major air bases at Torrejon near Madrid, at Zaragoza in northeastern Spain, at Sevilla in the south plus a Navy base at Rota on the southern coast. Each of these bases had a large contingent of U.S. military personnel and equipment, including highly visible jet fighter aircraft. In addition there were about a dozen aircraft control and warning (AC&W) stations dispersed around the country. It was the responsibility of USIS to put as good a face as possible on the American presence..

USIS worked closely with U.S. military authorities in handling the information aspects of in-country Air Force and Naval operations, cleared all military news releases with the Embassy and channeled those affecting U.S.-Spain relations through the Ministry of Foreign Affairs or the Ministry of Information. The Ministries released them, frequently unchanged, to the news media as official Spanish government information; and the Spanish press dutifully published these releases in their entirety. A joint Embassy-Air Force community relations committee, chaired by the PAO, sought to anticipate public relations problems affecting Spanish-American security relations and to resolve them before they got out of hand. Whenever necessary these issues were taken up with the Spanish government.

In addition to U.S.-Spain military cooperation, the Embassy also conducted a substantial economic aid program designed to strengthen the Spanish economy and further its potential for integration into the European Economic Community. The controlled Spanish press did little or nothing to inform the Spanish public about American economic aid, so USIS assumed responsibility for publicizing these activities. In this effort we worked closely with Milton (Mike) Barall, the Embassy's economic counselor, and Richard Aldrich, director of the U.S. Agency for International Development (AID).

Culturally, government xenophobia and censorship laws had long kept Spaniards intellectually isolated; but these barriers had been relaxed somewhat, and USIS audiences were displaying a strong interest in all aspects of American culture. Nevertheless, strict government control kept access to Spanish media uncertain at best; so USIS used a direct approach to Spanish audiences to handle non-political aspects of our relationships. One means of reaching them was through exhibits and films programs for which I was to be responsible.

USIS exhibits emphasized American culture and U.S. achievements in science and technology, topics very popular with the younger generation, and U.S.-Spain economic cooperation. Whenever possible we placed our exhibits in local fairs to maximize audiences, but the post sometimes organized solo shows such as an atomic energy exhibit that was just being inaugurated. Other means of direct access to audiences were lectures by our cultural officers, Casa Americana libraries, a book program which subsidized translations of American textbooks for sale on the Spanish market, and the films lending program for schools and for showing by a USIS mobile unit operating in provincial areas.

USIS had a good relationship with the Spanish National Radio (Radio Nacional de Espana) network that used our taped programs, primarily music. Spanish TV, just getting started, was using USIS documentary films until they could develop their own production. As films officer I was to develop a close relationship with the director of the Spanish newsreel agency.

I told Joe that my experience in Caracas and in Japan should prove very useful in handling this new assignment.

The USIS Team

USIS had 15 American officers and about 100 Spanish local employees, including those at three branch posts. I was pleased to learn that USIS operated as an integral part of the Embassy under Ambassador John Davis Lodge. Back in Takamatsu I sometimes felt like a one-man band.

As a member of the ambassador's country team, the PAO was responsible to him for the public diplomacy aspect of U.S. operations in Spain. Ambassador Lodge was an activist.[22] He spoke fluent Spanish and liked to be seen and heard in public. His wife, Francesca Braggiotti Lodge, was also publicly oriented. I would have ample opportunity to work with both of them.

In the USIS information branch Jack Higgins, as chief information officer, was responsible for our media output, maintaining contact with news media personnel and for supervising my work in films and exhibits and that of a radio officer. Jack's work in placing our output in the news media was hampered somewhat by the government-controlled press. Except for releases channeled through the government, newspapers seldom published the press releases we sent them. Even so, columnists drew on information contained in the releases, and papers frequently covered local events where the United States was involved.

We had two Embassy press attaches, Owen (Buck) Hutchinson a fellow Louisianan, and Herb Morales, a Puerto Rican. American news agencies and correspondents were well represented in Madrid because of the U.S. military presence, and they required special attention. Buck and Herb also served as speechwriters for the Ambassador who liked to

---

[22]. Lodge was a former governor of Connecticut. He had played lead roles in several Hollywood films, eg. as Marlene Dietrich's lover in "The Scarlet Empress." He was the son of Senator Henry Cabot Lodge (who engineered the Senate's defeat of U.S. membership in the League of Nations) and brother of US/UN Ambassador Henry Cabot Lodge, who later served as ambassador to South Vietnam and was the Nixon's running mate in the 1960 presidential elections. Ambassador Lodge enjoyed entertaining Hollywood personalities, many of who came to Spain to take part in movies filmed in Madrid studios. At one time he boasted of having Moses, Jesus Christ, and Abraham Lincoln all under the same roof.

make his frequent public addresses in Spanish. Herb made sure they were in correct Spanish; he also served as Voice of America correspondent for Spain.

John Reid (subsequently Jacob Canter) and two assistant cultural officers—Richard Phillips and Donald Mulligan—managed cultural activities and educational exchanges between the United States and Spain; later a third cultural officer, Allen Hansen with whom I had worked in Caracas, would be added to manage a book-publishing program.

Jim Drain was head of the local administrative staff. He was to be very helpful to me in running my films and exhibits section.

Branch public affairs officers were attached to three of the four the consulates in Spain: Steve Carney in Barcelona, Jay Castillo in Bilbao and Elmer Dorsay in Sevilla. The Consul in Valencia handled USIS affairs. The branch PAOs reported to the country PAO and coordinated their activities with their consuls. I would be working closely with each of them in field programs.

Finally, we were very fortunate in having highly competent local Spanish employees. I was lucky to have some of the best of them on my staff.

The Spanish Staff

Placido Caldevilla was head of the Spanish language information section. Jack described him as "our most respected local employee." Don Placido, as he was called, shared an office with Claudio Sanz, a translator who also served as a sounding board for Caldevilla's ideas. Like many Spaniards, both had endured severe hardships during the Spanish Civil War. Don Placido personified Spain's tradition for animated conversation and met regularly with his tertulia,[23] a group of friends, for political discussions. He made little effort to conceal his contempt for the Franco regime; but he explained that while the government exercised strict control over what appeared in the media, they did allow people to let off steam through group discussion—so long as it did not appear in the media. We were to spend many hours together talking about the Spanish psyche and the country's historical experience. I am indebted to Don Placido for much of what I learned

[23]. After Tertulian (cc 160-230 A.D.) a Latin church father born in Carthage .

about Spain during our three years in Madrid. USIS was fortunate to have a man of his character in its service.

Antonio Sacristan supervised our external films operation. We were to take many trips around Spain together. Antonio and his wife, Maria Luisa, the PAO's Spanish secretary, formed a USIS husband and wife team. Antonio apologized for his lack of English ability. "No importa," I said, "aqui todos hablamos espanol." (It's doesn't matter. Here we all speak Spanish.) I was grateful for having retained the Spanish I learned in Venezuela, even though it was somewhat marred by a Caraqueno accent. I vowed to refine it with more of a Madrileno enunciation.

My office was located in a partitioned-off section of what would-have-been the ambassadorial dining room. As we approached a slender, attractive woman in her early thirties rose from her desk. Her smile indicated I had been expected.

Mimi Echeverria greeted me with a pronounced Castilian accent. An artist, she designed USIS exhibits and supervised their construction and management. She would also serve as my assistant and secretary. Mimi was the daughter of a Basque civil engineer who had escaped the Spanish civil war by going to Brazil where he helped build that country's railroad network. Although she had grown up in Brazil and spoke Portuguese fluently, she still retained her strong Spanish characteristics. She was to become my mainstay during my tour of duty in Madrid.

Mimi introduced me to the men in the exhibits shop with whom I would develop an intimate working relationship over the next three years. They were Enrique del Campo, our exhibits shop foreman who was much loved by his co-workers (His deep blue eyes and gentle manners charmed Margaret); Julian Montes, equally handsome in coveralls or a caterer's tuxedo that he moonlighted in (he later worked for the film actress Ava Gardner during her Madrid years); Jose "Pepe" Camino, the "gypsy" who played the tambourine and gave life to staff parties; Antonio Rodriguez, tall, quiet and efficient; Ambrosio "El Chino" Wang, a skilled draftsman who gave a professional touch to all of our exhibits; and Jose (the bull) Toro, the invincible truck driver who transported our exhibit materials across the face of Spain dozens of times during my tour of duty. Last, but not least was Jose Maria Garcia Estecha who, studying independently, developed himself into an authority on atomic energy. He gave guided tours at our exhibits, became much in demand as a lecturer, and published a book entitled *El Atomo al servicio de la humanidad* (Atoms at the Service of Mankind).

Antonio Sacristan, with his intimate knowledge of the Spanish provinces and their key officials, complemented the team.

I look back with a justifiable pride on my association with this group of co-workers. Their help and cooperation enabled me to carry out a highly successful series of atomic energy exhibits and "American Weeks" in virtually every Spanish province, thus building bridges of friendship between the people of Spain and the people of the United States.

Settling In

By Christmas we were getting hotel claustrophobia, but since our household effects had still not arrived from Japan we moved into a fourth floor apartment across the street from Madrid's Bernabeu football (soccer) stadium. The apartment was light and airy and relatively quiet except for Sunday afternoons when a hundred thousand screaming Real Madrid fans showed up to cheer on their world champion "futbol" team. We figured we could either watch the games from atop our ten-story building or just not be home on those days. We borrowed a few items of furniture to hold us over, and spent the Christmas holidays getting to know more of Madrid, We particularly enjoyed the Prado, world famous for its collection of Goya, Velasquez, and Murillo paintings, but I got an overdose on a day-long visit and avoided returning for several months. When our household effects and car finally arrived in late January we unpacked and went for a long drive in the countryside. A year later we found a delightful house on the edge of town with a fireplace and an enclosed yard where our children could play in complete safety with minimum supervision. We lived there for the remainder of our three-year Madrid assignment. An unanticipated benefit was a nearby movie studio where we occasionally saw prominent American film stars coming and going and I served as an extra.

Atoms for Peace

I had barely moved into my office when Jack Higgins asked me to accompany him to Zaragoza to attend the opening of a new Atoms for Peace exhibit. The U.S. Air Force base in that city was cosponsoring it with USIS as a community relations project. Arrangements for the exhibit had been completed before my arrival, but since I was to be in charge of future showings Jack thought it desirable that I attend the opening.

We traveled to Zaragoza on December 1, 1957, my 38th birthday and my first trip outside Madrid. I felt a strong sense of the Old World as we drove through nearly 200 miles of Spanish countryside. In between occasional villages I observed herds of sheep grazing on the mountainsides, olive groves laden with ripe fruit ready for harvest, and leafless vineyards whose grapes were already fermenting for the year's new wine crop. At lunch in a small town we sampled the *vino corriente* (table wine) that I found quite delicate and thought better than California table wines (that have improved considerably since I became a Californian!). Irrigation farming near Zaragoza gave the area an appearance of prosperity, but northern winds off the snow-covered Pyrenees chilled the air. In Zaragoza itself remnants of an ancient city wall gave the place a medieval character and reminded me that it was famous as the home of King Ferdinand who married Queen Isabella. Their union led to the ousting of the Moors and the unification of Spain in the same year that Columbus discovered America.

As we pulled into the Zaragoza air base the sight of row after row of USAF jet fighter planes parked along the ramp put an abrupt end to my historical musings. The USIS exhibit we had come to inaugurate reminded me that I was living in the nuclear age.

At the time the world was painfully aware of the destructive power of the atom but knew little of its peaceful potentials. Public attention had focused almost exclusively on the atomic bombs dropped on Hiroshima and Nagasaki during World War II and on our subsequent A-bomb and H-bomb tests at Bikini Island in the Pacific. The Soviet Union's successful A-bomb tests and the ensuing nuclear arms race added to the climate of fear. Meanwhile, American nuclear scientists were beginning to reveal many beneficial uses of the atom, particularly in energy, medicine, and scientific research.

Under President Eisenhower the United States had made a calculated decision to demonstrate America's peaceful intentions by promoting popular understanding of the many ways in which the atom could benefit mankind. At home in the United States the Atomic Energy Commission was taking the lead to educate the public. Abroad, this task was assigned to USIA.

I had attended a USIS Atoms for Peace exhibit in Hiroshima, across the Inland Sea from my last post in Shikoku. While the people of Spain certainly could not compare with the people of Japan in experience with the power of the atom, there was no question that the theme was a popular one. I was delighted to become involved.

The Atoms for Peace exhibit, mounted by our USIS exhibits staff, was somewhat smaller than its counterpart in Japan. Although based primarily on photo panels, it was still impressive. Local VIPs turned out in force. In their opening speeches Ambassador Lodge and the USAF commander in Zaragoza expressed the desire of the United States to share its knowledge of atomic energy with Spain's scientific community. The Spanish base commander responded, welcoming U.S. assistance in scientific and technological as well as defense matters. There was a buffet lunch afterwards, hosted by the Air Force. I was miffed because they served sherry with the meal instead of a good red or white wine—but it was good sherry.

Jack returned to Madrid after the opening. I stayed over in Zaragoza an extra day to pay courtesy calls on local officials with whom I would be working. The Air Force flew me back to Madrid. I felt like a big shot.

In the spring of 1958 USIA Washington sent us a full scale Atoms for Peace exhibit with a realistic working model of an atomic power generator and a set of "magic hands"—remote controls for handling radioactive materials. Ambassador Lodge and the Spanish Minister of Mines inaugurated the exhibit at a major agricultural fair in Madrid. We made a big splash in the national press. ABC, Madrid's leading newspaper, carried a full front-page picture of the opening with me explaining to Spanish officials how the atomic power plant worked. In reality I knew little more than I had read in our brochures; but fortunately they knew even less, and Mr. Estecha was there to answer questions. Posturing made me uncomfortable so in future openings I let him take the limelight. During the exhibit's run in Madrid up to 25,000 people a day passed through our pavilion.

A similar pattern followed in each of Spain's other major cities—Barcelona, Bilbao, Sevilla and Valencia—where we held the exhibit in conjunction with our local Casas Americanas and the American consulates. Ambassador Lodge spoke at all of the opening ceremonies. Local newspapers covered these events and carried articles (provided by USIS) on the wonders of atomic energy to supplement their coverage. Amusingly, in Barcelona, as Ambassador Lodge, Joe McEvoy and Spanish officials toured exhibit, I followed them around snapping photos as the Ambassador posed with his Spanish guests. Eventually I ran out of film. When I whispered this information to Joe, he replied, "No matter. Keep shooting anyway."

Overall, hundreds of thousands of Spaniards of all ages visited the five showings with students taking assiduous notes on every detail. After the final showing at the annual fair in Sevilla in the spring of 1960, we up packed the exhibit and its models up and sent them off to another country, but we continued using our locally produced panels in our American Week programs (see below).

We promoted atoms for peace with vigor. This was President Eisenhower's special program, and we were driven by visions of a great new energy resource unhampered by the knowledge of the problems of nuclear waste. Our top nuclear scientists were gingerly testing the waters in this new scientific field, but even they did not anticipate such disasters such as Chernobyl. In retrospect, we were oversold on our own product; and, as a result, we went overboard in selling it to the Spanish public. For this, I can neither take nor place any blame. In promoting atoms for peace we simply reflected America's national hopes and aspirations.

American Weeks

For a number of years USIS Spain had used a program technique called "American Weeks" for promoting Spanish - American cultural relations in Madrid and in provincial capitals. A typical program would consist of a series of lectures by the cultural attaché or visiting American scholars, an art exhibit, documentary film showings, and an American music concert. Most often they were held in conjunction with a university or cultural organization.

About the time our major Atoms for Peace exhibits were winding down Captain George Spotswood, USAF public relations liaison officer, told a special meeting of the community relations committee that rumors were being spread that the U.S. aircraft control and warning sites were really disguised missile bases. Some people even believed the sites were equipped with atomic bombs and were afraid that their communities would become targets for a Soviet attack in case of hostilities. The mayor of Calatayud—a medium sized city north of Madrid—had asked the nearby AC&W base commander whether the rumors were true. The commander told him it was absurd; but the mayor said that's what people thought, and it was very difficult to squelch the rumors.

Frank Oram, who by then had replaced Joe McEvoy as USIS director, chaired the meeting. Others present were Jay Castillo, who had succeeded Jack Higgins as Information Officer, Embassy Political Counselor Bill Fraleigh and myself.

In reply to Oram's question whether the Spanish Air Force was doing anything to counter the rumors, Spotswood said the Spanish Air Force didn't even have a public information officer and that they believed people should accept without question whatever their government and the military forces did. Fraleigh remarked that Spain's rulers were more accustomed to governing through decree than through public persuasion and did not feel the same urgency Americans do about building public support for governmental decisions.

Spotswood was concerned about how the problem would affect American military personnel and was seeking assistance in alleviating a serious problem. The mayor was having trouble explaining the American presence, and American soldiers were being subjected to abuse in the towns where the sites were located.

Most of the Aircraft Control and Warning (AC&W) sites were near provincial capitals or small towns. About 100 American military technicians who lived there with their families staffed each site. The men operating the stations had been selected for their technical ability, and few of them spoke any Spanish. The location of the sites had been selected for technical and strategic reasons without regard to cultural or other considerations such as the proximity of a major city. Even the officers at the bases had minimal contact with the Spanish public or with the local officials.

The discussion about the AC&W sites reminded me of my own experience at an isolated Air Force radio weather station at Lanzhou in northwest China during World War II. I recalled that a single visit by a representative of Office of War Information (USIA's predecessor) who showed a documentary film on "Why We Fight" had boosted our morale and our prestige in the community.

The AC&W sites were very visible. I recalled that as Antonio Sacristan and I drove by one of the sites on a recent field trip and watched the two radar antennae go round and round and up and down he told me the Spanish people call them *la loca y la tonta*, the crazy one and the foolish one. Wouldn't it help, I asked Spotswood, if you invited some of the community leaders into the stations and let them see for themselves what kind of equipment you have there and what its purpose is?

Spotswood agreed that the idea might work, but with the Air Force being so secretive he would have to get it cleared with a higher authority.

After further consideration the committee decided to organize a series of "American Weeks" in the communities where the AC&W sites were located. At the end of each "Week" the site commander would hold an "open house" that would allow the local citizens to see for themselves what the Americans were doing and be reassured that *la loca y la tonta* held no danger for their community. The programs would use a combination of exhibits, films, lectures, and such cultural performances as we could organize. The committee assigned me the task of developing a community action program along these lines.

Since the "American Week" technique was broadly applicable to all USIS programs in Spain, Oram asked me to incorporate our other country objectives in the plan. These included furthering relations with the Spanish universities and promoting knowledge about U.S.-Spain economic cooperation in each of the communities to be included in the program. Thus, each unit of USIS Spain became involved, including our branch posts in Barcelona, Bilbao and Sevilla. I was grateful to get the support of other members of our USIS team, so vital to the success of the project.

Spotswood's military superiors and Ambassador Lodge approved the general program and Lodge authorized participation by top ranking Embassy officials as lecturers. Mimi Echeverria and our exhibits staff, with Air Force cooperation, prepared a large photographic display on the work of the U.S. Air Force at the AC&W sites. We also refurbished our old atomic energy exhibit, prepared new ones on U.S.-Spain economic cooperation, American agriculture, space exploration, and others on American life and culture that would convey an idea of what the American people were like in their own country. Our films section assembled a collection of relevant USIS documentaries.

In preparation for each American Week I visited mayors and other local authorities and explained our purpose and the type of program we proposed. In this, Antonio Sacristan, who seemed to know everyone, was invaluable in reaching the right officials or organizations. Then, working with them, we developed each week's schedule revolving around our exhibits with a special program each day—a lecture, a film showing, a concert depending on local interests and our available resources. Local authorities helped us with the publicity and we never lacked for audiences. The weeks culminated with an open house at the American base where the public got guided tours of the facilities conducted by Spanish speaking American personnel. These programs generally produced a sense of good feeling or, at least, a better understanding of what the Americans were doing there and why.

From September through December 1960 we put on 24 week-long programs, several simultaneously, in conjunction with local authorities in provincial capitals, at regional fairs, at universities and at city halls. We moved the exhibit materials around by our own USIS truck; our exhibits staff working nights and weekends to meet schedules. It was a very busy period for me. My transfer was in the offing, and I wanted to complete the project before leaving. In jest, Jim Drain, our administrative officer who was very helpful in finding ways to finance the weeks, dubbed the program "Harry's traveling circus."

The U.S. Air Force assigned a Spanish-speaking officer, a major from Puerto Rico, to work with me and loaned me the Air Force Band for a number of the programs. I recruited lecturers from the Embassy and visiting American scholars. I even gave lectures myself on the history of American painting, using slides combined with an Agency-provided exhibit on the same subject.

Margaret was amused at my audacity. "You never had any art training," she said. "How can you presume to talk to the Spanish, of all people, about art?"

I was not deterred. I took a formal slide lecture prepared by USIA, had it translated into Spanish, and sallied boldly forth. Of course I was careful to let the pictures speak for themselves and never allowed time for discussion. One of our more interesting art exhibits was a collection of original works by American artists resident in Spain. I still have several pieces in my personal collection presented me by participating artists who were grateful for the exposure.

In addition to the U.S. Air Force base programs we also conducted American Weeks in some of Spain's ancient cultural centers. One would really have to be jaded not to have his spine tingle a bit at the thought of lecturing in a site so steeped in academic tradition as the University of Salamanca.

I conducted programs in almost every province in Spain during the three years I was assigned there and became acquainted with many of the local cultural and political leaders. Spanish culture is much more formal than American, but my relationships with Spanish personalities enabled me to conduct these programs wherever necessary. In fact, when the Embassy was preparing a report on local elections, the chief political officer came to me for introductions to several town mayors.

How effective were we? At this distance that is hard to judge. But in my final report on the project I wrote:

"Public response to this series of American Weeks was exceptionally good throughout the country and particularly in those areas where the presence of U.S. military personnel have created an unusual amount of interest in America and Americans. How gratifying the results can be are indicated by a comment by Antonio Sacristan concerning a Week in Calatayud. 'In this region there is no longer any friction between the personnel at the (nearby) Inoges AC&W site and the Spaniards'."

At the end of the year shortly before our departure for a Washington assignment, I summed it up in our annual Christmas letter: "A lot of Spaniards who never saw an American before got glimpses of the real animal and heard him speak to them in their own language on topics of common concern. Judging by the public response they seemed to like what they saw and heard. It has been fun, almost as much as our Japan-America forums in Shikoku, though somewhat more expensive since all the forums cost were tea and cakes. We're going to miss these activities back in Washington."

Despite our efforts there continued to be minor frictions between American military personnel and the Spanish people near the bases, but these diminished over the years as U.S. forces were withdrawn. Spain became a member of NATO in 1982 and the bases agreement was renegotiated in 1987. The USAF contingent in Torrejon (Madrid) was withdrawn in April 1992, leaving only a USAF Base at Moron and a U.S. Naval base at Rota, both in southern Spain.

A Presidential Visit:

One of the most difficult but rewarding activities for USIS personnel at posts abroad is a state visit by the president of the United States, once rare but now much more frequent. Although these visits are very brief, usually lasting no more than a day, they can tie up the post for weeks in advance, especially if public exposure is part of the program. First comes the White House advance team with its secret service and media coordinators who must work out minute-to-minute details of the visit with the Embassy and local government representatives. There are such things as protocol, security, housing for the presidential party and accompanying newsmen, scheduling of events, publicity and hundreds of other details to be agreed upon.

The PAO and his staff play key roles in these arrangements. Once the public announcement is made from Washington, the PAO can focus on little else until the presidential party departs. The announcement will bring with it a deluge of media requests ranging from biographical data on the President to special favors in covering the visit. The visit itself will bring several hundred correspondents, both American and local and each with special needs. To handle these and the requirements of the local media the PAO must establish a press center and assign all his personnel to man it on a round-the-clock basis from the time the presidential party arrives until they depart.

President Eisenhower visited Madrid December 21-22, 1959, the first ever visit to Spain by a sitting American President. For the Franco government, trying to establish itself in a position of honor among nations, the visit was crucial. From the moment it was announced in mid-November, the Embassy, the Spanish Foreign Ministry and all Madrid began making fervent preparations, enthusiasm (and work) pyramiding with each passing day. Since Madrid was to be his last stop at the end of a ten-country trip we had time to build ourselves up to a white-hot heat, or a dreadful anti-climax. The portents were good, however, and the Spanish Government determined to make Eisenhower's visit to Madrid visit the most spectacular of all. On arrival, Eisenhower stepped to the door of his plane, raised his arms in an exuberant V for victory greeting and then, after greeting Generalissimo Franco, charmed his audience with a warm greeting that left Spaniards declaring, "Que simpatico. Que simpatico." Then, riding in a bubble-topped car with Franco, he led a spectacular parade before the hundreds of thousands who lined the route from the airport, through downtown Madrid to the Moncloa Palace, his White House for the night. There were other programs, each coming off without a hitch. The president stayed 18 hours.

When Air Force One (a Boeing 707 and the first jet passenger plane to visit Madrid) zoomed skyward from Torrejon Airbase we all breathed a deep sigh of relief. Half the Embassy staff went home, keeled over and slept for 24 hours straight. I recovered just in time to recoup my forces and get our Christmas tree and gifts ready for the children.

Election USA:

A year later we watched the Nixon-Kennedy campaign for the presidency with keen interest. Our ambassador's brother, Henry Cabot Lodge, was running on the Nixon ticket for vice president, but USIS information output focused on the democratic process itself with equal billing to the competing tickets. There was no CNN in those days. Trans-oceanic television was still in the future, so on election night we set up a scoreboard in the Embassy lobby. I spent the whole night monitoring returns over VOA, entering them on the board and answering hundreds of telephone calls that asked, "Who's winning?" It was nearly 10 o'clock Wednesday morning before we were able to respond that John Fitzgerald Kennedy had won.

After Hours

Tui Higgins' warning to Margaret about Madrid's active social life was well taken. Throughout our stay in Spain we averaged three or four nights a week carrying out official or unofficial obligations. These commitments involved everything from helping with ambassadorial receptions to escorting visiting firemen around the tapa[24] bars in Madrid's entertainment district or delivering lectures at our own exhibits. But even with official duties consuming a lion's share of our time, we still managed to enjoy Madrid's nightlife on our own or with friends. We had three factors in our favor: relative youth, a favorable dollar-peseta exchange rate, and a very dependable maid to look after our children.

We used official dinners and receptions as opportunities to introduce our Spanish counterparts to visiting VIPs from Washington and for informal discussions of Spanish - American relations. Margaret and I did more than our share of entertaining, both in our home and— while I was on the road—at restaurants. Our two most memorable and gracious guests from the United States were the late Senator Frank Church (Dem. Idaho) and his wife and the Hollywood actor James Stewart and his wife. We did not entertain either at our home, but we did escort them on sightseeing trips around Madrid and environs.

---

24. Appetizer or *hors d'oeuvre*. Many bars specialize in these delicacies, serving them with a variety of Spanish wines. One can easily make a meal of them.

Marlene Dietrich was another memorable visitor, although it was she who entertained us. One morning my office phone rang and a sultry voice came over the wire, "This is Marlene Dietrich," the voice said.

"Yes, and this is Harry Truman. What can I do for you?"

But it really was Marlene Dietrich. She was having a show that night in a tent in El Retiro Park (in central Madrid) and needed an amplification system. Someone had told her I was the person to contact. She said she would be happy to pay whatever the cost and invited me to be her guest at the show.

I arranged for one of our technicians, Jose Ochoa, to set up the amplification system on his own time, using USIS equipment. Margaret and I enjoyed the show, and Marlene gave me a hug and a kiss in gratitude for my help. But she never did pay Mr. Ochoa for his work.

The Common Bond

Madrid was a medium-sized USIS Foreign Service post at the time we were there (1957-1960) and might be considered a typical of the era. It was a relatively small organization operating with a common purpose within the larger Embassy community. We thought of ourselves as a team with each member having a prescribed role. The roles were relatively constant. Membership changed through transfers, often bringing together people who had worked together in some previous assignment.

In the Foreign Service one's closest relationships are with his working colleagues. You not only work together, you see each other at a continuing series of official and unofficial occasions. Spouses depend on each other for mutual support, both physical and moral. Children attend the same schools and develop their own interpersonal relations. Membership in the Embassy is the common bond, but the bonds in a sub-unit such as USIS are even stronger. Although personal animosities can develop, more often the close association promotes friendships that last a lifetime. Such was our case, and we cherish our ties with several couples we worked with during our time in Madrid.

The Spanish Experience

During our three-year assignment to Madrid—1957-1960—I made frequent trips around Spain in connection with my exhibits activities. I nearly always traveled in my own car, and Margaret went along whenever possible, leaving our children at home in care of our very dependable Sabina Chicharro. Together we observed Holy Week rituals in Murcia, Valladolid and Sevilla and explored Salamanca's 13th century university. We watched Castilian folk dances on Zaragoza's city wall at midnight while shivering in Pyrenean winds. We were awed by elegant Moorish architecture in Cordoba, Sevilla, and Granada—relics of the 700 years that Moors ruled Spain. We sampled Valdepenas wines in Ciudad Real, the land of Don Quijote, and relished savory suckling pig at a El Meson de Candido, a 16th century restaurant in the shadow of Segovia's still functioning Roman aqueduct. Two sample experiences:

On a visit to Valladolid: The governor of Valladolid, the ancient capital of Spain about 150 miles north of Madrid, gave a dinner to celebrate the opening of our Atoms for Peace exhibit. Margaret and I we were the guests of honor. Making conversation, Margaret casually mentioned that I was fond of dancing the flamenco, which was true though I was very much the amateur. Thereupon the governor sent out for a guitarist and a gypsy dancer and invited me to demonstrate my skill. He would have none of my feigned modesty, and I soon found myself stomping the floor with a gypsy partner until the wee hours of the morning, making up with enthusiasm what I lacked in skill. We spent the next day inspecting polychrome sculptures in the Valladolid museum and started back to Madrid about 5:30 in the afternoon. A light rain soon turned to heavy snow as we approached the Guadarama Mountains just north of Madrid. The roads had frozen over and our spinning wheels took us nowhere. We turned around, went back to a roadside inn—a summer hotel—where we sat around a pot bellied stove until late at night swapping snow stories with truck drivers and motorcyclists also stranded by the storm. Our room was icy cold. The toilet down the hall was a deep freezer. Next morning we got chains and crossed the mountains into a bright sunny day.

On Visiting a Spanish village: One Saturday we took Sabina to her village for the weekend. She had been talking to our children about her pueblo for a long time and they were excited about going. Sabina's family lived in Paredes, Guadalajara province, 125 miles north of Madrid. It was small, only 500 inhabitants and off the main highway. The people lived in the same way Spanish villagers have lived for centuries. They were hard-working, friendly and kind. Sabina's father welcomed me with a beer. Their houses, built of stones that lie around everywhere, had no windows and the doors were of heavy burlap.

Hence the inside was quite dark and contrasted sharply with the bright Spanish sunshine outside. Chickens and livestock lived in the village with them so there were an abundance of flies. Sabina made excuses for the poverty of the village, but her father, an active youngster of 81, chastised her for criticizing their pueblo. He had lived in the village all his life and was very proud of it. He showed us the "new church, only 70 years old." The previous one had burned down so all the church saints were also "new and not very interesting." He thought of an old church as one built in the 12th or 13th century. The dwellings were grouped together, and people went out each day to work their individual plots. They farmed wheat—only wheat—for a living and did it all by hand except that this year they had acquired a mechanical planter. We watched them winnowing wheat that had been flailed off the stalks. The men, using wooden pitchforks, tossed the wheat straw into the air. The wind blew away the chaff; the grain fell to the ground. The women came along behind, swept the wheat into a neat piles and sifted it to remove trash and dirt. I guessed that the whole season's work rendered the village less wheat than an American combine could cut and thresh in an hour. It's no wonder they were poor.

A Third Daughter

In 1959 we had extended our stay in Madrid for a year, making it one three-year tour rather than two two-year tours. The reason: Margaret was expecting our third child in November at the time when we would normally take home leave. Our third daughter, a spirited one, was born November 16, 1959, and we named her Judith Lynne. We had wanted a brother for our two girls but things didn't work out that way. She was a very pretty child, lively and bright eyed. We were sure she would rival her two sisters one day, and she has not disappointed us.

Adios a Espana

My transfer orders came in November 1960 at the end of my three-year tour. I had chosen to defer home leave so they authorized air travel to the United States for me and my family to Washington D.C. and instructed me to report for duty in January, at about the same time as the newly elected President John F. Kennedy. My replacement, Tom Grunwald, arrived December 2. PAO Frank Oram wanted us to have an ample overlap so I could show him the ropes, so my family and I left three weeks later, on December 29.

In good Foreign Service tradition there was a series of farewell parties, including a really heartwarming one given by the USIS staff. Margaret and I were especially honored by a farewell luncheon given us by Ambassador Lodge's wife, Francesca Braggiotti de Lodge, as she was called in Spain. It's an amusing story, but first a bit of background.

Francesca was a dog lover and intensely interested in a program for Seeing Eye dogs. At this time the Spanish had not yet developed a program of independent living for the blind who were entirely reliant on other individuals—often small children—to guide them about. There were a lot of stray dogs on the streets of Madrid, and Francesca had the idea that she could use some of them to develop a seeing-eye-dog program. But first she had to get Spanish social workers involved. One of her techniques was to show the workers documentary films on American training programs for seeing-eye-dogs. These I obtained through USIA Washington and screened them for her invited guests in the USIS auditorium.

At every showing Francesca would enter the auditorium in grand style with two or three dogs straining at the leash[25]. As a result of these activities I became rather close to her. Francesca's purpose was to get a Seeing Eye dog school started, I helped achieve that goal, and she appreciated it.

As we were preparing to leave Madrid, Francesca asked her husband to hold an official lunch in my honor. He agreed and she told me to invite anyone I wanted to, up to 22 people. So Margaret and I invited a number of our Spanish friends. Francesca gave a formal and very lovely lunch at the Embassy residence. Ambassador Lodge gave a toast in my honor to which I responded; and then Francesca said, "Mr. Kendall, I don't normally give toasts at these luncheons, but because you have been so helpful to me I want to say this, the dogs of Madrid will miss you!"

Well, I don't miss the dogs, but I do miss Madrid; and I also miss such episodes as this one that add spice to life in the Foreign Service.

---

25. Ambassador Lodge was tolerant of his wife's affectation. In his staff meetings he occasionally referred to it by remarking, "A dog's life? In my house dogs live wonderful lives."

USIS Spain in Retrospect

As one might easily deduct from the foregoing, I found my tour of duty in Spain one of highlights of my career in the Foreign Service. In this I am no different other FSOs who have been fortunate enough to serve there, particularly those with previous tours in Latin America who found on the Iberian Peninsula the undiluted roots of the cultures they may have puzzled over in earlier assignments.

But Spain under Franco was not the Spain of today. At the end of the 1950s when we were there, twenty-five years into the Franco dictatorship, the country was still emerging from the traumatic effects of its civil war. The economy was weak and the people suffered from their long isolation during their Civil War plus World War II and its aftermath. Spain had just been accepted into the United Nations, but its fascistic government made it a pariah in Europe and unwelcome in the North Atlantic Treaty Organization. The normalization of U.S.-Spain relations and the bases agreements, negotiated by the Eisenhower administration in 1953, were a first step for Spain back into the community of nations. The bases also helped reopen Spain for the Americans who came to operate them as well as many contract agencies, movie companies and individuals for whom Spain had hitherto been off base. The Spanish people welcomed them with open arms. Tourism got off to a slow start but eventually boomed.

As an instrument of American policy in Spain, USIS had two basic objectives. One was to reduce Spanish doubts about the American bases that served as a deterrent against Soviet aggression. The other was give moral support and encouragement to those forces that wanted to see their country become more democratic.

Did we succeed? History would say yes. There were plenty of obstacles, but we had a lot of help along the way.

Under the Franco dictatorship, public opposition to the bases agreement was artificially muted, and USIS had to avoid overplaying its hand. Community relations frictions developed, but opening the bases to public view as part of the American Week program helped iron out many of the problems. Even so, as inevitably happens, people grew weary of seeing foreign soldiers on their soil; and the bases became a serious irritant in our bilateral relations. After Franco passed from the scene Spain became a part of NATO, improved technology lessened the need for the bases, and the U.S. gradually closed them down. The irritant disappeared.

On promoting democratic ideals, the Fulbright and other exchange programs brought many Spanish intellectuals to the United States and American scholars to Spain, resulting in an interlocking network of ideas, thought and culture. Madrid was the focal point for these exchanges, but our USIS cultural affairs programs in Barcelona, Bilbao, and Sevilla and our American Weeks brought our participants face to face with a wide variety of Spanish audiences outside the capital, all avid for information about the United States, both scientific and cultural. I can say with some confidence that these factors helped Spain along the road to a democratic form of government. After Franco's death, however, it was the Spaniards themselves who chose democracy. Curiously, when the Spanish government was threatened with a military takeover and a tough choice had to made between democracy and another dictatorship, the person who made the difference was King Juan Carlos who had grown up under Franco's tutelage and had been exposed to a wide variety of influences from Western Europe and the United States. On October 2, 1987, I was honored to attend a special ceremony at which the University of California at awarded him the Berkeley Medal, its highest honor, for his achievements and leadership in the public interest.

Spain's minister of information, left, attends the Madrid opening of a USIS Atoms for Peace exhibit with Public Affairs Officer Joseph McEvoy, center and the Author

Commander William R. Anderson, USN, who took the nuclear powered Nautilus on
its historic voyage under the North Pole August 3, 1958, discuses the feat with author,
left, and USIS exhibits specialist Jose Estecha at the American Embassy in Madrid.

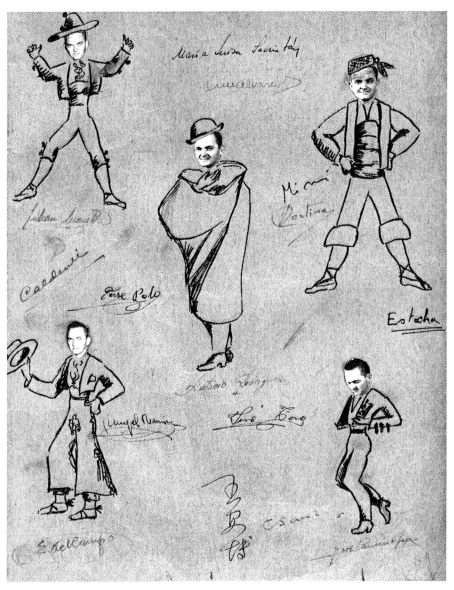

Sketches by USIS Madrid artist Mimi Echeverria evoke the author's love for Flamenco dancing. Signatures are by members of the exhibits staff.

V NASA - USIA'S Man in Space

*"I believe this nation should commit itself, before this decade is out,
to landing a man on the moon and returning him safely to Earth."*
*"We choose to go to the moon, and other things, not because they are
easy but because they are hard."*

John F. Kennedy - May 1961

We arrived back in the United States for our Washington assignment
ten years after I had joined the Foreign Service in January 1951. During
that time we had represented our country on three different
continents—South America, Asia and Europe. Now we were going to
be just another American family and lose ourselves in the anonymity of
the nation's capital. We liked the idea. Our children were thrilled. Except
for brief vacations they had never lived in the United States. Now,
instead of always being different, they were going to be just like
everybody else; and I was going to get myself re-Americanized.

In Washington it was the beginning of a new era. John F. Kennedy
had just been elected and was about to take office. We, like all our
colleagues, were seized up in the aura of excitement of a new beginning.
I had asked for a position in USIA's Policy Plans and Research (PP&R)
division without really knowing much about what its responsibilities
were, but it sounded good. I walked into an assignment as USIA's
liaison officer with NASA (National Aeronautics and Space
Administration) that was even beyond my dreams.

The exploration of space was becoming increasingly important in
our overseas information activities. The launching of Sputnik by the
Soviet Union on October 4, 1957, and of Explorer I by the United
States on January 31, 1958, had signaled the onset of a space race. Now,
as both of the world superpowers geared up for manned space flight, the
pace was quickening. The race was more political than scientific; but in
the public perception preeminence in space was equated with superiority
in military strength and technological achievement. Soviet Prime
Minister Nikita Khrushchev had bragged that if the USSR could send
Sputnik into orbit, it could certainly place a missile into America's
heartland. "We will bury you," he had said. The American leadership
could not let such a statement go unchallenged.

The United States was conducting two separate space programs—one military, one peaceful. Nevertheless, the basic technology was interchangeable. Rockets used for launching missiles could also be used for exploring deep space or sending a man into earth orbit. The Department of Defense military program was necessarily kept secret, but in the Cold War atmosphere neither country could afford to let the other appear to be ahead.

NASA, therefore, was assigned the public role of developing the peaceful uses of space. This would focus on putting man into space, on communications and meteorological satellites, and on the more esoteric scientific exploration of the solar system and beyond. In our open society, even failures had to be acknowledged and explained.

In promoting the U.S. space program, the Voice of America and USIS posts abroad were not talking to disinterested audiences. The popular demand for information on the U.S. space program was overwhelming. NASA was the primary source, and USIS officers needed all the help they could get to meet the demand. While all aspects of the space program were important, manned space flight was the center of excitement. USIA was challenged with the task of providing overseas audiences with details of the American space program by all means available.

Harold (Hal) Goodwin, the USIA science advisor and a member of PP&R had primary responsibility for overseeing the agency's output on space. He had recommended the appointment of a Foreign Service Officer familiar with overseas requirements to serve as a full time liaison officer with NASA. In Hal's concept a person operating out of NASA's office of public information could keep himself apprised of new developments and feed information to the various USIA elements on a continuing basis. To Hal fell the task of finding the right individual. Since I had asked for an assignment to PP&R my name was one of those he considered. Hal asked Walt Nichols who had been USIS field supervisor in Tokyo while I was in Takamatsu whether this guy Kendall would be able to act independently without the necessity for close supervision. Walt gave me a strong recommendation on the basis of my record in Shikoku, and I got the job.

On January 9, 1961, I checked in with Hal at USIA Washington, then located at 1776 Pennsylvania Avenue. After a briefing me on my new assignment he walked with me over to NASA headquarters, at that time in the Dolly Madison House just off Lafayette Square. (Later

NASA moved to the Department of Education building on Independence Avenue.) There Hal introduced me to Joe Stein, then chief of NASA's Office of Public Information, and to my new job as USIA's space man. Thus began a brand new phase in my career.

My "adventure into space" would continue for a full decade, well beyond my three-year Washington assignment and into my next three overseas posts. This chapter will give a personal account of how one Foreign Service Officer helped USIA to fulfill its role of informing an avid world audience about America's initial steps in exploring the frontiers of space.

The New Washingtonians

My new job was exciting but my initial task was to find a home for my family. Purchasing a house proved more economical over the long run than renting so we chose that route. When we went overseas again we could rent it out and have a place to return to when the time came. After a two-week search we found just the place we wanted in Wood Acres, a neighborhood on Massachusetts Avenue in the Montgomery County suburbs of Washington. It was a two-story American colonial style white brick house. Its three bedrooms, two baths, kitchen, dining room, living room, a nice study converted from a garage, ample basement and a large back yard were just what my family needed. The best part about it was the location, back to back with a community park and playground. On the other side of the park was the Wood Acres elementary school. Our children could walk safely across the park and be in school in less than five minutes. For me bus service into Washington was only two blocks away. The price of the house was $22,500 with a mortgage interest rate of four and a half percent, well within our range. (I include these details for historical interest. Twenty years later we sold the house in a sluggish market for $150,000.)

USIA - Policy, Plans and Research (PP&R)

Shortly after John F. Kennedy took office as President of the United States he appointed Edward R. Murrow as director of USIA. This was a tremendous shot in the arm for all of us who were members of that organization. Murrow was undoubtedly the country's leading broadcast journalist. He was highly respected at home and abroad for his performance as the CBS wartime correspondent in Europe and his subsequent role in exposing McCarthyism. In naming Murrow as director of USIA, the President sent a message to the country and to the world that he was giving a high priority to telling America's story abroad in an honest and factual manner. We were proud to work under Murrow. Years after he had passed from the scene people were still referring to USIA as "Ed Murrow's organization."

Thomas Sorenson, younger brother of Theodore Sorenson, was appointed head of USIA's Office of Policy and Plans under the new administration. Ted was President Kennedy's speechwriter and one of his principal advisers. Tom was a middle grade USIS officer in Greece when he was named to the position. To my knowledge he had a good but not outstanding reputation. It was widely assumed he was given the job to facilitate connections with the White House.

The role of PP&R was to provide USIA Washington media elements and our posts abroad with policy guidance on how to treat matters affecting U.S. foreign policy. Fast news media guidance was particularly important. Media research specialists kept a close watch on overseas reaction to major events involving the United States, giving high priority to the U.S.-Soviet space race. They analyzed daily reports from overseas posts and sent summaries to the White House for the information of the President and his staff, to the National Security Council and to the Department of State. PP&R also conducted public opinion surveys abroad to determine foreign reaction to important policy issues.

The USIA science advisor was one of several specialists who maintained liaison with other government departments concerned with foreign affairs and provided input for USIA's policy guidance channels. The more important of these entities were the White House and the National Security Council, State, Defense, Treasury, the Atomic Energy Commission, NASA and the National Science Foundation.

In taking on the job as USIA/NASA liaison I did not kid myself that I knew anything about space exploration. But I did know that among our overseas audiences there was an ever-increasing demand for information about science and technology and especially about the U.S. space program. I would have to serve as a channel for that information from NASA to USIA's media services and posts overseas. In the Cold War competition with the Soviet Union, President Kennedy had made American leadership in space a prime objective. A major psychological effort to convince the world public of American superiority in space would produce a spin off effect of demonstrating U.S. leadership in all aspects of science and technology.

The commercial news media could be counted on to keep the American public informed about developments in space exploration. USIA, especially the Voice of America, had its job cut out in informing overseas audiences about fast breaking events. The Agency's press, motion picture and television services would provide background information to help achieve our psychological objectives abroad.

I began reading everything I could lay hands on about the NASA program and soon became a space addict. I paid particular attention to keeping USIA media informed about forthcoming developments within the space program, assisting them in coverage of major events and in adapting NASA's information output to our Washington and field requirements. I soon became the prime point of contact between USIA and NASA personnel in arranging media interviews and handling special requests from overseas posts. I also set out to educate the NASA information staff about their tremendous overseas audience and the potential for reaching them through USIA.

Within USIA's media elements a handful of experienced science writers and reporters carried the major burden. Charles Schroth and Walter Froelich did the job for the press services, providing overseas posts with a continuing supply of backgrounders that supplemented spot news coming from commercial news agencies. In the Voice of America, Joseph Lubin, Edward Hickey and Wayne Hyde distinguished themselves with a worldwide audience for their English language broadcasts. VOA's Spanish to Latin America, Russian to the Soviet Union, and other language services also had their star figures. The motion picture service worked overtime turning out newsreels and documentaries on the space program to capitalize on public interest.

The National Aeronautics and Space Administration

NASA was less than three years old when I became USIA-NASA liaison officer. The space agency, formed out of its predecessor, the National Advisory Commission for Aeronautics, had come into being on October 1, 1958. During NACA's 43 years of existence its scientific and technical staff had made significant contributions toward the development of the nation's aircraft industry, enabling the United States to achieve preeminence in both civil and military aviation.

Until NASA was established the Army, Navy and Air Force had competed for primacy in America's space exploration program. The Navy bragged noisily that its Vanguard rocket was superior to the Army's Redstone. But when the Vanguard blew up on the pad in its attempt to launch the United States' first satellite, the Army asked for and was given permission to do the job with a Redstone developed by Werner von Braun's team at the Huntsville, Alabama, research center. The Redstone performed perfectly, sending Explorer I, America's first satellite, into earth orbit. The Explorer's instruments made the important scientific discovery of the Van Allen radiation belt. The Redstone, eventually chosen for Project Mercury's sub-orbital flights, was the precursor of the giant Saturn rocket that sent American astronauts to the moon.

Despite the Army's initial success the military's need for secrecy unnecessarily complicated the job of newsmen and USIA in trying to inform the American public and the world about U.S. efforts in space. President Eisenhower remedied this situation by creating two separate agencies—one military and one civilian. The Advanced Research Projects Agency (ARPA) within the Defense Department was given the role of coordinating the military's space projects, permitting secrecy as necessary. NASA, the civilian agency, was assigned responsibility for non-military space programs and giving an open and peaceful face to America's exploration of space.

Eisenhower appointed his science advisor, Dr. T. Keith Glennan, director of NASA and Dr. Hugh Dryden, former director of NACA, as deputy director. In the words of Dr. Dryden, NASA's mission was "one of joining all governmental agencies, the academic community, and industry in a national program for the peaceful conquest of space for the benefit of all mankind."[26]

Cape Canaveral

The Cape Canaveral (Spanish for cane brake) launch site was carved out of a 15,000-acre triangle of deserted, snake-invested palmetto flats

---

[26]. *Aeronautics and Astronautics - An American Chronology of Science and Technology in the Exploration of Space 1915-1960,* by Eugene M. Emme, NASA Historian, Foreword by Hugh L. Dryden, Deputy Administrator, National Aeronautics and Space Administration, 1961. p. iii

located in Brevard County, halfway down the Florida Atlantic coast, eight miles north of Cocoa Beach. One of the chief reasons for the site's selection was the existence of a chain of islands that stretches from the Bahamas southeastward to the Lesser Antilles off the coast of South America. Tracking stations on these islands would permit the monitoring of test missile launches.[27] During the decade of the fifties the Department of Defense converted Cape Canaveral into a missile test range and built Patrick Air Force Base nearby to provide air access and administrative services for the test site.

When I first visited the Cape early in 1961 in for the launching of the chimpanzee "Ham" on a sub-orbital flight, Canaveral was already on its way to becoming a legend. The town of Cocoa Beach had been converted from a sleepy fishing village into a complex of motels to house visiting newsmen and contract personnel associated with NASA and Department of Defense launch programs. Its broad beaches provided ample recreation and camping space for missile watchers and curiosity seekers who poured into the Cape whenever a major space launch was imminent. The town and its environs would expand many times as NASA developed the Saturn launch site for the lunar landing program.

To Go to the Moon

NASA was preparing for Project Mercury's first manned sub-orbital flight when the startling news came that a Soviet cosmonaut named Yuri Gagarin had orbited the earth on April 12, 1961. This was shortly after the Bay of Pigs fiasco, and Western prestige was at low ebb. We badly needed a space success. We got it three weeks later on May 5 with the flight of Alan Shepard in Freedom 7. Though less impressive than Gagarin's orbital flight, the event was emblazoned in headlines around the world. Both the United States and the Soviet Union were amazed at the public reaction to space exploration. The propaganda value of success in space was enormous and the race was on in earnest. Then, on May 25, 1961, with 15 minutes of manned space flight to our credit, President Kennedy set for America the task of reaching the moon; and

---

[27] William Roy Shelton. *American Space Exploration - the First Decade*, Little Brown & Co, Shelton, 1967, p. 6 ff.

manned space flight became an instrument in the Cold War.[28] In the subsequent months and years, through the completion of Project Mercury and the beginning of Project Gemini, I felt myself in a very privileged position of helping inform the world about America's achievements in space.

The moon race, which turned out not to be a race at all when the USSR dropped out early in the game, totally overshadowed America's other space achievements in which I was involved. These included the Telstar, Syncom, and Intelsat satellites that revolutionized world communications networks, and the TIROS weather satellites that enabled meteorologists to view for the first time weather patterns as they developed.

In December 1961 E. C. Welsh, executive secretary of the National Aeronautics and Space Council, wrote USIA Director Edward R. Murrow saying "Of all the U.S. space accomplishments so far, the weather satellite program presents the best vehicle for a factual story, based on the immediate practical benefits." He asked whether USIA was getting the necessary data and whether the story was getting out. I was asked to prepare a reply with factual data. My response, based on a survey of USIA media services and geographical regions, came to five single spaced pages, was a resounding yes. Both NASA and the Weather Bureau, I wrote, "have cooperated with us as splendidly as have the TIROS satellites themselves."

The space technology to which these pioneering earth satellites led has now become so much a part of our daily lives that we often forget that before the decade of the sixties these instruments existed only in the fertile imagination of science fiction writers such as Arthur C. Clark and Isaac Asimov. Other space marvels were the deep-space probes that provided a completely new view of our solar system and the worlds beyond and were to lead to new concepts on the origins of the universe.

To borrow a phrase from Dean Acheson, I felt especially privileged to be "present at the creation."

---

28. Tim Furniss, *Manned Spaceflight Log*, Jane's Publishing Company, United Kingdom, 1963, p.9.

NASA Public Information

President Kennedy named James E. Webb, an Oklahoma lawyer and former director of the Office of the Budget, to succeed Keith Glennan as head of NASA. Hugh Dryden stayed on as deputy director and chief scientist. Webb proved to be a dynamic and effective administrator during a time of tremendous growth. He brought in O. B. (Bill) Lloyd as his director of public information. Joe Stein, originally NACA's information director, remained for a time as Lloyd's deputy, focusing primarily on aeronautical projects, particularly the X-15 that achieved sub-orbital flights. Lloyd named public information specialists to handle NASA information output on each space exploration project. Of these the most important was Paul Haney, information officer for the manned space flight program. At Cape Canaveral Lt. Col. John (Shorty) Powers served as the spokesman for Project Mercury and became widely known through his announcements of NASA's manned space flight launches. It was he who gave fame to the phrase "A-OK." Shorty's deputy, Jack King, also played a prominent role in handling newsmen at the Cape. As the space program grew so did NASA's public relations hierarchy, but these are the people with whom I worked most closely.

In preparation for each of the launches NASA's public information specialists prepared press kits that contained a wealth of information about the component parts of the launch vehicles and the spacecraft together with their respective functions. They also provided names and background on the principle scientific and technical personnel involved, including the astronauts in the case of manned space flights. I had not seen the kits until I began working at NASA. At the end of January I looked over the material on Samos 2 that was scheduled to study the effect of micrometeorite impacts in space. I was fascinated. On inquiring about their distribution I found they were going only to science writers in Washington area, at the NASA research centers and to correspondents at Cape Canaveral. I explained to Joe Stein (this was before Bill Lloyd had come aboard) that there were many science writers abroad, especially in advanced countries, who would give their eyeteeth to get the kits. I proposed asking USIA's press services to send the packets overseas to USIS abroad for selected distribution to science writers. Joe agreed. USIA surveyed its posts to determine the requirements and in a short time requests came back from USIS posts around the world for the NASA packets. I was pleased to hear somewhat later from journalists who came to Cape Canaveral to cover

John Glenn's orbital flight that they were getting the service regularly through USIS.

Project Mercury

During the three years I was with NASA I shuttled back and forth from Washington to Cape Canaveral for each of the Project Mercury launches, with occasional side trips to the Houston flight control center. For each launch, from "Ham" through the Alan Shepard and John Glenn flights to end of the program I spent long hours helping USIA media personnel and members of the foreign press cover the events. VOA had huge audiences around the world for its English and foreign language broadcasts live from trailers at the launch site as well as from its Washington studios.

Publicity on each of the Mercury flights began well in advance with major newspapers and radio and TV networks reporting on every detail. Anticipation about what the Russians would do next added to the suspense. The first orbital flight by Astronaut John Glenn was particularly suspenseful. Two Russian cosmonauts, Yuri Gagarin and Gherman Titov had already circumnavigated the earth, and the world was eagerly watching to see when the United States would catch up. Cape Canaveral became the center of world attention. Early each morning on the announced flight dates, hundreds of reporters and TV network personnel with all their paraphernalia gathered at the launch site to cover the launch while thousands of anxious spectators lined the nearby beaches to witness the historic occasion. But NASA engineers took no chances. Originally scheduled for December 20, 1961, Glenn's flight was postponed first to January 16 then, for technical and weather reasons, several more times until February 20 when he was launched from Cape Canaveral in a Mercury spacecraft aboard an Atlas rocket for America's first manned earth orbital flight. The five-hour, three-orbit flight in the glare of worldwide of publicity made Glenn a national hero and eventually landed him (pun intended) in the United States Senate. Years later, at the age 77, he took his second flight aboard a space shuttle.

NASA and USIA exploited Glenn's orbital flight to the utmost. While the nation went on an orgy of hero worship that left us all somewhat groggy, I found myself assisting in the production of newsreel coverage for TV and theatrical distribution world wide. John Glenn bore up well under it all. There were to be more orbital flights but after this one they would all seem somewhat routine.

Two months after Glenn's flight, he met with Titov in Washington under the auspices of the International Space Flight Association. The association's Dutch president presented each of them half of a pair of wooden shoes. The same afternoon I found Glenn in his office, both feet on his desk, admiring his shoe. His comment: "Titov got the left one.

As NASA's Mercury program progressed through orbital flights by Astronauts Scott Carpenter, Wally Schirra and Gordon Cooper, there always seemed to be more and more to do in my job. Space was perhaps the single most important item in USIA's overseas information output, and I was involved in every bit of it. Mariner probes to Venus, communication satellites, weather satellites, manned space flights, all occupied the attention of the public everywhere; and I seemed to be the focal point for channeling this information to USIS posts overseas. It was exciting, interesting and rewarding.

On May 15, 1963, NASA sent Astronaut Gordon Cooper on Project Mercury's final manned flight for 22 earth orbits in 34 hours and 20 minutes. Some 500 media representatives, including 50 foreign correspondents who were my responsibility, assembled at the Cape for the occasion. VOA broadcast its coverage around the clock. As space flights go Cooper's flight was a fairly easy, but an automatic control malfunction that made manual reentry mandatory provided the melodrama needed to make the flight memorable rather than being relegated to comparative oblivion. NASA held parades in Washington, New York and Houston to impress Congress with the public approval of space flight, but they were sincere manifestations toward a popular hero. Project Mercury was over, and NASA began preparing for Project Gemini, but I would be observing that from overseas.

Foreign Correspondents

NASA's Office of Public Information was well organized for handling the needs of domestic newsmen but not for foreign correspondents. The project specialists paid special attention to media representatives, particularly science writers and network correspondents, providing them with details on forthcoming launches and arranging interviews with NASA personnel. American journalists also knew their way around the aerospace industry and frequently recurred to NASA's program information specialists to confirm what they already knew. When covering major launches at Cape Canaveral they were well informed about what was supposed to happen, and their questions at press briefings kept NASA officials on their toes. Many, in fact, would already have their stories written and came primarily to cover the drama of the occasion.

On the other hand most foreign correspondents covered U.S. space exploration as only one of many aspects of their work that usually focused on U.S. political and economic relations with their home countries. They tended to be novices in the space field and were almost totally dependent on NASA handouts or monitoring TV networks for information. Those coming from abroad to cover manned space launches—and there were many during the early dramatic days of Project Mercury—were even in a worse situation. Some would arrive at the last moment expecting to get all the information they needed on the spot. In those hectic moments NASA information specialists would be so busy with the press of events that they had virtually no time to give foreign reporters the attention they needed.

Thus, caring for overseas correspondents covering NASA's manned space flight program fell to me by default. Two incidents are representative:

A Mexican television crew, headed by Miguel Aleman, Jr., son of the then president of Mexico, came to Cape Canaveral to do live coverage of John Glenn's flight for the Televisa TV network. Although Aleman and his colleague, Jacobo Zabludovsky, both spoke good English, they needed more assistance than NASA could give them. The American Embassy in Mexico, vitally interested in having the broadcast go forward, asked me to assist them with appropriate contacts, which I did. The time was January 1962, years before satellite TV became commonplace. The event was John Glenn's three-orbital flight. Curiously, there had never before been a direct U.S.-Mexico telecast, and arrangements were time consuming. Fortunately, delays in the launch gave Aleman the time needed to organize a connection through San Antonio via NBC, the National Broadcasting Company, and John Glenn's flight was seen in Mexico live from Cape Canaveral. More such telecasts were to follow with each manned space flight. In 1966, when I was in Mexico City escorting the Gemini V spacecraft on a Latin American tour Aleman and Zabludovsky did a telecast from the exhibit site. They interviewed me on the program and recalled our earlier experience at the Cape.

A Spanish correspondent, sent by his paper from Madrid to cover Wally Schirra's six-orbit flight, arrived late in evening before the launch. He spoke little English, had no place to stay, and had read only news reports of what was to happen.

"Harry," Paul Haney shouted across the pressroom, "can you take care of this guy? I can't understand a word he says."

The reporter was vastly relieved to find someone who understood Spanish. Somehow I managed to get him a shared room with a Mexican correspondent and filled him in on the next day's schedule. He stuck by my side through the launch and most of the flight as I translated progress reports for him. I never saw the story he filed with his paper, but I hope it was at least minimally accurate.

I was grateful for letters from correspondents thanking me for helping them cover the space program. The most gracious were from Ernie Wiener, then chief of USIA's Foreign Press Center, who commended my services to resident foreign correspondents, and from Reginald Thornhill, BBC science correspondent who I first met during the long wait for John Glenn's flight. He wrote Bill Lloyd: "Again we gave live coverage to the (MA-7 Scott Carpenter) shot on BBC sound and television programmes, and the success of these broadcasts was largely due to all the help and cooperation I was given at the Cape by your officers... particularly Mr. Jack King and Mr. Harry Kendall, who were endlessly patient in helping me to obtain recorded interviews for use on the day of the shot."

Because my frequent absences for the launches left my position at NASA Headquarters uncovered at critical times USIA gave me a secretary/assistant who could respond to media requests while I was away. The person was Lula Asberry, an African-American lady who was not only highly competent but also a wonderful person to work with. Our NASA co-workers appreciated her very much, and she always made me look good, even when I blundered.

NASA International Programs

Although the American public looked upon NASA as being "national" as the name implies, it was and is to a large extent international. NASA's world wide tracking network and the nature of many scientific experiments involved participation by government officials and international scientists from around the world. Without the many scientific contributions from abroad the American space exploration program could never have developed as rapidly as it did. The foreign participation, in turn, drew attention by the media and the public at large in each of the countries concerned. It was natural, therefore, that USIS posts in these countries emphasize the local connection with NASA to develop public support for the American space program. NASA, for its part, vitally needed international public support in order to operate its overseas tracking network.

NASA's International Programs Division was charged with negotiating agreements with the many countries where the space agency conducted its activities, particularly those where NASA had tracking stations for both manned and unmanned flights. These included Australia, Bermuda, Chile, Nigeria, Madagascar (now The Malagasy Republic), Mexico, and Spain—among others. The division also managed NASA's relations with the hundreds of international scientists who took part in NASA experiments and the agency's participation in international conferences on the peaceful uses of space. NASA coordinated its overseas activities through Department of State's Bureau of Science and Technology and American Embassy science advisors in the countries concerned.

Separate bilateral agreements had to be negotiated with each country for the operation of the satellite tracking stations. The more industrialized societies such as Australia welcomed the NASA installations that could be operated by local technicians with a minimum American presence. In Third World countries such as Nigeria the stations had to be built and operated by American technicians. In these countries the presence of a foreign tracking station managed by foreign technicians, unless properly explained to the public, could arouse intense local opposition, endangering both the personnel and the installation.

The many public relations aspects of its international operations led NASA to request that USIA assign a second Foreign Service Officer to work with its International Programs division, particularly with international conferences. Allan Funch, the person designated, was a former newspaperman who had previously served with USIS in Rome, Naples and Calcutta. A New Yorker by birth, Al was proud of his Danish heritage, and we became good friends—as did Margaret and his wife Ruth. He frequently lent me a hand attending to the needs of foreign correspondents during manned space flight launches at Cape

Canaveral. On one occasion he played nursemaid for a week to a specially invited Nigerian editor, a difficult personality, from a newspaper in Kaduna where the Nigeria tracking station was located. After a year and a half at NASA Allan felt International Programs no longer required his services, and he returned to USIA to work in the press services branch.

USIA became deeply involved with NASA in conducting educational campaigns on the U.S. space programs at two different levels: the industrialized societies and Third World countries. As USIA/NASA liaison, I was the coordinating point for both. In the modern industrial societies we simply provided local science writers and scientific organizations with the information on which to base their output on the space program, and they took care of the rest. In most Third World countries materials had to be more refined. USIA's media services handled most of this work with press articles, films, radio and TV documentaries which could be channeled directly to end users.

Africa required a more direct approach. USIA's African branch cooperated with NASA in a joint solution—the Spacemobile, patterned on USIA's mobile films units as described in my chapters on Caracas and Madrid. USIA recruited two highly qualified and adventurous young black men too operate these units. John Twitty handled the Anglophone countries; and Elton Stepherson, completely bilingual, covered the Francophone countries. Their vans were equipped with motion picture projection equipment, a supply of 16-mm documentary films, and literature on the space program. Each man traveled from town to town showing his films, lecturing on the American space program and explaining the role played by African tracking stations. NASA funded the whole operation. The program's success was measured in increased appreciation for the space program and by diminished opposition to the NASA installations. Subsequently both Twitty and Stepherson moved on to other Foreign Service assignments.

As I was preparing to leave NASA for reassignment, the chief of the Spacemobile Services Branch, John E. Sims, wrote Edward R. Murrow expressing his appreciation for "Harry Kendall's many invaluable contributions (which) have helped create a most excellent rapport between the two agencies... Such fine cooperation," he wrote," is not peculiar to Washington alone. In the ten countries where our Spacemobiles have operated or are now operating all-out assistance and cooperation has been the 'order of the day' for all USIS personnel. Again, the result of Harry Kendall's results in our behalf."

Acting USIA Science Advisor

As my three-year Washington tour of duty with NASA drew to a close I began shopping around for a new assignment. My request for a post where I could use my space experience brought no results. In fact, outside of Washington there was no such position. Project Mercury had been completed, and further manned space flights had been suspended while preparations for Project Gemini moved forward. Lula Asberry, my former assistant, was handling my USIA/NASA liaison job quite competently. By now Hal Goodwin had resigned as USIA Science advisor to join the National Science Council. From his new position he wrote a "Well Done" letter to the deputy director for policy and plans, commending my services as USIA/NASA liaison. Hal wrote: "(Harry) has occupied a difficult and often frustrating position with considerable distinction (and) has represented USIA in a manner that has consistently reflected credit on the Agency... Operating with no real supervision, he consistently exploited space events and opportunities for USIA's benefit, usually anticipating the Agency's needs long in advance."

Simon Bourgin, a science writer for Life Magazine, succeeded Hal, but since he would not assume his duties until mid-April. I took over as "acting science advisor" pending a new overseas assignment. My NASA experience had given me a good introduction to the scientific world and I felt at home among the professionals. I represented USIA at scientific conferences, at meetings of the National Science Foundation and the Academy of Sciences, read imposing science literature and, after consulting the real experts, issued USIA scientific policy guidances with a sense of authority. I thoroughly enjoyed acting like a scientist and relinquished my science advisor duties only reluctantly when Bourgin came aboard.

Telling the Space Story Abroad

At the end of April 1964 I was still looking for an overseas assignment when one came up rather unexpectedly from Panama. In January there had been a nasty flag incident in the Canal Zone that resulted in a break in diplomatic relations. The Department of State and USIA had withdrawn all except a skeleton staff, including Carl Davis, the Public Affairs Officer. Now, nearly four months later, the two countries had reestablished diplomatic relations. But bitterness remained, especially in Panama, and Davis urgently needed an experienced, Spanish speaking information officer. I was available and was given two weeks to report. Before getting into that part of my story, let me complete my space adventure.

During my more than three years as USIA/NASA Liaison Officer I had been deeply involved in conveying information on America's space exploration program from its source at NASA to a world wide audience. Though unaware of it at the time I was soon to get equally immersed at the other end of the line in disseminating this information to foreign audiences. This time I would be in direct contact with the public.

In Panama I put space in the back of my mind while working with Davis and Jack Vaughn, our newly appointed ambassador, to get the local situation under control. However, when NASA resumed manned space flight in March 1965 with astronauts Gus Grissom and John Young aboard Gemini III, my enthusiasm for the program regained its old fervor. I had gotten to know both of the astronauts in Washington where Young had briefed Si Bourgin and me on the Gemini program. Later, in Panama I encountered all of the Gemini astronauts when they came there for jungle survival training. When the astronauts emerged from three days in the jungle, Bourgin—their escort officer—and I joined them for an evening's excursion on the Panama Canal aboard the Canal Company's guest launch to the accompaniment of lively Panamanian music.

I was pleasantly surprised to find Panamanian reaction to the U.S. manned space flight was every bit as enthusiastic as the American response. Shortly after the Gemini III flight I was invited to give a talk on America's lunar landing program at the Instituto Panameno Norteamericano, our binational center. It was a new but welcome experience for me. In preparation I obtained a set of slides showing a step-by-step artist's concept of the entire lunar landing process from launch through astronaut recovery and drew up a lecture based on NASA's press packets. With these I set out to explain, in Spanish, how the United States would carry out the mission President Kennedy had laid out in his dramatic proposal of "landing a man on the moon and returning him safely to earth within this decade." The student audience and my USIS colleagues pronounced the presentation a resounding success.

Thus began my space-lecturing career that continued throughout the Gemini and Apollo lunar landing program as I met with audiences all over Latin America and even Vietnam.

Escorting a Gemini Spacecraft

Overseas tours by NASA astronauts were one of the most effective means USIA had for capitalizing on widespread interest in the American space flight program. But astronauts could only be made available on a short-term basis. For more extensive use USIA, with NASA cooperation, employed exhibits of spacecraft and artifacts such as space suits and waste disposal equipment that had been used in space flights. Both were useful in helping to convince foreign audiences that the United States was indeed leading the Soviet Union in the space race.

Thus, shortly after John Glenn's dramatic orbital flight, NASA loaned USIA his Mercury spacecraft, "Friendship 7," for an extended show-and-tell trip to leading cities around the world. I had helped arrange it from my position as USIA/NASA Liaison. USIA's exhibits division, working with NASA, provided supplementary visual materials explaining the flight; and audiences numbering in the hundreds of thousands, most of whom had seen television coverage of Glenn's flight, turned out to marvel at his spacecraft.

The overseas tour of "Friendship 7" was repeated by tours of Gemini and Apollo spacecraft with accompanying exhibits. But the real pieces de resistance were rocks from the moon brought back by Apollo 11. I would take one of these on tour later.

Many USIS posts, using materials provided by USIA Washington, built their own exhibits of rockets, spacecraft and even lunar landing vehicles. They supplemented the impact of astronaut and spacecraft visits by arranging press, radio and TV interviews and by providing local media with informative materials that saw widespread use everywhere. This highly effective technique was repeated throughout the Gemini and Apollo programs.

My first experience in this program involved the Gemini V spacecraft flown by astronauts Gordon Cooper and Pete Conrad on an extended eight-day orbital flight in August 1965. In November USIA sent their spacecraft and an exhibit on U.S. manned space flight to Brazil, Argentina, and Mexico—for six weeks in each country. USIA invited me to serve project as information officer for Argentina and Mexico. Since I did not speak Portuguese I did not go to Brazil. In preparation for the tour I refreshed my knowledge with a visit to the Houston Space Flight Center and to Cape Canaveral for a Gemini launch. My responsibility was officiating at the exhibit and informing news media and the public about the spacecraft itself and the NASA lunar landing program. William (Bill) Bergstrom, on leave from USIS Hong Kong, served as transportation officer to insure that the spacecraft and the exhibit were handled properly as they moved from one exhibit site to another.

Argentina: In January 1966 I met Bergstrom with the exhibit in Buenos Aires. The USIS post had done its work well in publicizing the show. John McKnight, the PAO, assigned two of his officers to work with us—Mel Blum and Forrest Fischer (with whom I was to work later in Vietnam).

We set our exhibit up on the Costanera (shores) of the River Plate. The Argentine Air Force took advantage of our exhibit to display its own space research activities. Gemini V was housed in a brightly colored, specially designed tent. The approach to the spacecraft took visitors through the Argentine Air Force exhibit and past a series of photographic panels and objects portraying aspects of the U.S. space program. These included photos of the earth taken from Gemini V, Astronaut Ed White (Gemini IV) space walking, a space suit, space food samples, and human waste disposal equipment. After looking at these exhibits the visitors stepped up on a platform from which they could view the cramped interior of the spacecraft where Gordon Cooper and Pete Conrad had sat during their eight-day flight.

The Argentines turned out in droves. One Sunday we counted some 25,000 persons as they paraded past to get a glimpse of Gemini V. I responded to hundreds of questions, often repetitive but always interesting, from visitors who poured through the exhibit every day. They would stand there a few moments with looks of puzzlement coming across their faces, then turn to me and say, in embarrassed tones, "Excuse me, senor, a question, how do they handle the problem of human waste in such a small space? And for eight days!?"

I quickly learned to anticipate the question by the looks on their faces. Often I was tempted to make facetious remarks, but I usually confined myself to saying, "They eat low bulk foods which reduce the amount of human waste. They also carry special bags for urine and solid waste disposal. You will find samples of these items on the exhibit panels."

"Oh, gracias senor." And the viewer would move on.

Most of the questions about space flight gave me no trouble, but university engineering students sometimes asked complicated technical questions that taxed my knowledge. These sent me scurrying back to my space flight manual for answers and added interest to my long days at the exhibit.

All went well until early one morning about 4:00 o'clock when one of Argentina's infamous blustery windstorms awoke Bill and me in our hotel. Bill banged on my door shouting, "The tent! The tent!" We rushed out to the exhibit site expecting the worst. Our exhibit panels were askew and a trailer containing part of the Argentine exhibit had been overturned. The Argentine police guards were struggling to keep the tent from being blown away. A few minutes after we arrived the wind died down almost as suddenly as it had begun, and together we managed to restore a semblance of order by the time the public arrived at 8:00 a.m.

Mel Blum arranged for me to give several slide talks for university and technical school groups on "Science and Technology in the United States," and USIA backed me up with a prepared lecture on the topic. The lecture was pure Cold War rhetoric, reflecting Washington's determination to convince the world that the United States was way ahead of the Soviet Union, not just in space but in every aspect of science and technology. I toned down the propaganda thrust, added some lunar landing drama and moved boldly forward, relying heavily on my Panama lecturing experience. The audience turnout and favorable response left me with a warm feeling.

But the best part of the Buenos Aires showing of Gemini V had nothing to do with space flight and everything to do with food. Each evening after closing down, Bill, Forrest, Mel and I headed for one of the many beef bistros along the Costanera where we enjoyed delicious barbecued Argentine steak (*bife*), a glass or two of red wine, and rehashed the events of the day before heading back to our hotel.

Besides Buenos Aires we also exhibited Gemini V in Mar del Plata, Argentina's second largest city. There people were more interested in enjoying the splendid beaches than in space flight, but many did take time out from sunning themselves to visit our exhibit in their bathing attire.

Mexico: In April I met Bergstrom and the Gemini V exhibit again in Mexico City. USIS Mexico had also given the exhibit wide publicity and people responded enthusiastically, turning out by the thousands to see the spacecraft in our tent on Mexico City's Polo Grounds. I was particularly pleased when, as mentioned earlier, Miguel Aleman and Jacobo Zabludovsky of Televisa—whom I had met at Cape Canaveral during the John Glenn flight—showed up with a mobile TV unit to do a live broadcast from the exhibit. They invited me to give their TV audience a guided tour.

Margaret joined me for the final days of the Gemini V showing in Mexico City and accompanied me to Guadalajara where we showed the exhibit for another week.

Astronauts in Panama

In the fall of 1966 Astronauts Richard Gordon and Neil Armstrong, later to become the first man on the moon, went on a public relations tour of Latin America with Panama as their final stop. I was control officer for Panama. They arrived late Sunday, October 30, and spent all of 18 hours with us. Their allotted program time was 7:00 a.m. to 1:00 p.m. Monday, and they followed their schedule like a carefully timed space launch They began with breakfast at the residence of Ambassador Charles Adair, then after a motorcade through the city, they laid a wreath honoring Panama's first president, called on President Marcos Robles, held a press conference and gave a lecture for students. The most memorable event was at the Embassy Residence.

We had just finished breakfast when Carolyn Adair, the Ambassador's wife, rose from her seat and said, "Gentlemen, I know you have undergone an unusual experience orbiting the earth in your Gemini spacecraft, but I want to present you with one made in Panama for which you will never find an equal." With that Mrs. Adair unfolded a colorful *mola* (appliqué) emblazoned with a Gemini spacecraft, made by Panama's Cuna Indians of the San Blas Islands, and presented it to the two astronauts. My own souvenir of the astronaut's visit is a thank-you letter from Neil Armstrong.

Chile: The Chet & Harry Show

In the summer of 1967 USIA transferred me to Santiago, Chile, again as USIS information officer. Chile had a special interest in the United States space exploration program because NASA, together with the University of Chile, operated a scientific satellite tracking station near Santiago. The director, Chester Shaddeau, was a genial, bilingual space scientist known to all as Chet. He and I were to develop a close personal relationship and become local celebrities during the Apollo lunar landing program.

When the Apollo lunar flights got under way, Catholic University's Channel-13 (Canal Trece) decided to carry live satellite feeds from NASA's Houston space flight center. These feeds, all in English, were the same as those used by American networks, the only difference being that the U.S. networks employed their own science correspondents as commentators to interpret action on the screen for their TV audiences.

Channel 13 had no one with sufficient knowledge of the U.S. space program to fulfill the commentator's role for its Spanish speaking audiences. The director knew of my NASA background and asked me to fulfill that role for the Apollo flights. I agreed but suggested that he also invite Chet who spoke excellent Spanish. Chet accepted with alacrity. He brought a set of models of the Saturn rocket and the lunar landing vehicle to the studio, and between us we put on what we jocularly called the Chet and Harry show, a take-off on the Chet Huntley-David Brinkley TV news program then popular in the United States.

We warmed up on the Apollo 8 lunar circumnavigation flight and the subsequent Apollo 9 and 10 earth orbital flights as the astronauts practiced their docking maneuvers. Often we spent as much as two hours straight in front of the TV cameras using the models to explain what was happening with the rocket, with the Apollo spacecraft, and what the astronauts were doing at any given time. During lulls when nothing particular was happening—and there were many such occasions—we took turns answering questions phoned in by the audience and passed on to us by the regular TV announcers.

The real marathon came during the Apollo 11 moon landing. A few days after the event I wrote my mother:

"I would never have believed a people could get so wrapped up in an event as the Chileans did with our manned lunar landing. For two weeks the papers have published practically nothing else. The radio stations and the TV have inundated the public with every detail. The people we meet on the street, at parties and in friends' homes talk of nothing else. I thought at first it was my own involvement, but other Embassy officers tell me they encounter the same thing. During the flight I was on the air before the TV cameras on eight separate occasions in programs ranging from thirty minutes to five hours on the night of the lunar walk. Since everyone was looking at nothing else but that program my face became a rather familiar scene in everyone's living room. Questions from the TV audience came by the hundreds and covered virtually everything from how the astronauts dispose of human waste to scientific theories on the makeup of the moon. As a result of all this Chet and I have become a celebrities around town, the type that people point out in crowds, ask for autographs, and say hello to as though you were an old friend. It is awfully good for one's ego, but it can also be rather trying. Now that Apollo 11 is over, I hope memories will fade in a hurry."

My performance on the Apollo telecasts led to numerous invitations to lecture on the U.S. space program for audiences ranging from scientific groups and university students to Rotary clubs and high schools. The demand was insatiable, and I found myself lecturing three and four times a week, often twice in one day, mostly but not exclusively on my own time. I accepted one high school invitation expecting a classroom audience, only to find 1200 students awaiting me in a huge auditorium. I was gratified that my performance evoked more than just polite applause.

Lecturing in one's non-native language can lead to some amusing and sometimes embarrassing experiences. On one occasion, speaking to an audience of university students, I was explaining how NASA's space research had produced many spin-off products for everyday use. My example was Teflon. "This product," I said, "is now widely used for kitchen utensils because food doesn't stick to it. For example, every morning my wife cooks my eggs in a Teflon frying pan." The expression I used in Spanish, *mis huevos*, brought a burst of laughter that puzzled me. Later I learned that mis huevos is a Spanish euphemism for "my testicles." I should have said *los huevos.*

The demand on my time for lecturing on the U.S. space program seemed never to let up, and after several weeks Carl Davis, then PAO in Chile, reminded me that I had other duties to perform so I began playing hard to get.

Travels with a Moon Rock

My TV performance produced another unexpected result—a trip with a moon rock as a resource person on lunar exploration. Anxious to take full advantage of the favorable publicity generated by the Apollo ll lunar landing, USIA obtained from NASA six lunar rock samples for showing in the major world geographical areas. To enhance their presentation the Agency's exhibits division put together identical displays on the American lunar landing program with the moon rocks as the centerpiece. In each exhibit a walnut-sized moon rock was mounted like a jewel in a vacuum-sealed, top hat-shaped Plexiglas case filled with protective nitrogen. The case itself was mounted on a slowly rotating pedestal inside a large plastic globe. The moon rock looked just like any earthly lava rock with the exception of some tiny glass specks that shone under a bright spotlight that dramatized the exhibit in the darkened display room. A continuous play tape recording explained the rock's origin. USIA assigned Foreign Service officers to accompany the priceless moon rocks wherever they went for exhibition.

The Latin American version of the moon rock exhibit had a limited first showing at a geology conference in Caracas and was then moved to Lima for its first public showing. Just after Thanksgiving 1969, Bob Amerson, then USIA assistant director for Latin America, asked me to accompany the moon rock exhibit from Lima to Bogota and then Mexico City. My job was to advise the posts on exhibit techniques and to serve as "moon rock information officer" for media news coverage.

In Lima, as a portent of things to come, I found long lines waiting to see the rock at an annual Pacific Fair. My anxiety level was at a high pitch as I left for Bogotá with the moon rock beside me in its specially designed case, traveling incognito in a diplomatic pouch and on a half-price ticket. The first courier to carry a moon rock had checked it into the baggage compartment. When he reached his destination he found that vibration had shaken the rock loose from its setting so he had to go back to Houston to get it reset. Thereafter the rock was accorded favored passenger treatment alongside its escort officer.

USIS Bogotá, like me, had received only three days' notice that they would get the moon rock. They were eager but poorly prepared. Nevertheless, the staff rallied to the cause and mounted the exhibit in the binational center (BNC). I drew on my Santiago and earlier Panama experience in handling radio and TV publicity. The public responded far better than we had good reason to expect. After the BNC exhibit, a one-day showing at the Bogota airport in conjunction with a U.S. Air Force acrobatic display drew a record day's audience of 17,000 people.

Bob Amerson was in Mexico City for a hemispheric meeting of American ambassadors when I arrived. After seeing the opening and my performance Bob asked if I would be willing to continue through the remainder of the Latin American tour. That would take me to 16 countries in Central and South America and keep me on the road until the middle of May 1970. With Carl Davis's concurrence I agreed. The Mexico City exhibition was completed just before the Christmas holidays. From there it would go to Guatemala City after Christmas.

Margaret and I had planned a year-end vacation in Punta Arenas at the tip end of Chile. I shifted my family vacation plans from Punta Arenas to Mexico City and Guatemala. Margaret flew up from Santiago with Nancy and Judy, and Betsy flew down from Indianapolis where she was then in high school. Moon rock magic gave us an unforgettable Christmas and New Year enjoying gala Mexican and Guatemalan festivities unique to those countries. During the next five months I would see my family only three times—twice in Santiago and once in Montevideo. Margaret joined me for a week in Buenos Aires.

After Guatemala the rock became my constant traveling companion around Latin America. USIA scheduled moon rock showings to take advantage of major local events such as national festivals or fairs that would enhance attendance. This resulted in a zigzag course through Latin America and frequent backtracking. Transferring the moon rock exhibit from country to country involved more than just a diplomatic pouch. I also had to oversee the shipment of the four huge wooden crates containing the display unit that was essential to proper exhibition of the rock. The crates would fit only in large jet aircraft with wide doors. To meet our tight schedule, the crates had to take precedence over all other freight. No matter how many assurances cargo agents had given us that the shipment would get priority treatment, the loaders' automatic reaction was to push the large crates aside in favor of less bulky items. At each airport I had to use all the moon rock's influence to insure we traveled together. Working with the individual USIS post control officers, many of them old friends from prior assignments, I made every one of our 28 showings in 21 cities in 16 Latin American countries on time, setting it up and taking it down at each stop.

Security was a primary concern. No one overlooked the possibility that some revolutionary group, seeking publicity for its own cause, might try to "kidnap" the rock to draw attention to themselves. A widely reported theft of moon dust in Los Angeles didn't help matters any. I was met at each airport by armed security guards and then taken, often with a motorcycle escort, to the American Embassy where the rock was stored until ready for display. Guards were always present during the showings, sometimes the bare minimum of a single policeman and once even a detachment of soldiers, a ridiculous excess. Each evening I returned the rock to the Embassy for safekeeping until the next day's showing.

As USIA/NASA Liaison Officer I had learned a lot about space exploration but practically nothing about selenology (lunar geology), so I devoted most of my in-flight time between countries boning up on the moon and moon rocks. Geological dictionary in hand, I pored over official NASA reports on the rock studies to prepare myself for that unexpected tough question which always seemed to pop up.

We opened each showing with a press conference where I was the central figure; I appeared on 40 TV shows and an equal number of radio programs, answering hundreds of listeners' questions ranging from the scientific to the inane, from those wanting to know the geological structure of the moon or whether it was really made of green cheese to those who thought the whole moon landing episode was a fake. And there were many, many questions at the exhibit itself. I also took part in scientific forums and gave lectures at universities on "The Scientific Results of Lunar Exploration." After the first three or four countries many things became repetitive; but there was always some new element, and the totality was a highly interesting and productive experience. I was gratified that reports from the field to Washington gave me and the exhibit high marks.

As part of the same program, the Department of State and NASA sent each of our ambassadors in Latin America a small lunar fragment imbedded in Lucite and mounted on a simple but decorative stand together with the host country flag that had accompanied the Apollo 11 astronauts to the moon. Our ambassadors presented these gifts to the chief of state in the name of the people of the United States, and several made the presentations in connection with the moon rock exhibit. On these occasions I gave a little spiel about the lunar exploration program for the president and assembled cabinet officers. I have photographs of myself with the presidents of Argentina, Brazil, Bolivia, Costa Rica, Ecuador, Nicaragua, Panama, Paraguay, and Uruguay.

While I was escorting the Apollo 11 moon rock around, Apollo 12 Astronauts Charles "Pete" Conrad, Richard Gordon, and Alan Bean also made a tour of Latin America. They arrived in Chile ahead of my exhibit and one-upped me by presenting President Frei with the lunar fragment and a Chilean flag that had been to the moon to President Frei.

In summary my moon rock trip involved:

* 28 public showings of the moon rock with the display unit and 35 private showings without the unit in 21 cities for a total audience of more than 1,106,000 persons, most of whom stood in line anywhere from 15 minutes to an hour to see the rock.
* Private showings for the presidents of nine of the 16 countries visited. Several of them invited their full cabinets and the diplomatic corps to be present.
* Participation in 40 prime time TV programs ranging from 5 minutes to an hour each; 40 radio programs; and 18 press conferences and press previews, thus reaching millions.
* Five university level lectures on "The Scientific Results of Lunar Exploration" and participation in two public forums on the same subject.

In retrospect, despite the deadlines that had to be met, despite the impossible hours and continual travel for nearly six months, I found the duty as "moon rock information officer" immensely rewarding and frequently enjoyable. Everywhere I found a high degree of receptivity to the information I had to impart, and only occasionally did I encounter skepticism about the U.S. lunar exploration program. Nowhere did I find hostility. Curiously, despite all the television exposure, I found that many people regarded the lunar landing program as another case of American gimmickry and still seriously doubted that man has reached the moon.

The greatest pleasure of the whole trip was working with a dedicated group of USIS Foreign Service professionals who knew how to extract the best possible benefit for the United States from the small Apollo 11 moon rock. At every stop they showed their appreciation for my efforts with warm and generous hospitality. I could not possibly mention every one to whom I am indebted, but I am deeply grateful to them all.

Space Lectures in Vietnam

I was hardly back from my moon rock experience before orders came from USIA assigning me to Vietnam as economic programs planning officer. More of that later, but at the time the assignment struck me as a fatal blow to my 'adventure in space." Surely, no one in that beleaguered country would be interested in the U.S. space program. In fact, it was not until July 1971 and I had already been in country nine months that I was asked to give a space lecture. Astronaut David Scott's

Apollo 15 lunar landing inspired the director of the American Cultural Center in Cantho, who had heard of my Santiago TV experience, to invite me to give a talk on the Apollo program.

I was a soft touch. A year earlier during my moon rock trip around Latin America I had spent the better part of a week in Panama with David Scott who was there representing President Nixon at the 1970 InterAmerican Olympic Games. That was before his walk on the moon, and I found him to be a warm and outgoing individual who charmed his Panamanian hosts. The moon rock showing was scheduled to take advantage of widespread interest in the Games.

When I started preparing for the Cantho lecture I was appalled at how rusty I had become after being off the space flight lecture circuit. I didn't trust myself to give an extemporaneous talk so I took a day off and drafted a slide presentation on "Apollo on the Moon: The Scientific Results." I had an audience of about 50 people who seemed attentive and interested, but I was disappointed when the only question I got came from an American soldier. In Saigon I repeated the lecture several times at the Vietnamese American Association. There, although university students in my audience showed a lot of interest, the vagueness of their questions manifested lack of exposure to the massive TV coverage people got in other countries. I gave my final space lecture on June 7, 1972, shortly before the end of my Vietnam tour of duty. After that I became an interested spectator but an inactive participant in the American space program.

A Look Back in Space

When President Kennedy established the moon-landing program as an American goal for the sixties, we in USIA had our work cut out for us. Our job was to get the story of that effort out to the world. Though portrayed as peaceful exploration of space, the moon-landing program was really a highly effective Cold War campaign designed to demonstrate to the world American superiority in science and technology. Audiences everywhere equated space flight supremacy with military capability. In the intense competition of the Cold War the Soviets had gained an initial edge with the launch of Sputnik and the first man in space, and they kept the world guessing about what they would do next. We were doing well with the scientific space exploration, but manned space flight was what caught and held the public eye. The

123

audacious challenge of a moon landing told the Soviets to put up or shut up.

For USIA the manned space program was a natural. We did not have to "sell" the program. Audiences at all levels everywhere were avid for information. All we had to do was to get it to them. The openness of the NASA program provided a stark contrast with Soviet secretiveness, and we exploited that difference to the hilt.

The three years I was at NASA coincided with the Project Mercury program, the beginnings of U.S. manned space flight. There was no CNN to take live coverage to the far corners of the globe. Satellite communications technology was still in the experimental stage. American TV networks and other news media informed domestic audiences. Overseas, for real time information, audiences turned to USIA's Voice of America. Foreign print media relied mainly on wire services to provide news coverage of the major events, but they turned to USIS for backgrounders on the NASA program. For follow up information, NASA and USIA documentaries found ready outlets among television stations around the world.

NASA's cooperation in sending its spacecraft and astronauts overseas increased the impact, enabling USIS posts to arrange public appearances both for scientific communities and for hero-worshiping audiences. They were seen and heard by millions.

The Apollo 11 landing on the moon on July 20, 1969, was an event of world proportions. By that time satellite TV had become a reality, and the feat held history's largest TV audience awestruck for days.

My six years of direct contact with tens of thousands of people all over Latin America during the Gemini flights and the Apollo lunar landings left no doubt in my mind that the USIS information programs were achieving their objective of convincing the world public of America's leadership in space as well as in science and technology.

I am grateful to have been USIA's point man at NASA during the initial years of the space flight program, and I am proud to have been a part of USIA's overseas team in telling audiences all over the world the story of America's conquest of space. It was indeed an unforgettable experience.

At Cape Canaveral Mexican TV Correspondent Miguel Aleman, Jr., right, and the author review an Aleman article on space exploration beside a model of a Mercury spacecraft while they await Astronaut John Glenn's earth orbital flight February 20, 1962. Aleman's live coverage of the Glenn flight was the very first direct telecast from the U.S. to Mexico City.

At Houston Space Center Astronaut Gordon Cooper, right, who, with Charles Conrad, circumnavigated the earth in Gemini V for eight days in August 1965, describes its characteristics to the author as he prepares to escort the spacecraft on a tour of Argentina and Mexico.

Members of Argentine Air Force Academy examine interior of Gemini 5 spacecraft as the author looks on. On one Sunday alone in Buenos Aires more than 25,000 persons visited the exhibit.

Chile's President Eduardo Frei and his wife get details of the Apollo 11 lunar landing in Spanish from the author during the live telecast from the moon. (Photo: Washington Gonzalez, El Mercurio).

The author's long hours before Chilean television camera explaining the Apollo lunar landing program motivated this cartoon by a USIS Santiago artist.

On December 12, 1969, Mexico City's Mayor Alfonso Corona del Rosal, second from right, and U.S. ambassador to Mexico Robert McBride inspect the Apollo 11 moon rock on exhibit at Mexico's Museum of Natural History, at right is USIA Director Frank Shakespeare, at left under the lamp is the author. During the six months the he traveled with the moon rock Kendall presided at 28 public showings in 21 cities for a total audience of 1,106,000 persons spectators stood in line up to an hour to see the rock.

Jacobo Zabludowsky, left, and colleague of Mexico City's Televisora Nacional interview author Kendall about the Apollo 11 moon rock during his stay in that city. The cartoon spoofs security aspects of the rock.

In Buenos Aires, Argentine President Juan Carlos Ongania, left, gets details about Apollo 11 moon rock from the author in the presence of U.S. Ambassador John Davis Lodge and USIS Director Frank Oram (with glasses). Ambassador Lodge, previously U.S. envoy to Spain, presented the president with a chip from the moon on behalf of the American people. The author gave similar showings for presidents of nine of the 16 Latin American countries where the rock was exhibited.

In Asuncion the author explains details of the Apollo 11 moon landing to Paraguay university students. During his moon rock tour Kendall gave five university level lectures (in Spanish) on "The Scientific Results of Lunar Exploration" and participated in two public forums on this topic.

In Panama City the author welcomes Astronaut David Scott to the Apollo 11 moon rock exhibit on the grounds of the Legislative Palace. Scott, who was later to command Apollo 15 and walk on the moon, was in Panama representing President Nixon at the 1970 Interamerican Olympic Games.

VI Panama - Picking up the Pieces

The Flag Incident

Less than two months after he took office following the assassination of President Kennedy, President Lyndon B. Johnson encountered his first foreign affairs crisis. It came as a result of a flag incident instigated by American students at Balboa High School in the Panama Canal Zone.

Earlier, in 1960, after embittered debates and massive efforts by Panamanian students to implant their flag in the Canal Zone, President Eisenhower had ordered that both the Panamanian and the American flags be flown at designated sites in the Canal Zone to recognize Panama's titular sovereignty. The high school was not one of the sites. For the Panamanians, Eisenhower's concession had been a big victory. The Panamanian flag had not flown in the Zone since 1903.

At the heart of the dispute were the "perpetuity" and "sovereignty" clauses in the 1903 Hay—Bunau-Varilla Treaty. The idea for the treaty had been sold to the United States Senate by a French citizen, Philippe Bunau-Varilla, anxious to save his investment in the failed French effort to dig a canal across the Isthmus. Under this treaty the United States acquired the right from the newly independent Panama to construct a canal within a ten-mile wide zone and to govern the zone "in perpetuity... as though it were sovereign." Panama, at the instigation of the United States and hoping to gain major economic benefits from the canal, had declared its independence from Colombia of which it had been a part. When Panamanian leaders reached Washington to negotiate a treaty they found the Bunau-Varilla treaty an established fact.[29]

Patriotic Panamanians contended that the treaty had been foisted upon them as a fraud. The sovereignty and perpetuity aspects poisoned U.S.-Panamanian relations from the very beginning. Panamanians looked upon the canal as their major natural resource for which the United States derived a lion's share of the income. They argued that the

---

[29]. For a detailed description of the negotiations that led to the Hay-Bunau Varilla Treaty see Edmund Morris, *Theodore Rex*, New York, Random House, 2001,

Zone cut the country in half and limited Panamanian access to the southern part.

On the American side, the construction of the canal and 50 years of operation by the Panama Canal Company, a subsidiary of the U.S. Army, had developed strong vested interests to which both the Pentagon and the "Zonians" clung tenaciously. The PanCanal Company employees who sought to defend their sinecures were the most adamant. The Pentagon was equally firm in upholding the vital importance of its military installations in the Canal Zone.

On both the U.S. and the Panamanian sides flying the national flags had become all-important symbols of sovereignty, not to be toyed with.

On January 9, 1964, in defiance of official orders and urged on by their parents, the students at Balboa High raised the American flag in front of their school.[30] Word of the action went out quickly to nearby Panama City. Some 200 Panamanians marched peaceably into the Zone to protest the absence of their flag. Zone police allowed the marchers to display their flag; but a scuffle broke out between the two groups, and the Panamanian flag was torn and trampled upon. When the demonstrators returned to the city emotions flared quickly. A highly incensed crowd climbed the mesh wire fence separating the city from the Canal Zone, tore down the American flag and burned it. In the melee twenty Panamanians and four Americans were killed. Protest riots broke out all over Panama City and a mob burned the USIS library.

As a result of the incident Panama broke diplomatic relations with the United States. There was no U.S. ambassador in Panama at the time. The previous ambassador, Joseph Farland, had resigned several months earlier and had not yet been replaced. Given the hostile environment, the Department of State and USIA transferred most of their Embassy personnel out of the country, leaving only a charge d'affaires and a skeleton staff. In the case of USIS it was PAO Carl Davis, a Latin America veteran.

Assistant Secretary of State for Latin America Thomas Mann, at the direction of President Johnson, took charge of discussions aimed at

---

[30]. Good accounts of these events and the negotiation of the 1978 Carter-Torrijos Canal Treaty are given in Walter LaFeber, *The Panama Canal - The Crisis in Historical Perspective*, Oxford University Press, updated edition, 1989. Shelton B. Liss, *The Canal - Aspects of United States-Panamanian Relations*, Notre Dame, 1967, carries a detailed account of the flag incident.

resolving the dispute. At the same time Johnson announced that the United States would begin studies for a sea-level canal in Central America and Mexico. Concerned about possible loss of income through competition from another canal, Panamanian President Roberto Chiari agreed to the restoration of diplomatic relations, but only after the United States accepted his demand to renegotiate the 1903 Treaty. On April 3, 1964, the United States and Panama resumed diplomatic relations.

Information Officer, Panama

With the restoration of diplomatic relations Carl Davis asked USIA to assign a qualified, Spanish-speaking information officer to the post on an urgent basis to help pick up the pieces. The Latin America Area offered me the job. I had really wanted to go back to East Asia, but there was still no post in sight. The Panamanian incident had been in the top of the news for weeks, and the position presented the kind of challenge I liked. I called Margaret. She was agreeable. I accepted immediately.

The Agency asked me to arrive in Panama within two weeks. I had two choices: I could pull up stakes in Washington and take my family with me, or I could leave Margaret and the children behind while they finished the spring school term and then join me in Panama. Margaret and the girls objected to being left behind. We decided to go together. We left our house in charge of a neighbor who managed rental properties, the movers came; and almost before we realized what had happened we were heading for Panama. On the way we stopped in Mexico City to visit USIA's Regional Service Center[31] where I assured myself of publications support at my new post.

Arrival in Panama

On April 24, 1964, we stepped out of our Pan American Airways plane at the Tocumen international airport into a Panamanian steam

---

[31]. USIA ran two Regional Service Centers, one in Mexico City that published books and pamphlets in Spanish for distribution by USIS posts in Latin America, and one in Manila that provided a similar service in a variety of languages for USIS posts in East Asia and the Pacific. Significant economies were achieved by this centralized publishing.

envelope that was to surround us during our whole three years in that tropical country. Carl and Joye Davis greeted us at the airport.

Carl apologized for the short notice he had given me but said he needed my help in getting USIS back into business. We went swiftly through customs as Margaret chatted animatedly with Joye, a gentle, soft-spoken mother of two, about schooling for our girls. Joye took Margaret and our three girls into Panama City with the USIS driver while Carl and I went in his personal car. On the way he briefed me on the latest developments.

Things had calmed down a bit since January, but for about a month after the riots the atmosphere had been really hostile. It was not a pretty situation, and the Panamanian media's inflammatory reporting didn't help any. Mobs in Panama City had fired more than 2000 bullets at the Tivoli Hotel, just inside the Canal Zone. In northern Panama the American consul in Chiriqui escaped lynching only through the help of a Panamanian friend who put him in the trunk of his car and drove him across the border into Costa Rica. Carl, Joye and their two children spent most of their time in the Canal Zone waiting for tempers to return to normal.

The USIS Panamanian employees had been forced to lay low. None had agreed with the action that set off the protest, but neither did they agree with the violent turn it took. They had stayed at home during the break in relations but were all were back at work and had been very helpful in reestablishing USIS cultural and media contacts.

Carl's previous post had been in the Dominican Republic under Ambassador Joseph Farland. When President Eisenhower appointed Farland ambassador to Panama he brought Carl with him as public affairs officer. President Kennedy had kept Farland on. Carl said Farland had been very popular with the Panamanians but got fed up with the inability of the State Department and AID (Agency for International Development) to take any positive action on Panama's demands to renegotiate the Canal treaty. He resigned and returned to his old business in West Virginia[32]. The Senate had not yet confirmed his designated successor, and the United States was represented by a charge d'affaires when the flag incident occurred.

With the resumption of diplomatic relations President Johnson had personally chosen Jack Hood Vaughn as ambassador, and he had just

---

[32] Subsequently he was appointed U.S. ambassador to Pakistan.

arrived. Vaughn was a former head of the Peace Corps for Latin America and before that director of the USAID Mission in Chad. Johnson had met Vaughn while traveling in Africa as vice president and liked his down-to-earth approach to African problems. Carl described Vaughn as a "gutsy guy" who spoke a very colloquial Spanish that he learned as a student at the University of Mexico. He had been a golden gloves lightweight champion and earned his way through college by boxing.

Other Embassy personnel were coming in gradually. State and the White House wanted to have a new staff take a fresh look at the Panama situation. USAID had also allocated a larger budget to support the Alliance for Progress effort and assigned a new director, James Magellas, who had a reputation for problem solving. I would be working closely with him.

Except for myself, Carl had asked USIA to postpone sending any further USIS personnel pending a decision on what to do about the burned library. The books had been completely destroyed, but the shell of the building remained. We would have to decide whether to rebuild or look for a new site. Meanwhile, he and I and the local staff would have temporary offices in the chancery. As Carl said, we were cramped for space, but at least we were in business.

Getting Settled

Carl had reserved a two-room suite for us at the Continental Hotel in downtown Panama City. A fair-sized pool greeted us as we entered the hotel premises. Several children of hotel residents were splashing about. Our girls were delighted. The Embassy was using the Continental Hotel for other incoming officers, so Margaret and our children had ample companionship as we searched for a more permanent place to live. The Embassy paid tuition to the Canal Zone schools for its officers' children but not for Panamanian schools that taught only in Spanish. We enrolled our children in the Zone schools, and they went back and forth by bus.

I went to work immediately, taking time out whenever possible to house hunt. It took us two months to find a suitable place within my living allowance. It was a nice three-bedroom house in the Bella Vista section a block up from Panama Bay and five blocks from the Embassy. I could walk to work and home for lunch.

Weather was a major fact of life in Panama. There were two seasons—wet and dry. The rains began in April and lasted until early December. The humidity varied considerably between the wet and dry seasons, but because the temperature remained fairly constant the year round it was easy to lose track of time. Torrential rains of ten or twelve-inches in a couple of hours were commonplace. No one seemed unhappy with all the rain. The Panama Canal operated entirely on fresh water, and rains were what kept it going. Every ship passing through the canal used up 52 million gallons of water, and upwards of 30 ships passed through every day—sometimes as many as 48.

Picking up the Pieces

Carl wasted no time in introducing me to the Panamanian news media. After protocol calls on Ambassador Vaughn and top Embassy officials, he accompanied me to the major newspapers to meet the editors and leading journalists. At that time the leading papers were *El Panama America* and its English version, *The Panama American*; *La Estrella de Panama* and its English version, *The Star and Herald*; *The Panama Tribune* (English), *Critica*, and *Ultimas Noticias*. (Here I should note that while Spanish is the official language of Panama, English is used widely, both in the Canal Zone and in the Republic where it is the first language for the many West Indian immigrants who helped dig the Canal and their descendants. For example, *The Panama Tribune*, edited by a highly respected West Indian intellectual, circulated almost entirely in that community. When I left Panama in 1967 there were twelve papers being published in Panama City, an unusual number for a city that size. We also visited the two television stations and the major radio stations. Panamanian journalists knew Carl well, and they received us warmly.

The media calls completed, Carl had me sit in on his regular weekly meeting with Panama Canal information officers, both from the Canal Company and the U.S. military. A week after these introductions Carl gave a reception in my honor at his home and invited many of those we had met during our courtesy visits. I was pleasantly surprised to see that most of them came. Officially I was off and running.

The day after the reception I asked Carl how it was that the very people who ran inflammatory campaigns against the United States during flag incident saw no contradiction in greeting him like a long lost brother when we called on them, or in accepting his invitations and drinking up his whiskey.

Carl explained that Panama had a love-hate relationship with the United States, that there was hardly any journalist or anyone of importance in the country itself who did not travel frequently to the United States or have relatives there. He said the Embassy had always enjoyed good relations with the news media, and he fully expected that Jack Vaughn would be as well received as Ambassador Farland was during his tenure.

As Carl explained and I was to learn first-hand, most of the Panamanian animosity was turned against the Canal Zone and the Zonians (American residents) whom they saw as enjoying special privileges at the expense of Panama. The fact that any one of the journalists would grasp these privileges for himself if he could didn't change their resentment. They saw the Zonians as living in a virtual paradise where everything was provided for them—housing, health care, education for their children, food at subsidized prices, and recreation, to mention only a few. On top of this the Zonians received higher salaries than the average American and many times higher than most Panamanians. All they had to do was to keep that canal running. That they did very well, but many acted as though the Republic of Panama didn't exist, spoke no Spanish at all, never bothered to learn. Some had never set foot inside Panama and looked down their noses at Panamanian citizens. The fact that many of those living and working in the Canal Zone were fourth generation Zonians and still held these attitudes helped to explain the Panamanian's resentment.

Paradoxically, next to the government itself, the Canal Company was the country's largest employer. Panamanian workers were valued employees, and they had continued to work even during the January uprising. They lived in the Republic and went back and forth to the Canal Zone to perform their duties, but they did not enjoy the special privileges or the high pay scale bestowed upon the Americans. In effect, there were two payrolls—the American and the Panamanian. In the early days of the Canal they were distinguished from each other as the gold and the silver payrolls.

These, however, were all symptoms of the major issue. What Panama really wanted was not just a bigger share of the take from the traffic on the Canal and not just a bigger voice in running it. Ultimately what they wanted was the Canal itself.

Just how much control the United States was willing to cede to Panama to achieve peaceful bilateral relations was a major question and became the subject of intense negotiations. Presidential elections were coming up in both Panama and the United States, so neither side was willing to make concessions that might damage the chances of either Lyndon Johnson or Marcos Robles in the forthcoming presidential elections.[33]

Reflecting on the foregoing information I observed that the only remedy would be to change the system, but that would have to come on a much higher level than ours.[34] The question was what Carl and I as lower level officials could do.

President Johnson had Assistant Secretary Tom Mann working on the problem from the Washington end, and Ambassador Vaughn was working on it in Panama; so the best thing Carl and I could do was to help promote an atmosphere of conciliation to facilitate both sides of the negotiations. Thus, our role was to maintain good relations with the journalists to insure that information about the U.S. position on the canal reached the Panamanian people.

USIS Reconstructs

After Carl had introduced me to our key contacts, he and I made a detailed inspection of the burned-out USIS building. Though known as the USIS library, it had actually contained the whole USIS operation. It was a two-story structure. On the lower floor were the library, a radio studio, and documentary film lending section; on the upper level were the USIS offices and a modest auditorium used for lectures and film screenings. The location was favorable and the institution was well known to USIS clientele, primarily educators, students and the news media.

We had to decide whether to rebuild or seek another location. It was a leased property so the Panamanian proprietor was also involved. Carl had already looked at several possibilities; but the owners, for obvious

---

[33]. Robles was supported by then President Roberto Chiari. He was subsequently elected by an ample margin and served a four-year term, throughout our stay in Panama.

[34]. See LaFeber, p. 158 ff. In 1977, under the Carter Administration the United States and Panama concluded a treaty, effective December 31, 1999, that gave Panama full possession of the Panama Canal, free of American military bases. Since January 1, 2000, Canal territory has remained neutral. Panama has primary responsibility for its defense, but the United States military has the right to defend the canal's neutrality.

reasons, were not interested in renting to USIS. The burned out building had been untouched since the fire. While the flames had damaged or destroyed most of the its contents, the basic structure seemed to be in good shape. Carl had asked a construction engineer to look it over. He had pronounced the framework as solid.

After discussing the alternatives we decided to offer the building's owner a long-term lease in exchange for rebuilding the library to our specifications. He accepted, and within a fortnight a construction crew went to work on the building. We moved back in at the beginning of September and named the restored library the Biblioteca Amador-Washington, after the first presidents of Panama and the United States. I wrote my mother about the move:

"The USIS building has now been completely renovated. This week we have been busy as pack ants moving our equipment, books, pamphlets and office furniture into our new-old building. For me it is completely new. For the others, especially our Panamanian employees it is 'going back home.' They are all quite happy about it. During the four and a half months I have been here we have just been trying to keep things going. As of next week we hope to be back in full-scale operation. There is certainly plenty to be done in this country, especially in my line of work."

About the time we moved back into our USIS quarters, Charles (Chuck) Meyer arrived from Tegucigalpa with his wife and two children to become our Cultural Affairs Officer. (He had been director of the Panama City binational center when the riots broke out in January and had been given a temporary assignment in Honduras.) Our basic staff was now complete, and our daughters had two new playmates.

With President Johnson taking a personal interest in the canal negotiations—State officials referred to him as the Panama Desk Officer—USIA put Panama at the top of its priority list. While most USIS posts had to struggle to get Washington to grant them sufficient budget and personnel to fulfill their program obligations, we were given all the operational funds and personnel we could effectively use. A country the size of Panama, two million population at the time, would normally have had a USIS staff of three or at most four American officers. By 1965 we had six Americans and fifteen local employees. This is not to say that we were overstaffed. Given our country objective of "promoting an atmosphere of conciliation for the negotiations" there was ample work for all.

The Embassy/USIS Team

During my three years in Panama I worked under two ambassadors and two public affairs officers. Ambassador Vaughn headed the U.S. Mission from April 1964 to June 1965 when he was named Director of the U.S. Peace Corps. In that one year he became extremely popular as a tough negotiator who also understood the Panamanian common man and was able to speak to him in his own language. He was succeeded by Charles Adair, a career Foreign Service Officer who spoke fluent Spanish but without the vernacular flair that made Jack Vaughn so popular. Adair conducted his office with dignity and was well respected by both the government and the public. I was fortunate in being able to work closely with both men and the Embassy staff they headed. The Embassy benefited from a highly competent political staff, notably Deputy Chief of Mission Rufus Z. Smith, Steve Bosworth and Diego Ascensio, all of whom later became ambassadors on their own.

In August 1965 USIA transferred Carl Davis to Miami to supervise the Agency's programs directed at Cuba. (We joined forces again in Santiago, Chile, in September 1968.) Hoyt Ware, who had spent a good part of his early career with the Associated Press in Brazil and spoke Spanish with a pronounced Portuguese accent, succeeded Carl. Both men were highly competent in dealing with the public and enjoyed the confidence of their ambassadors and co-workers. My other USIS colleagues were all hard-working officers who gave a good account of themselves in Panama and went on to various degrees of distinction in subsequent assignments. Our Panamanian employees, who had served USIS loyally for many years, provided us the specialized knowledge and contacts that enabled us to conduct our mission. In working with us they took the attitude that they were serving not only the interests of United States but also those of Panama, and we never asked them to do anything to the contrary.

The Wolf Pack

Because of the Canal, the American media devoted a disproportionate share of attention to Latin America, particularly during and immediately after the January-April 1964 diplomatic rupture. Press agencies retained regular stringers in the country. Major American newspapers, newsweeklies, and radio and TV networks all had correspondents with Latin America as their beats, and airline schedules made Panama a natural north-south stopover. Any hint of student demonstrations or unusual political activity brought immediate telephone inquiries to Carl Davis or myself. If anything more "promising" developed the correspondents would smell blood and descend upon us. They were so persistent we began calling them "the wolf pack."[35] When the political situation grew hot, there might be as many as 15 to 30 American correspondents in that small country, all asking for briefings by the American Ambassador or Embassy officers on the current political situation. It was part of our business and we enjoyed our contacts with them; but we spent hundreds of hours, often evenings and weekends, helping these professional newsmen get the information they needed for their American audiences.

Vacations - Escaping the Heat

My boyhood in Louisiana adapted me to hot clammy weather, but Panama City's heat is so oppressive even the natives seek relief whenever an opportunity arises. Our weekend solution was a family outing at Summit Gardens, a 30-minute drive from the city. There Canal Zone authorities had developed an attractive park area with exotic tropical flora and a variety of zoo animals native to the tropics, including brightly colored macaws. Our children loved climbing in the shade trees, fishing for guppies in the ponds and watching the monkeys at play. Amador Beach, also in the Canal Zone, offered relaxed swimming inside protective shark nets and some relief from the heat. The island of Taboga, an hour's boat ride from Panama City, offered diversion.

To really escape the heat within Panama, there was only one solution—the mountains in Chiriqui, Panama's richest agricultural province, bordering on Costa Rica. Its capital is David, Panama's second largest city. To the west, on the Pacific coast, the United Fruit Company operated huge banana plantations. To the east lies a mountain range that traverses Central America and Panama with peaks rising up to 6,000 feet. The western slopes of the mountains, gifted with a temperate climate and moderate rainfall, lend themselves to coffee growing,

---

[35]. Later the term "parachute journalist" came into vogue for describing newsmen who drop in, get their story and then move on to another hot spot. The system is not necessarily one to their liking; it developed because of the cost of maintaining qualified correspondents overseas.

vegetable farming and dairying. Boquete, an hour's drive east of David, is the principal town of this region and the fiefdom of the infamous rabble—rousing politician Arnulfo Arias (thrice elected president, thrice deposed). Flowers grow in abundance everywhere in Boquete, and there are several good hotels so it is a pleasant place to visit for a short or extended stay.

Getting to Chiriqui required a half-day drive from Panama City over the Pan American Highway, a large section of which was a rocky and unpaved, but was worth it. We found our favorite vacation spot at the nearby village of Cerro Punto, named for a mountain peak that dominates the scenery. Margaret and I took our daughters there twice during our stay in Panama. We hiked on the mountain trails, picnicked alongside the trout stream, and dangled our feet in its icy waters.

We spent another vacation over the Christmas-New Year holidays in 1965-1966 in the San Blas Islands, an archipelago off Panama's Caribbean coast. They are the home of Panama's Cuna Indians who have maintained their ethnic purity over the centuries in the face of Spanish colonialism by never allowing Spaniards (as they referred to Panamanians) to remain overnight. They are famous for their colorful hand-stitched appliqué *molas,* one of which Ambassador Adair's wife presented to Astronaut Neil Armstrong as related in the previous chapter.

The Alliance for Progress

President John F. Kennedy introduced the idea of an "Alliance for Progress" between the United States and the countries of Latin America. The concept was an outgrowth of President Franklin D. Roosevelt's Good Neighbor Policy and Brazilian President Jucelino Kubischek's idea for an "Operation Pan America." The program called for American economic and technical assistance to Latin America to help resolve their many economic and social problems. Panama's President Roberto Chiari embraced the scheme, as did his successor Marcos Robles who introduced his own Plan Robles for economic development. David Samudio, Panama's director of economic planning and heir apparent to Robles, had responsibility for Plan Robles activities. James Magellas, newly assigned head of USAID, joined forces with Samudio in reactivating the Alliance for Progress. Between 1964 and 1968 the United States injected over $65 million into a socio-economic program to boost agricultural production, improve rural living conditions, and to slow rural-urban migration. As USIS Information Officer my role was to publicize Alliance for Progress achievements in Panama. In this I had the close cooperation of the Ambassadors Vaughn and Adair as well as Jim Magellas and his USAID staff. I became deeply involved in stimulating media coverage of events as well as in publishing pamphlets and distributing films explaining the benefits of the Alliance for Panama.

Whenever possible we also brought the Panama Canal Company into the picture, usually through exhibits at rural fairs. Our USIS/USAID exhibits portrayed the social and economic achievements of the Alliance while PanCanal exhibits focused on the contributions of the Canal to Panama's economy and presenting Panamanians as equal partners in operating the canal. I was pleased at the Canal Company's readiness to cooperate.

USAID focused its major efforts on joint US-Panamanian projects to construct schools, hospitals, model housing, water supply systems, and farm to market roads. Besides helping finance the projects, USAID also brought in technicians to work with Panamanian government officials and private companies involved in the Alliance program. Magellas was careful to have each of his many projects identified with the Alliance for Progress. In fact, we promoted the "Alliance for Progress" term so vigorously it became virtually synonymous with USAID. Every site displayed highly visible blue and white signs bearing the Alliance logo and the statement that this was *"Otro proyecto de la Alianza para el Progreso"* (Another project of the Alliance for Progress). Panamanian information personnel, in their output, also identified the projects as part of the Plan Robles.

The vast majority of the Alliance projects were in the countryside, distant from the usual haunts of Panama City journalists. In terms of news coverage the best stories occurred at the time of project completions when the government and USAID held joint inaugural ceremonies, thus giving journalists photo opportunities and a news peg. Local communities turned these events into gala occasions that they celebrated in conjunction with agricultural fairs. Festivities frequently included judging handsome livestock specimen plus colorful parades and folk dances in native costumes. President Robles and one or more Cabinet officials as well Ambassador Vaughn or (later) Ambassador Adair attended major events accompanied by Panamanian journalists who provided coverage for newspapers and evening TV newscasts. When that happened the Plan Robles got a lion's share of the credit.

For most project inaugurations, however, the principals were Jim Magellas, representing USAID, a government minister (education, health, or agriculture), local officials and myself. Since Panamanian editors were reluctant to spend money to send reporters out of town I made it a practice to take along a USIS writer and a photographer to provide coverage of these events. Our stories and photos got wide usage in the Panama City press. We also used them in our own publications on the Alliance and dramatized some of the projects in our radio output for Panamanian radio stations.

Getting a busy government minister out of Panama City was not easy, so Magellas usually scheduled several inaugurations a day and perhaps as many as a dozen over a two or three-day period. The events were grueling and repetitive. There were long jeep trips over dusty roads; hearty salutations to local officials who may have been waiting hours for our arrival; a ribbon cutting ceremony; speeches by both sides—the locals thanking the Alliance for Progress for making this fine new school (or whatever) possible, the visitors congratulating local authorities on their vision for the future—a hospitality period and then on to the next site.

It was those demonstrations of hospitality that got to me. They were invariably the same, a plate of *sancocho* (a typical Panamanian dish—chicken or beef stew, yucca, corn on the cob) served with a tortilla and a tepid soft drink. Though tasty, after consuming several of them at different sites in one morning, it is hard to feign pleasure over the next two or three in the afternoon. I shall always remember these excursions as "*sancocho* sagas."

Alliance for Progress - Postscript

In return for its economic assistance, Washington asked that Panama enact tax reforms so that previously tax-exempt corporations would bear their fair share of the costs. President Robles and David Samudio (Robles' designated successor) cooperated in carrying out Alliance programs, and the people in rural Panama obviously benefited from them. As the public diplomacy arm of the American Embassy we in USIS promoted cooperation under the Alliance for Progress by demonstrating how it was benefiting Panama both socially and economically and fostered friendly relations between the Zonians and Panamanian citizens. In general the media was also relatively free and cooperative in publicizing Alliance projects. What neither the Embassy nor Washington could control was the widespread corruption that sucked off large amounts of USAID funding for Alliance projects and the unwillingness of Panamanian oligarchs to contribute a fair share of their income toward the economic growth of the country.

In 1968 the Alliance for Progress received a double blow. First, the U.S. Congress sharply reduced the American contribution[36]; and, second, the Panamanian government's efforts to impose taxes on the previously tax free sugar and cement industries so enraged Panama's oligarchy (five per cent of the population received more than one third of the national income) that they sided with Arnulfo Arias in the 1968 election. This right wing support enabled Arias, with the complicity of National Guard Commander Bolivar Vallarino, to defeat Candidate Samudio. After taking office as President of Panama on October 1, 1968, Arias attempted to neutralize the National Guard by sending some of its key officials abroad. Eleven days later the National Guard ousted him and established a dictatorship under Colonel Omar Torrijos, former commander in the province of Chiriqui. Torrijos remained in power until he was killed in a plane crash in July 1981, the reasons for which are still unknown. Thus, the oligarchy's acts of utter selfishness led to the two-decade (1968-1989) hiatus in Panamanian democracy that was restored only with the ousting of Manuel Noriega by strong U.S. action under (the first) President Bush.

I had called on Omar Torrijos on many occasions when he was National Guard commander in David, Chiriqui. His brother, Monchi, whom I also knew in my capacity of USIS Information Officer, was a well-known columnist for the left-leaning Panama City daily *Critica*. As with many other Panamanian journalists, Monchi's talents were available to the highest bidder. Omar sent Monchi as Panamanian ambassador, first to Buenos Aires and then to Madrid.

---

[36]. LaFeber, p. 119 ff. The Congressional reduction of funds occurred as the United States was becoming more deeply involved in the Vietnam conflict. Coincidentally, Jim Magellas was transferred from Panama to Saigon in 1968. I was transferred to Chile in 1967.

The Peace Corps

The Peace Corps was an integral part of the Alliance for Progress in Panama, and Jack Vaughn was its hero. As former Peace Corps director for Latin America, then Ambassador to Panama, and subsequently overall director of the Peace Corps, he contributed much to its success by inspiration and example.

The volunteers carried out their work on an entirely different level from that of USAID. Individual volunteers lived and worked with their Panamanian counterparts in community projects—health, schools, sanitation, farming, housing, and many others. They lived spartan lives, with a minimal living allowance, and were not allowed access to Canal Zone privileges. All spoke Spanish, most fluently. During our stay in Panama there were some 150 volunteers in country, and I was forever encountering them in out-of-the way places. All were loved and respected in their communities. It is worthy of note that during the virulent anti-Americanism following the January 1964 flag riots, none of the volunteers were harmed.

Margaret and I had close relations with many of the volunteers. Our favorite was Julie Gevedon, a bright, attractive young blonde who worked in the slums of Panama City. Julie and her many friends often visited our home and were invariably starved for American home cooking. Our house acquired the reputation of a place where a Volunteer could get a good meal. They were all outstanding young people and a continuing source of great stories about life in Panama. We relish the memory of the times we spent with them.

Visitors

Louisiana and Panama have much in common, especially the weather, and we had many Louisiana visitors during our stay in that country. Two of them caught the public eye: Senator Allen Ellender and LSU President John Hunter. Ellender, a power in the U.S. Senate in his time, came for a three-day stay while visiting Alliance for Progress projects around Latin America. While the ambassador and his top deputies normally handle Congressional visits, I was involved in the Ellender visit because of my Louisiana origins and my association with the Alliance for Progress. Unfortunately, the senator's reactions to Alliance expenditures in Panama (and other Latin countries) were negative and contributed to the massive Congressional cuts referred to above, to the defeat of Presidential Candidate David Samudio and, paradoxically, to the Omar Torrijos dictatorship with all of its unpredictable fallout—including Manuel Noriega.

President Hunter came to Panama twice on trips promoting LSU's educational programs designed for Latin American students. As an LSU alumnus and fellow "Tiger" I was delighted and honored to host receptions for President Hunter and to coordinate his meetings with the Panamanian minister of education. We worked out a sister university relationship between LSU and Panama's Catholic University that strengthened the latter's scientific curriculum.

Another LSU visitor was Professor Jane Lucas DeGrummond, counselor of my student days at LSU who had also visited us in Caracas. She came for research on her biography of Renato Beluche, the pirate Jean LaFitte's deputy who had become an admiral in the Venezuelan navy and left numerous descendants around the Caribbean.

Kaoru Nishimura, my former colleague in Takamatsu who was on a USIA orientation trip around the United States, extended his visit to Panama to see us. He marveled at the Panama Canal as he watched a Japanese ship transiting the Miraflores Locks, but when he looked for Panamanian souvenirs to take home he could only find objects "Made in Japan." He finally took home several molas. My daughters remember him teaching them the Awa Odori, a folk dance of Tokushima prefecture.

Quest for a Sea-Level Canal

Like thousands of others who have visited or lived in Panama, I found the Canal a continuing object of fascination. Standing on Paitilla Point overlooking the Bay of Panama in the early morning one can look east and see the sun apparently rising over the Pacific and, at the same time, count ships waiting to enter the Canal. Surprisingly, the Canal doesn't run east—west at all, but southeast to northwest, and the Atlantic (really the Caribbean) entrance is farther west than the Pacific entrance. Most intriguing, though, was the operation of the Canal itself. We never tired of watching huge ships being raised or lowered silently through the locks as they entered or left Gatun Lake, the artificial waterway across the isthmus. Built in 1914, the locks still operated as smoothly and efficiently as they did then even though over the years traffic had multiplied more than ten times from the three or four ships a day when the canal opened.

At the time there was much talk about the Canal becoming obsolete in 15 years. A sea-level canal was cited as the answer, but no one had yet determined where nor how it should be dug, whether by conventional earth-moving means or by atomic explosives. High cost hindered the ditch digging approach, and the atomic test ban hindered the nuclear approach. If a completely new site were chosen what would happen to the existing canal or its two terminal cities of Balboa and Colon?

Following up on the commitment President Johnson made upon the resumption of diplomatic relations, the U.S. Government established a Sea Level Canal Study Commission, with offices in the Canal Zone, in an effort to determine some of the answers to these and other questions. The study, an entirely American operation, was conducted under a joint U.S.- Panamanian agreement. Even so, the Panamanian government imposed strict secrecy measures about it because officials were nervous about the effect the results of the study might have on the populace. The lack of public information on details of the agreement and how it was being carried out gave rise to acrimonious debate in political and press circles about its legitimacy. Nevertheless, Panamanian officials stubbornly resisted our arguments in favor of opening up the project to the press.

After numerous surveys the Commission decided on the most appropriate site for the sea level canal. They chose the straits of Darien, some 150 miles east-southeast of the existing canal—from the Gulf of San Miguel (Puerto Quimba) on the Pacific to the San Blas island of Mulatupo on the Caribbean side. There the geological elevation is at its lowest and the Isthmus relatively narrow in width. The area is pure jungle; seasonal rains are torrential. During the 1965-1966 dry season— November to May—teams of life scientists spent several months in the area studying the potential effects of nuclear fallout on the food chain of plant and animal life, from microscopic insects to monkeys and crocodiles and the resident indigenous tribes.

While the Panamanian government was still resisting publicity, the BBC got word of the project and sent a TV team to produce a documentary. At first Panama resisted, but finally accepted our argument that an objective report by the BBC would be in their best interest. I went with the BBC team as escort officer. We tramped through miles of jungle on the Pacific side, now dry, filming the scientists at work. For me the most interesting aspect was watching the ornithologists as they trapped hundreds of tropical birds in mist nets, took careful note of characteristics of each, and then released them. Next we flew east across the Isthmus to Mulatupo to film another area that would be affected by any nuclear excavation. Everywhere life was abundant in multiple forms.

Subsequent to the BBC visit the Embassy was able to persuade Panama to lift the lid on the survey. With that Peter Mygat, the Sea Level Canal information officer, and I put our heads together and came up with our own plan. We arranged for the chief of the canal studies to brief media representatives on the canal survey and provided them with an illustrated backgrounder on the studies and progress to date. We followed this up with a press tour of the sea level canal area, inviting journalists thought to be responsible. Their observations, supplemented by our backgrounder, saturated the Panamanian news media. After that the public debate virtually ceased.

In the end the scientific studies concluded that the risks from nuclear fallout made digging a sea level canal with atomic explosives completely untenable. This conclusion was tragically confirmed many years later by the explosion of the Chernobyl reactor. With the Carter-Torrijos Treaty and the subsequent transfer of the Canal to Panamanian jurisdiction the project for a sea level canal has been abandoned and enlargement of the present canal to handle increasingly larger ships is unresolved for multiple reasons, not the least of which is the huge expense involved.

Canal Epilogue

The prime objective of USIS Panama during my period of service there was to help provide an atmosphere in which the United States and Panama could negotiate a treaty to replace the outmoded Hay - Bunau-Varilla Treaty of 1903 that had been responsible for so much friction between our two countries. While the negotiations were carried on largely in secret between our two governments USIS used every opportunity to stress American goodwill, a job frequently complicated by accusations of bad faith by firebrands such as Congressman Daniel Flood on the American side and former President Arnulfo Arias in Panama.

Paradoxically, it was the seizure of dictatorial power by General Omar Torrijos that gave Panama a leader strong enough to negotiate a new canal treaty with the United States, though he, too, faced stiff domestic opposition to the draft treaty. It was only coincidental that his opposite number was President Carter who had sufficient foresight to recognize the need for a revised U.S.-Panamanian relationship. (Carter's successor, Ronald Reagan, staunchly opposed the treaty.)

President Carter charged Ambassadors Ellsworth Bunker and Sol Linowitz with working out a draft treaty. The President and his team, with the cooperation of Senate Majority Leader Harry Byrd and Minority Leader Howard Baker, pushed it through a reluctant Senate. They succeeded only after lengthy debates, a massive publicity campaign, and then only because the canal was no longer considered vital to American security. On October 17, 1977, Presidents Carter and Torrijos signed the treaty that was to formally transfer the canal to Panama on December 31, 1999. In the interim the Panama Canal Commission, a U.S. Government agency, operated the Canal and helped prepare Panama for full possession. On January 1, 2000, Panama took control of its unique national treasure in a major national celebration, bringing to an end nearly a century of contention between the two nations over its ownership.

Journalism Seminar

To label Panamanian journalism standards as "low" would be an understatement. They were atrocious. I shall never forget watching an unnamed journalist at work on a local crime story and asking him whether he had verified his facts with the individuals involved.

"No," he replied, "That would spoil my story."

Unfortunately it was not a joke. Much of what they wrote as news was pure hearsay embroidered by their own fertile imaginations. This was vibrantly evident in their coverage of the January 1964 riots. At USIS we made elevating Panamanian journalistic standards one of our country objectives. Relying on my own status as an LSU journalism graduate, I broached the idea of a journalism seminar to Jose Cajar Escala, editor of *Critica* and president of the national *Sindicato de Periodistas* (Newspapermen's Union). The response was enthusiastic. With the cooperation of Senor Cajar Escala, then Cultural Affairs Officer Sam Dieli and I organized a three-month "Journalism Techniques Seminar" in Panama City and Colon. Our lecturers were visiting American correspondents—who spoke on a professional level—and journalism professors, including LSU's John Merrill, recruited by USIA. I cannot measure the degree to which our seminar improved Panamanian journalism, but it did bring USIS closer to the journalism community. When we were about to leave Panama the Sindicato showed their appreciation by giving me an *agasajo periodistica* (affectionate journalistic reception) accompanied by several columns of newsprint about the affair.

Although I was too involved in all the activities related above to be completely unbiased, it was my impression that within the period of my tour (1964-1967) we were able to erase much of the ill will caused by the 1964 flag incident. I also felt that we significantly improved our institutional and interpersonal relations with the Panamanian media that had been so volatile at that time. Even so, there was no guarantee that a similar incident would not again inflame them against the United States.

Farewell to Panama

In March 1967, three years after our sudden transfer from Washington to Panama, I received word that my next assignment would be as USIS Information Officer in Santiago, Chile, a larger post. As we prepared to leave I reflected on the emotional events of the past three years. I would never forget picking up the pieces after the January 1964 riots and striving to keep the lid on the Panamanian cauldron while our negotiators sought to work out a substitute treaty for the one that had caused so much grief. It seemed then that a solution was in sight, but it would be another ten years before the two sides finally agreed upon the terms of the 1977 Carter-Torrijos Canal Treaty.

Although I was becoming accustomed to these moves from one country to another, I always left a bit of me behind. Panama was no exception. I had been especially fortunate in having two superb ambassadors, Jack Vaughn and Charles Adair, who treated me with respect and dignity. I gave of my best to them and if we did not accomplish all we attempted it was not for not trying. Of my Panamanian friends, who had seen many American Embassy officials come and go, I liked to think they will remember me as fondly as I remember them, forgetting names perhaps, but never our joint efforts to bring our two countries closer together.

On May 13, 1967, Ambassador and Mrs. Adair and a crowd of Panamanian and American friends saw my family and me off at the airport. During our home leave we visited Margaret's family and mine before heading for Santiago.

VII Chile - Before Allende

"The Well Known Yankee Imperialist"

Home leave was sweet that May and June of 1967. Three years of constant stress in Panama had left me on the edge of burnout. I desperately needed a rest. In Washington I raced through a pro forma debriefing on Panama and pre-departure consultation on Chile. I had learned from experience that Washington country desk officers are always happy to see folks in from the field—for a short time. If you stay too long their eyes begin to glaze over or to wander back to the "immediate action" cables on their desks. It is wise not to try their patience—or waste your own time. While in Washington we ordered a new Plymouth sent to Santiago and bought a second-hand Chevvy for use during home leave. Expo-67 was under way in Montreal. I particularly wanted to see the NASA exhibit of its new lunar landing spacecraft, so we spent several days there and then drove back down to Louisiana and Texas to visit relatives.

In Lake Charles Betsy, Nancy and Judy got reacquainted with their Louisiana cousins while Margaret and I relaxed. Our departure date came all too soon. On July 2 we flew to New Orleans and caught a plane for Santiago, Chile. Overnight we traveled from mid-summer to mid-winter, from 30 degrees north latitude to 27 degrees south latitude. As we approached Santiago we could see the snow capped peaks of the Andes. One stood out above all others. It was Mount Aconcagua. At 22,000 feet it is the highest in the Andes and in the southern hemisphere. Ski resorts at its lower level offer a major attraction for sports enthusiasts.

Arrival and Getting Settled

Bill Miller, the USIS executive officer, greeted us at the airport and escorted us to the Hotel Carrera where the boxes of winter clothing we had shipped ahead awaited us. We had not seen most of the items for three years, and our girls found opening the boxes to be almost like a Christmas morning. Miller had pre-enrolled our children in the "Nido de Aguilas" (Eagles' Nest) International School used by the American Embassy. Margaret went with the children to school on their first day, and I went several days later. It was a beautiful ride with a view of the snow on the mountains and a rushing stream to cross before coming to the school buildings that sat majestically in the Andes foothills. We were sure our girls would be happy at Nido.

After a brief stay in one of the Embassy's transient apartments we found permanent quarters in a two-story duplex located in the relatively smog-free upper section of the city. Our daughters moved into the upper floor where each had her own bedroom and painted it to suit her fancy. Margaret and I took over the downstairs apartment where we had ample space for my frequent official entertainment responsibilities. The location also brought us within easy access to the children's school.

In Chile, south of the equator, the seasons were reversed from our previous post. It was mid-term at the Nido de Aguilas, and our girls encountered some difficulty in adapting to their classes and to a new circle of friends. This is a predicament that faces many Foreign Service families. There is no easy solution. Children adapt because kids do, but they suffer. Two years into our tour we sent Betsy, our oldest, to high school in the United States.

Meeting the USIS Staff

The American Embassy occupied four floors in a tall building across the street from the Hotel Carrera; USIS was on the tenth. Country Public Affairs Officer Jim Echols greeted me, noting that I had arrived just in time for his weekly staff meeting. About six feet tall, lean and athletic looking, he had the appearance of being more at home on the ski slopes where he had spent the July 4 holiday than in an Embassy office. He said he and the staff had looked forward to my arrival because Holley Mack Bell, my predecessor, had left nearly six months previously and that a lot of important work had gone by the boards because there weren't enough bodies to go around.

With the staff assembled, Echols announced that I would be his second in command and head of the Information Section. Bill Miller, whom we had already met, was administrative officer. Those under my direct supervision would be Bob Cohoes, press officer who had been acting IO pending my arrival and Ed Elly, AID information officer. Yet to arrive was Bob Meyers who had been a junior officer trainee with me in Panama. He would be our radio, TV and films officer.

The cultural section consisted of CAO Bob Ebersole, a professional artist who had arrived shortly before me; Lucie Adams, the assistant

CAO who coordinated binational center (BNC) activities and handled cultural exchanges with the help of Louise Kelleher,[37] a junior officer trainee; BNC Director Berton Bailey, head of the Instituto Chileno Norteamericano; and Aurelius Fernandez who devoted full time to working at the BNC with the highly politicized Chilean university students. Not present were BNC directors in Conception (southern Chile) and in Antofogasta (northern Chile). I was to work closely with each of these individuals in one capacity or another. This narrative will not dwell on our personal or working relationships, but we became good friends with everyone and we have kept in touch with several despite having moved on to other assignments, other careers.

During my three-year stay in Chile there would be an almost complete changeover in USIS American personnel, including Echols who would leave within the year and be replaced by Carl Davis, my PAO in Panama.

The USIS staff also included nearly a hundred Foreign Service Nationals (FSNs), Chilean citizens on whom we relied to get our job done. I would be working with many of them but most closely with our press chief Alfredo Middleton and our publications chief, Adriana Hernandez, both splendid professionals who had devoted many years to work with USIS. My secretary was a lovely young Anglo-Chilean named Margaret Rogers who looked after my correspondence during my many absences on behalf of the U.S. space program. Her sterling qualities did not go unnoticed by our Marine guards, one of whom made her his bride and took her away to the United States.

In addition to the three binational centers with American directors, there were fifteen centers with Chilean directors in various parts of the country. These operated as English teaching institutions with only minimal USIS support, mostly in the form of teaching materials.

Jim Echols had come out of USIA's English teaching program, and he never felt quite at home with the problems we confronted in dealing with Santiago's highly politicized society. He had a difficult ambassador, Ralph Dungan, a former special assistant for foreign affairs to President's Kennedy and Johnson, who had a reputation for being tough

---

[37]. Since our first meeting in Santiago, Louise—now Louise Crane—has risen to the top ranks of USIA. In 1996 she was appointed Public Affairs in Tokyo. Subsequently she became vice president of AFSA, the American Foreign Service Association.

on USIS. I am unable to judge how much of the Dungan's attitude toward USIS can be attributed to his relations with his PAO, but his successor would frequently bypass Echols and come to me. This did not happen after Carl Davis arrived in September 1968.

Carl had been a professional journalist and congressional aide before joining USIS. His previous service included La Paz, Ciudad Trujillo, Panama City (with me) and head of USIA's Cuban affairs office in Miami. He had received the Agency's meritorious service award for his work during the 1964 Panama riots and superior honor award for his work in Miami. He could be tough but was also quite fair with his subordinates. We got on well together both professionally and socially.

The Top Echelon

Edward Korry, former ambassador in Ethiopia, succeeded Ralph Dungan shortly after my arrival and remained as ambassador to Chile until December 1971, a year and a half after my departure. He had two deputy chiefs of mission (DCMs), Robert Dean and Harry Schlaudeman, with whom I worked closely. They were both superb Foreign Service Officers who performed brilliantly in Chile and in subsequent ambassadorial assignments.

Korry had been a correspondent for *Look* magazine when President Kennedy appointed him to the post in Addis Ababa. Although President Johnson named Korry to Santiago, Nixon kept him there; and he always liked to remind people that he was named ambassador by three presidents, two Democrats and a Republican.

Korry understood the news media as few ambassadors I have known. He steadfastly refused to react to press criticism "simply because some nitwit journalist took it in his head to write a critical article about me or about the United States." He also turned down numerous requests for interviews and let it be known that, "When I have something to say to the press I will let them know, but I will do it in my own good time, not theirs."

Ambassador Korry was undismayed by the power of television. When he held his first big Embassy reception a TV station called me to ask if they could film reportage for the evening newscast. I checked with DCM Bob Dean. "Yes, I don't see why not," he said. (This had been done under the Dungan regime.) I gave the TV station the go ahead, and they sent a mobile unit with all its paraphernalia to the Embassy residence. When Korry came down from his living quarters and saw the cameras and the cables strung across his living room, he was furious.

"Get those people out of here!" he exclaimed. "When I invite people to my home, it's because I want to see them, not to show everybody in Chile who has been to an American Embassy reception."

Fortunately the TV reporters took it with good grace and left.

I enjoyed working with Ambassador Korry. He was an excellent public speaker and a writer who knew the value of humor and satire and how to use them. He typed up his own dispatches and they were considered favorite reading in the State Department. Unfortunately his promising ambassadorial career ended in the bitterness engendered by prolonged Congressional investigations into the CIA involvement in the Chilean elections in which the Marxist candidate Salvador Allende was elected president and then murdered by his opponents in a military coup. Korry eventually left government service and went into the private sector. He died at age 81 as this memoir was going to press.

The Chilean Political and Economic Scene[38]

Chile had long enjoyed a tradition of democratic government, one of the few Latin American countries to do so. Eduardo Frei, a Christian Democrat and father of a later chief of state, was president of Chile during my tenure. In 1964 he had succeeded Jorge Alessandri, known as the business president.[39] Unfortunately, Alessandri had been unable to resolve Chile's continuing economic and social problems. Frei made a valiant but futile effort. His six-year term as head of a government overburdened by foreign debt, persistent inflation—at times reaching 35 per cent—and subject to continuing vituperative attacks from political enemies, even from within his party, left him a disillusioned man and the nation at odds with itself. On leaving office in 1970 Frei compared Chile to the patient who calls the doctor but then refuses to take the medicine. "The problem is mainly political," he said. "Everyone wants the sacrifices to be made by others (than themselves)."

---

[38]. For this chapter I have drawn factual data from *Chile Since Independence*, edited by Leslie Bethell, Cambridge University Press, 1993, chapter 4, "Chile Since 1958."

[39]. Chilean presidents cannot succeed themselves but may run again as Alessandri did in the 1970 election, but he came in second to Allende. Interestingly, he was owner of the building in which the American Embassy was located, and we frequently encountered him going to and from his office in the same building.

Much of Chile's foreign debt was owed to the United States. It grew out of credits received to finance industrial, economic and infrastructure development; social programs such as education and housing, and reconstruction from a disastrous 1960 earthquake. There were also credits for agricultural products that, with proper management, could have been produced domestically. In fact, during the decade of the 1960s Chile received more than a billion dollars in overt U.S. aid, more per capita than any other country in the hemisphere.

American companies, particularly Anaconda and Kennecott, had heavy financial investments in Chilean copper mining for which the country derived major income; but fluctuating copper prices were patched over by increased foreign indebtedness. Anti-management agitations by communist dominated labor unions and pressure for Chileanization of copper were a continuing source of friction and concern for the United States. This objective was eventually achieved, but the copper companies profited more than Chile.

The United States gave agrarian reform urgent priority both because of the need for improving agricultural production and over concern for rural guerrilla activity. Betting on President Frei's Christian Democrat party, USAID invested heavily in a land reform program through the Alliance for Progress. Agricultural production grew but not enough to remedy the long neglect that would not be fully overcome until after the 16-year Pinochet dictatorship.

In the late 1960s the country's political parties quarreled incessantly among themselves. Often it seemed as though the country's large central European immigrant population had brought with them their inability to agree on anything of substance.

During those pre-Allende days Chilean society, especially in Santiago, was highly politicized. The five major political parties—the ruling Christian Democrats, Radical, Socialist, National and Communist—bickered incessantly over internal politics. Competing American and Soviet influences, both private and official, lurked on the sidelines promoting their own special interests at every opportunity. Chileans, well aware of these, played them off against each other, seeking American or Soviet help to promote their own special causes. The USSR invested heavily in supporting the socialist and communist activities. Soviet and Soviet satellite state representatives were in Chile all out of proportion to their legitimate economic and diplomatic interests in the country. I encountered many of them at diplomatic receptions, all eager to garner information about American operations in Chile.

I will not attempt to assess the United States' role in the collapse of Chilean democracy. That happened after I left, and the U.S. Congress conducted hearings ad nauseam on the matter. But certainly the United States and the now defunct Soviet Union share blame for the tragic outcome of meddling in Chile's internal affairs.

The USIS Role

Many Chileans, with their immigrant backgrounds, were culturally oriented toward Europe. Nevertheless, there was a strong sense of community with the United States that derived in part from common economic interests and in part from a common historical experience. Although attitudes toward the United States were generally favorable, Chileans found much to criticize, especially the U.S. role in Vietnam and what they thought to be our excessive economic presence in their own country. We sought, wherever possible, to strengthen the favorable attitudes and to temper the critical ones.

We worked closely with the multiple media outlets, with Chilean cultural and education institutions and with American organizations engaged in promoting closer relations with Chile. (For more than a year I served as program officer for the American Society scheduling events for this purpose.) Our Chilean-American Institutes (Institutos Chileno-Norteamericano) in Santiago, Conception and Antofogasta not only taught English but also were centers of intense activity promoting Chilean-American cultural relations. Our BNC directors and personnel working in these centers, such as Aurelius Fernandez, maintained contact with large numbers of students of every political hue, responding to their concerns about the United States and assisting many in their desires to continue their study at American universities.

In the information field we had both failures and successes. We worked closely with USAID and Embassy economic officers to further the objectives of the Alliance for Progress until Congress drastically cut USAID funds. We also worked at exposing international communism, managing somehow to avoid involvement in Chilean domestic intrigues. Our foremost failure was in convincing the Chileans that America was on the right track in Vietnam, but this was really beyond our control. Our primary success was in conveying an image of America as a leader in science and technology, thanks in large part to NASA's Apollo program. In this, as recounted in a previous chapter, I was privileged to play an important role.

The Media

The Chilean media was free and influential. USIS maintained contact with all elements, but we tended to focus most of our attention on those we felt we could influence. There was no point in wasting our time or resources on extremist media.

The newspapers covered the political spectrum from right to left. We worked most closely with *El Mercurio*, one of the top newspapers in Latin America and close to the Frei administration, and the paper's two afternoon tabloids—*Las Ultimas Noticias* and *La Segunda*. We also worked closely with *La Nacion*, the government newspaper, but it had a smaller circulation and was less influential. Each of the major parties had its own newspaper: *El Diario Ilustrado* represented the National Party; *La Tercera de la Hora*, a popular tabloid, represented the Radical Party; *Ultima Hora* represented the Socialists; *Clarin* was an independent leftist tabloid; and *El Siglo* was the voice of the communists. The Soviet Embassy reputedly subsidized *El Siglo* heavily, and the paper was available all over the country though it was questionable how many people actually read it. A healthy magazine industry covered a similar spectrum of political and cultural tastes.

There were three television stations—two in Santiago and one in Valparaiso, all run by universities. In Santiago the University of Chile station had a strong socialist bias. We worked with them but found the Catholic University station and its sister outlet in Valparaiso more cooperative.

There were 118 radio stations in the country, all commercial except for four university stations and a state-owned one in the northern city of Arica. There was no radio censorship. We had our locally produced and Voice of America programs on many of the stations.

Getting to Know Chile

In our Christmas letter for 1967 I described the Chile we had come to know at that time:

"Santiago is a beautiful city of wide boulevards, beautiful, well-kept parks and lovely homes. It lies about 75 miles inland at the top of a valley that extends some 700 miles southward with the Andes on the

163

east and the Cordillera of the Coast on the west. The capital itself is near the geographical center of this 2,600-mile long string bean-like country that extends from the hot rainless Atacama Desert in the north to the cold Antarctic climes of Cape Horn in the south. Its total land mass is equivalent to that of Texas but never more than 221 miles across at its widest point. Santiago, at 2000 feet altitude, has ideal weather and four distinct seasons. The summer is not very hot, and winter temperatures seldom drop below freezing. Summer nights are cool enough to require a blanket. A two-hour drive to the east will take you to some of the world's best ski slopes for winter sports or, west, to beaches for summer sunning. The frigid temperatures of the Humboldt Current that runs northward along the coast are not inducive to bathing, but girl watching on the beaches is a favorite sport during the summer. With its great variety of scenery and climate there is really no place in the world like Chile, except possibly California. Chile's Pacific coast resembles the western coastline of the United States but upside down."

My description was overly generous in not mentioning Santiago's persistent winter smog that settles in downtown Santiago, the lower section of the valley, and remains there for weeks on end. Most of the better residential areas are located on the relatively smog free mountain slopes.

I devoted a good portion of my first six months in Chile to developing interpersonal relations with our news media clientele, both in and out of Santiago. I had found this useful in each of my four previous overseas assignments and was determined to continue it in Chile. In doing so I was following the prescription of Edward R. Murrow who liked to say, "The most important part of intercultural communications is the last three feet."

In Antofogasta, BNC Director Frank Florey took me to visit the local newspapers and radio stations. We also visited Chuquicamata, the world's largest open pit copper mine operated by the Anaconda Mining Company. Copper was Chile's prime source of foreign exchange, but the mine was also the source of some of the country's worst labor relations problems between the American owners and communist labor union leaders. The resultant labor strife was a matter of continuing concern to our Embassy.

Driving across the desert to the mine I was amazed to see ghost towns from the era of Chile's pre-World War I nitrate industry that brought prosperity and all of its trappings (e.g. an opera house) to that region. With the development of synthetic nitrates by Germany in the First World War[40], both the industry and the trappings had evaporated like water in the desert. Now many relics of the nitrate industry can be found in Antofogasta's museum and decorating the city's picturesque restaurants.

In December 1967 Alfredo Middleton[41], our Chilean press chief, accompanied me on a trip to southern Chile to pay courtesy calls on newspapers and radio stations located in the country's fertile agricultural region. We sent a USIS driver with a carload of our publications ahead and flew to Puerto Montt whose eastern skyline is dominated by an extinct snowcapped volcano. Located on the Gulf of Ancud, more than twice the size of the San Francisco-Oakland Bay, Puerto Montt is the focal point for the logging and fishing industry of southern Chile. Its architecture and traditions might be compared to those of Alaska, although its winter is milder.

On our drive northward the splendid scenery, the lakes, rivers fascinated me as did the green pastures, all so vastly different from the desert wasteland of northern Chile. I resolved to return with my family on a vacation at our first opportunity.

Middleton knew many of the newspaper editors in the cities we visited, if not personally at least by name. He had been with USIS for many years but had infrequent occasion to visit the area. My notes from the trip indicate some success in placement of USIS press and radio services, including relays of VOA news programs. They also indicate considerable concern about communist activities among the students of the region. Subsequently, Bob Meyers, in follow-up visits to the radio stations, significantly increased placement of the radio programs for which he was responsible.

A year later Middleton and I made the trip in reverse order, driving down from Santiago. It was shortly after the 1968 election of President Richard M. Nixon. This time I was received as an old friend, and my notes, much more extensive, manifest a notable increase in use of our

---

40. Nitrates were necessary for the production of ammunition. Denied further access to Chilean nitrates by the Allied blockade, German industrialists developed the technology for synthesizing them.

41. Middleton's ancestors had lived in Chile for several generations; despite his English name he was not comfortable speaking English. We communicated entirely in Spanish.

USIS information output. The editors expressed a deep interest in Mr. Nixon's views toward Latin America and asked many questions about the incoming president. Although I had personally supported Hubert Humphrey, I played the good Foreign Service Officer and put a favorable face on Nixon's potential Latin American policies, most of which proved to be wishful thinking.

After Mr. Nixon had been in office for several months, I asked Ambassador Korry if he could define Nixon's Latin American policy for me. His answer was succinct and to the point, "When I find out what it is I'll let you know."

"The Well Known Yankee Imperialist"

I encountered communist editors and journalists on frequent social occasions, and my name occasionally appeared in their columns identified as "the well known Yankee imperialist." I have vivid memories of a communist editor asking me for an interview. "If I give you this interview, how will you use it?" I asked.

"Oh," he said, "against you, of course."

Despite his disarming frankness, I knew that if I didn't answer his questions he would make up something vicious and publish it anyway.

"Check with me tomorrow," I said.

I asked Carl Davis for his advice. Carl queried Ambassador Korry who said, "OK but keep it brief." The result was an innocuous piece; far more forgettable than the accusations the editor would have leveled against the Embassy and me had I refused.

We managed to get our point of view across in the non-communist press, but it was hard work. We tried but we certainly didn't succeed in countering the heavy communist influence. It was difficult to make any real mark in that highly politicized society. You couldn't open a conversation, any kind of conversation, no matter whether it was about art and literature, or culture and travel abroad, anything, without local politics raising its ugly head.

"Representation"

Margaret and I entertained a lot, officially known as "representation." Our large residence had plenty of space. The unofficial rate of exchange[42] was in our favor; and we had good domestic help, so I invited many media people to our home—usually with an important visitor or other Embassy officers—where I was able to talk to them in depth about issues that concerned both the United States and Chile. The best I was able to do was maintain good personal relations to keep the dialogue open. That in itself was important, but I never really felt that we achieved as much as we could have in a less volatile situation.

Our colleagues from the "other agency" (a euphemism for CIA) were also very active with the news media. For USIS it was difficult trying to conduct an out-front type of operation where you knew that press outsiders in fact planted commentaries that appeared to be locally originated. You could be fairly certain that the anti-American, pro-communist materials were originated by communist, possibly Soviet agents; but you would just have to guess who was placing the other kinds of material. As in many Latin American countries the Chileans also had their journalists for sale.

During the third year of my Chilean assignment I spent six months traveling around Latin America with a moon rock so my deputy, Bob Cohoes, carried on our work with the Chilean newspapers. Bob was politically savvy and deserves a lion's share of the credit for whatever we were able to accomplish in that arena. Ed Elly gets credit for what we were able to achieve on Alliance for Progress programs. Bob Meyers handled radio, TV and motion pictures in a creative and imaginative fashion and placed our programs on virtually every important radio and TV station in the country. I take a small amount of credit for his achievements because he had trained under me as a JOT (Junior Officer Trainee) in Panama, but most of it was due to his own intelligence and ability.

Cerro Tololo

My personal interest in science and space exploration got me involved with the inauguration of the Cerro Tololo Interamerican Observatory being installed on a mountaintop east of La Serena, 100 miles north of Santiago, on the southern edge of the Atacama desert. A

---

[42] The official dollar-escudo rate of exchange was so unrealistic Embassy personnel traveled regularly to Argentina to change money at the black-market rate, something U.S.-Chile bilateral agreements prohibited us from doing in Chile.

consortium of Interamerican universities had selected the site after an extensive search of the southern hemisphere for an appropriate spot from which to observe the skies. The Cerro Tololo site provided an amazing clarity of the atmosphere, and its remote location eliminated artificial light that might interfere with the observatory's work. The University of Chile, as the host country's prime educational institution, would play an important role in operating the observatory.

The inauguration was a significant event for the Chilean scientific community and the Interamerican University Consortium. The director, a bilingual Puerto Rican astronomer, came to USIS for assistance in handling the public information aspects. For me, with my NASA experience, it was a natural.

When I first I visited Cerro Tololo I expected something interesting, but the spectacular naked eye view of the star studded night skies from atop Cerro Tololo took my breath away. As a boy growing up in the Louisiana countryside, I had frequently studied early morning skies, but I had never seen anything to equal the view from Cerro Tololo. With the assistance of a USIS photographer, the director and I developed publicity releases to announce the official opening, scheduled for dusk on a moonless night.

President Eduardo Frei arrived at the observatory precisely at the appointed time to cut the inaugural ribbon in the presence of the American ambassador and a large contingent of Chile's news media. As Ambassador Korry and I toured the facility with the normally articulate President, peering through the telescopes at the night skies, he could only describe his impressions as "fantastic," "incredible" or "awesome." The Chilean media reacted in kind, and we chalked up a score for the reputation of American science in Chile.

The Cultural Scene

The Chileans were and are justly proud of their cultural life that manifests intensive activity in all fields of the arts—theater, dance, music, graphic and plastic arts, to mention but a few. The University of Chile and Santiago's Catholic University organized many of the programs, but there were also independent professional groups. Chilean novelists and poets were among the foremost in Latin America; the most famous was Pablo Neruda, a Nobel prize winning poet whose affiliation with the Communist Party kept getting him into trouble.

USIS conducted an active exchange program that brought American students, professors, and performing artists to Chile and assisted Chileans visiting the United States. During my tenure there were frequent visits by American groups, ranging from pop singers to leading opera stars. Some came under USIS sponsorship, but more came under commercial contracts. I have fond memories of listening Count Basie beat out popular jazz tunes on Carl Davis' piano in the PAO residence. Carl had once played the piano in Basie's orchestra and the two were close friends.

As the Embassy's press attaché, I became involved in providing the news media with information about visiting American artists. There were few prima donnas. Most were hard working professionals who left good impressions of themselves and of the United States. Barry Morrell of the Metropolitan Opera was one of our visiting performers during the Chilean opera season. I was backstage with him once at intermission. I thought he looked rather uncomfortable.

"Mr. Morell," I asked, "is there anything I can do for you.

"Yes," he replied. "Singing has left my mouth very dry. Please get me some chewing gum."

Another visitor was Duke Ellington who was touring Latin America with his orchestra under a commercial agreement that included concerts in Buenos Aires and Santiago. At Ellington's request I arranged a press conference for 7:00 a.m. on his arrival from Buenos Aires following an evening performance in the Argentine capital. The 70-year old orchestra leader charmed the sleepy Chilean reporters with his lively responses and then said, "Good night."

"Mr. Ellington," I said in an aside, "please remember that Ambassador Korry has organized an Embassy reception in your honor for 7:00 o'clock this evening. I am to pick you up at 6:45 and take you there."

"OK, call me at six," he said.

He appeared in the hotel lobby with his traveling companion a few minutes after 6:45, looking like death warmed over.

"My God, this is going to be a disaster," I said to myself. And then I asked his companion, "Is he OK? Shall we go ahead?"

"Yes, yes. He'll be all right. Let's go on."

I wasn't convinced, but took her word for it. The two remained quiet, exchanging few words during the 15-minute drive to the Embassy residence. I prepared myself for the worst.

When we stopped at the Embassy steps, a guard opened the back door. Mr. Ellington bounded out of the car and up the steps like a 19-year-old, greeting the Ambassador and his wife as old friends. Within minutes he was at the piano, playing his favorite tunes, enlivening the party like fireworks.

"What happened?" I asked his companion.

"Oh, he was just conserving his strength."

Vacations

One of the special perquisites of Foreign Service life is the opportunity for exotic travel at minimum expense during your regular summer vacation. In Chile, as in other countries where we were assigned we took full advantage of these occasions.

January and February in Chile are like July and August in the northern hemisphere, time for a summer vacation. In late January 1968 we realized my aspiration to return to the Lake Region of southern Chile that had so enthralled me on my first visit to the area. Margaret, the three girls and I drove southward through the fertile Central Valley, admiring the verdant hills and picturesque lakes in the dairying centers of Valdivia and Osorno, a stark contrast to Santiago's arid cityscape. In Temuco, the cultural center of Chile's Araucanian Indian population, we stocked up on colorful knitted wool ponchos, jackets and rugs. At nightfall, following the day's drive from Santiago, we reached our destination, the Hotel Chollinco on the banks of a delightful lake of the same name. There we spent a restful ten days fishing, reading, horseback riding and just relaxing. We ran short of money and, simultaneously, the rains came so we returned to Santiago for the last several days of our vacation.

On our arrival Bill Miller told us his standard poodle had produced a litter of puppies. I had already put in my bid. We chose a black male and named him Chollinco that soon transformed itself into a more natural "Charlie." Despite his mischievous ways or perhaps because of them, Charlie was a sheer delight from the start. He became a favored member of our family and a splendid companion for all of his 12 too-short years.

In February 1969 we went on another two-week family vacation, this time north to Bolivia and Peru. While I could write a separate chapter on that fascinating adventure, suffice it to say this prime educational experience gave us first hand knowledge of the region's geography and of the life and culture of the Indians who inhabit the 14,500 foot high

Bolivian altiplano. Equally fascinating were crossing Lake Titicaca, the world's highest large body of water, visiting the ancient Inca cities of Cuzco and Machu Picchu in Peru and that country's capital city, Lima, where Pizarro and several dozen Spanish adventurers toppled the Inca Empire. A memorable vacation over, we returned to our real world in Santiago much better informed and more appreciative of the vastness of South America and its Indian civilizations.

Vietnam Vietnam

The Vietnam War, in full swing during our stay in Chile, constituted the focal point of anti-Americanism among the Chilean populace and the cutting edge of communist attacks against the United States. It was also our major obstacle in getting across an image of an America that knows what it stands for, what it is doing, and where it is going. As the official voice of the United States in Chile, we felt compelled to convince Chileans that America was on the right track in Vietnam.

USIA was using the strategy of sending prominent journalists to Vietnam to see for themselves. There, the Joint U.S. Public Affairs Office (JUSPAO) gave them full briefings and answered all their questions. We sent several from Chile. On their return, if not fully convinced, they usually gave us the benefit of the doubt.

Not all would go. We invited El Mercurio's foreign affairs editor, the best known and most respected journalist in Chile, to take the trip. He accepted and was eagerly looking forward to the experience. As an advance orientation, I obtained and showed him a prize-winning French combat film on the Vietnam War. It was counter-productive. It scared him. He decided he didn't really want to go after all. He had no idea about the ferocity of the combat before seeing the film. In fact, I hadn't either.

During that period USIA was also sending its country public affairs officers to Saigon to see for themselves, the theory being that with a fuller understanding of the U.S. role in the war they could better explain it to their USIS audiences. From Chile USIA sent first Jim Echols and, near the end of my tour, Carl Davis.

Much of the Chilean opposition to the U.S. role in Vietnam came from Chile's Institute of International Studies. Its members wrote prolifically and almost unanimously condemned U.S. Vietnam policy as another form of American imperialism with which Latin Americans were all too familiar. Many of the authors were either communists or openly supported the communist line. But even those who were not pro-communist disagreed with the United States' Vietnam policy. Their repetitive denunciations, appearing daily in the news media, made it difficult for any educated Chilean not to question American motives in Vietnam. Nevertheless, we worked closely with the Institute and frequently took visiting American professors there to lecture and to interact with its faculty. After Echols' trip to Vietnam the Institute invited him to report on his findings. He made a good presentation of the official U.S. position, but they did not buy it. In fact they were so vociferous in their denunciations that Jim vowed never to return to the forum.

Our next major effort with the Institute was to schedule Douglas Pike for a lecture there on the U.S. Vietnam policy. A USIS officer who had been in Vietnam since 1960, Pike was the author of *Viet Cong,*[43] a definitive book on the Vietnamese communist underground He came to Chile on a USIA-sponsored world lecture tour in which he met with hundreds of groups similar to ours.

Pike made an even stronger presentation than Echols to the Chilean institute on the U.S. Vietnam policy. He had all the facts at the tip of his tongue and mobilized his information into convincing arguments. The questions put to him were very emotional and heated. Pike answered them all in a factual, non-emotional manner, but he was unable to win anybody over. To Pike's credit he gave his audience satisfaction because he answered their questions, but as he later agreed he won no converts.

The essence is that we made a valiant effort to convince Chileans that the United States was on the right track in Vietnam; but they did not agree, and we could do nothing convince them otherwise. Vietnam had become a losing issue in Chile. Everything we said on the subject was used against us. Carl and I went through an agonizing reappraisal, weighing the importance of the Vietnam War against the need to focus on Chilean-American issues. We decided that our only solution was to withdraw from the Vietnam arena in our official output and simply respond to questions when asked. We took the matter up with Ambassador Korry, and he concurred that this was the best way to handle the matter.

---

43. MIT Press, Cambridge and London, 1966, 466 pp.

Reassignment Saigon

My moon rock tour that had begun in November 1969 ended in La Paz, Bolivia, on May 12, 1970. After returning the rock to the Houston Space Flight Center I went to Washington to make my final report. Since my Chilean tour would be up in July, I also used the occasion to lobby for my next assignment. The Latin America area office virtually promised me a Washington job at the Voice of America. That suited me fine.

"Incidentally," my control officer said, "the Vietnam personnel office would like you to drop around."

"Why? I'm not interested in going to Vietnam."

"Oh, it's routine. They want to see everybody coming in from the field."

So I went.

"How would you like to go to Vietnam?"

"In what role?"

"As economic policy officer."

"But I don't know beans about economics."

"Never mind. You can learn."

I reflected on the question for a moment. A number of officers who had refused to go found themselves forced to resign from the Foreign Service.

"I won't volunteer, but if I'm assigned I guess I have no choice."

"OK. That's all I wanted to know."

There had been no agreement so I thought no more of the brief interview. I returned to Santiago and took over as acting PAO while Carl Davis went to Vietnam on the orientation trip mentioned earlier in this chapter. One morning, when I had been back in Santiago for less than a month and was finally getting rested up from my arduous travels, John Benson, then our executive officer, entered my office.

"I'm glad you're sitting down. I have a cable from Washington that concerns you."

I could hardly believe my eyes. The cable read, in essence: "You are hereby assigned to Saigon for a period of eighteen months without family."

"John, let me think it over a bit."

It was June 1970. The Vietnam War was still raging. During the past six years, in both Panama and Chile, I had been defending the U.S. role in Vietnam. Some of my colleagues had been there and spoken passionately about events in that beleaguered country. I would not be going as a soldier, but as a diplomat. Rightly or wrongly, regardless of the outcome of the conflict, Vietnam would play an important part in American history. By going I would become an actor in that drama. In any case, I had two choices, accept or resign. Finally I said to myself, "Harry, that's where the action is. Why don't you try it?"

I cabled my acceptance.[44]

Did We Make a Difference? A Retrospective View

Even though I left Chile at the end of my three-year tour with a strong sense of accomplishment my immediate inclination is to answer this question in the negative. Despite the major effort and resources the United States expended in trying to sustain Chile's democratic government, the election of Salvador Allende and the brutal military overthrow of his government constituted major setbacks for U.S. policy in Latin America and certainly for the people of that country.

Yes, we of USIS did all we could to promote good bilateral relations and the sanctity of the democratic process. In this chapter I have pointed to many positive achievements as well as some significant failures in our exercise of public diplomacy. But we had little or no control over many of the external and internal factors at work.

Chile's leftist politicians had a continuing love affair with Cuba, and Fidel Castro sent many of his agents there to conduct missionary work among the communist-led labor unions. The USSR poured large amounts of cash into support for Allende and his socialist party, certainly enough to have made the difference in his slim margin of victory over Alessandri (36.2 vs. 34.9 per cent). In 1971, after the Allende election, Castro himself spent a prolonged visit in Chile, much to the annoyance to the Chilean military establishment.

On the American side the Nixon Administration (through the CIA) and certain private organizations, especially ITT,[45] worked hard and not

---

44. USIA was under great political pressure to keep JUSPAO staffed, and as many as one fourth of the Agency's Foreign Service personnel served in Vietnam at one time or another. The Vietnam personnel officer told the Latin American area office I had volunteered for the assignment. This statement was untrue; but my Latin American colleagues were irritated with me because they had worked hard to get me an assignment with VOA.

45. In 1970 ITT owned 70% of Chitelco the Chilean Telephone Company.

always with the greatest discretion, first to prevent the Allende election and then to overthrow him; but USIS seldom knew what they were up to. Because of the CIA's secrecy Chileans often blamed them for evils where they were not the slightest bit involved. After Allende's election the United States began a series of economic road blocks in an effort to overturn his government. In this climate USIS continued to operate but had difficulty gaining access to anything but opposition media. Back in the United States liberal sympathy for Allende further complicated USIS efforts to promote American policy objectives.[46]

But the ultimate reason for the collapse of the Chilean democracy was internal. The Chilean constitution did not require that a presidential candidate gain a majority, only that Congress approve the one with the largest plurality. The Chilean Congress accepted Allende as chief of state only after exacting his agreement to strict conditions that he immediately proceeded to ignore in his efforts to impose a socialist economy on the country. It was the resulting domestic turmoil that led to Allende's downfall, the brutal military dictatorship and the 16-year hiatus in the Chilean democracy.

The Chilean experience with socialism and its punishing outcome taught Chileans a hard and bitter lesson. When they had another chance they chose democracy.

The 1988 Chilean plebiscite to end the dictatorship and the election of President Patricio Alywin in 1989 were carried out in a free and open manner and expressed the overwhelming desire of the Chilean public to reestablish their democratic traditions. The subsequent 1995 election of President Eduardo Frei (son of the former president) reaffirmed that desire. Today Chile is prospering economically, and U.S.-Chilean relations have never been better.

Perhaps the democratic seeds we sowed in the pre-Allende days were simply in their gestation period during the Pinochet dictatorship and have now taken firm root.

I would like to think so.

---

[46]. Oral history interview with James J. Halsema, USIS Public Affairs Officer in Chile, 1971-1975, conducted by G. Lewis Schmidt, August 19, 1989, ASDT Collection, Arlington, VA.

VIII Vietnam - Economic Program Planning Officer

In Washington they say nothing's too good
for our guys in Vietnam,
and that's exactly what we get.
(Saigon complaint)

Santiago to Saigon

The realization that I would be going to Vietnam took several days to settle into my subconscious. I had rationalized my acceptance of the assignment as good for my career. But having just returned from six months of continuous travel with the moon rock on USIA's behalf, I could not help resenting further separation from my family. Nevertheless, I resolved to be the good soldier and put the best face possible on this new phase of my life in the Foreign Service.

Family separation was not subject to appeal. The American Embassy in Saigon was taxed to the utmost just caring for essential personnel. The war and rampant terrorism made security a prime consideration; but housing was scarce, there were no schools available for children, and health facilities were dedicated to the needs of military combat personnel. Dependents were required to remain in "safe havens" chosen by the families themselves. Favorite places were the United States or in nearby cities such as Bangkok, Hong Kong or Taipei. Officers whose families chose to stay in the United States or Europe could visit them at government expense for three weeks every six months. Those whose families chose to live in nearby countries could visit for five days once a month under a similar arrangement, and during lulls in violence wives could visit their husbands in Vietnam. In either case the personnel affected received a separate maintenance allowance (SMA) to help cover the cost of maintaining their families away from their post of assignment. Family visitation time, called "SMA leave," did not count against annual leave but was added to one's length of duty in Vietnam. Since Vietnam was classified as a hardship post, officers assigned there also received a 25 per cent differential pay.

Margaret and I debated the pros and cons of both plans and decided that it would best for her and the children to remain in Washington where they could live in our own home, and the children could attend the excellent Montgomery County schools in our neighborhood.

We had made many friends in Chile and it seemed everyone wanted to give us a *despedida* (farewell party). A Chilean magazine publisher honored us with a fantastic dinner featuring virtually all of the country's many kinds of mariscos (shell fish), some of which I tasted for the first and last time. Carl Davis, back from his own trip to Vietnam, hosted an official farewell attended by Ambassador and Mrs. Korry and most of the Embassy and USIS staff.

On July 9, 1970, Margaret and I, together with Nancy, Judy, and our dog Charlie set sail from Valparaiso on the Grace Lines Santa Mariana. (Betsy was attending high school in the Indianapolis and would meet us in Lake Charles.) As it happened, this was the final voyage for the Grace Lines passenger steamers. Luxurious ocean travel had succumbed to more economic and efficient airline competition. Refreshed by the relaxing voyage, we left the ship in Balboa, Panama Canal Zone, and flew to Lake Charles for an all too brief reunion with my extended family. There Charlie romped to his heart's content in the fields around my mother's house. Then, all of a sudden it was over.

Back in Washington I used the remainder of my home leave to reestablish my family in our Wood Acres residence. As September began Betsy, Nancy and Judy returned to school, happy to be reunited with former classmates. Margaret once again became a suburban American homemaker, which meant no maid and a multiplicity of obligations, including taxi service for three lively girls.

Home leave over, I checked in at USIA where I learned that my new job title would be "Economic Program Planning Officer" for the Joint U.S. Public Affairs Office (JUSPAO) in Saigon. I was concerned that my lack of training in economics (I had only a year's undergraduate course) left me ill prepared for the job. Nevertheless, Art Hoffmann—who had just returned from Saigon where he had been instrumental in establishing the position—and Otis Hays, then Vietnam desk officer, reassured me that I had all the necessary qualifications. An economist, they said was the last person needed to fill the job. I immediately began a series of consultations related to my future duties, including a three-week Vietnamese area-training program at the Foreign Service Institute. There, State, USIA and AID officers who had already served in Vietnam indoctrinated me and my classmates on official U.S. policy and on how to avoid becoming a victim of Viet Cong terrorism, a topic which held our rapt attention.

Despite having long been an advocate for the U.S. role in Vietnam, the more I learned the more I began to wonder whether it would not be best for the United States to withdraw and let the opposing sides settle their own affairs. I was encouraged when Wilson Dizard, a former colleague who would be my immediate supervisor in JUSPAO, wrote me that Vietnamization was beginning and USIS was "planning to shift to more normal USIS activities."

On October 6, 1970, I bid my family goodbye at the Dulles International Airport and boarded a plane headed for Asia. It had been 25 years since I left China following World War II and 13 years since I left Japan at the end of my Takamatsu assignment. There was no way I could have known it at the time, but Asia would dominate the remainder of my professional life. This was but the first of many trans-Pacific trips that I would be making over the next 25 years. Stopovers in Japan and Hong Kong to visit old friends restored my sense of identity with the Asian scene. Soon I would become fully immersed in the maelstrom called Vietnam.

JUSPAO - A Prefatory Note[47]

In 1964, during the initial period of American involvement in Vietnam, the U.S. Army conducted its media relations separately from the Embassy. However, the variance between the Army's version of ongoing events and the position the Embassy wished to convey resulted in considerable confusion among newsmen about who to believe. In early 1965, Barry Zorthian, then Public Affairs Officer for the American Embassy in Saigon, developed the concept of a Joint U.S. Public Affairs Office as a means for bringing some order into the U.S. Government's media relations. He sold the idea to USIA Director Carl Rowan and Army Chief of Staff Harold Johnson while the two were in Saigon on an official visit, and they took the matter up with the National Security Council (NSC).

In April 1965 NSC issued a directive creating the Joint U.S. Public Affairs Office (JUSPAO) under USIS leadership and charged it with control of all U.S. propaganda operations in Vietnam. Zorthian was

---

[47]. For this prefatory note I have drawn on an oral history "Interview with Barry Zorthian" conducted by Cliff **Groce,** October 20 and 26, 1988, ADST Archival Collection, Arlington, VA

named director with two deputies, one military and one civilian. Besides USIA, the new organization drew its personnel from the Agency for International Development (AID), the Central Intelligence Agency (CIA) and the Military Assistance Command Vietnam MACV).

Initially, the new arrangement worked well with JUSPAO as coordinator for communications with news media covering the Vietnam War. Since MACV was issuing a written daily press report on military action but not responding to questions, Zorthian set up a daily press briefing to which he invited MACV spokesmen to answer queries and help newsmen understand what was going on. He chose five o'clock as a convenient time. However, with the growing size of MACV and its concern for psychological operations (psyops) "the tail soon started wagging the dog" (Zorthian's words). After Zorthian's departure people who took over the briefings handled them less successfully than he had, and the briefings became known as the "five o'clock follies." Vietnamese participation was but a fig leaf. Most of the information about the war came from American sources.

MACV's overbearing requirements transformed JUSPAO from a coordinating agency into a support organization for its psychological warfare (psywar) operations. JUSPAO coordinated its provincial operations through USIS psyops chiefs assigned to each of the four regional headquarters of CORDS[48] (Civilian Operations Revolutionary Development Support), and they, in turn, supervised the psyop representatives assigned to the 26 provinces. USIS personnel, thus, found themselves engaged in psywar operations for which they were never trained. Even so, many proved more skilled at the trade than their military colleagues.

In Saigon JUSPAO was, in effect, running a surrogate ministry of information for the Vietnamese government. While the Vietnamese were nominally in charge of the various media, they depended on the United States for virtually everything from radio and TV equipment to the paper and ink for their publications. JUSPAO's output, written in English and translated into Vietnamese, carried a "made in the USA"

---

[48] Vietnam was divided into four military regions, designated MR I (Eye Corps) with its headquarters in Danang; MR II headquartered in Nha Trang; MR III, in Bien Hoa just north of Saigon; and MR IV (Four Corps) at Cantho in the delta.

tone that reflected very unfavorably on the Vietnamese government as a puppet of the United States.

JUSPAO put massive effort into developing psywar leaflets that were printed at the Manila Regional Service Center (RSC); and the U.S. Air Force dropped tons of them over enemy territory, enough to paper Vietnam from one end to the other. The leaflets did, indeed, produce some defectors, but the program's critics said they did little more than provide the Viet Cong with toilet paper. Other techniques were to airdrop inexpensive transistor radios set at JUSPAO broadcast frequencies or to fly low over known Viet Cong or North Vietnam positions and broadcast appeals to defect over loudspeakers.

One USIS officer told me of participating in such an exercise. He had arranged for an airplane with loudspeakers to fly over an area where a defector indicated his friends operated. He went with the man to the area and had him broadcast a message—from the ground up to the plane and down into the jungle—saying he had been well treated and calling upon his friends by name to turn themselves in. Several days later on a visit to the Chieu Hoi[49] center he found three men who had heard the broadcast and deserted. Why? Not because of the good treatment they expected to get but for fear of being punished by their officers after their names were called out.

According to Zorthian, USIA became disillusioned with psychological operations within a year after the creation of JUSPAO. Many within the Agency said wartime propaganda was not USIA's job. Besides, USIA was a relatively small organization with worldwide responsibilities and JUSPAO was causing a heavy drain on the agency's resources and personnel that were sorely needed in other world areas. Nevertheless, successive U.S. Ambassadors—Maxwell Taylor, Ellsworth Bunker and Graham Martin—as well as the Departments of State and Defense found JUSPAO a convenient tool for the conduct of the war and kept it functioning as a psyops organization for eight years, well into Vietnamization of the war and the drawdown of U.S. forces.

In 1968 shortly after the Tet offensive, Ed Nickel, former PAO in Japan, replaced Zorthian as JUSPAO director. Nickel's managerial style did not allow for much familiarity with his subordinates. In fact it was

---

48. Viet Cong defectors to the SVN government; the name was also applied to the program that encouraged defection by enemy soldiers.

quite the opposite of Zorthian's, who made it a point to know all of his people in the provinces and visit them at their posts as frequently as possible[50]. Ed delegated this responsibility to his deputies. In August 1971 Robert Lincoln came to Saigon with orders to disband JUSPAO and convert it into a USIS establishment. I worked under both Nickel and Lincoln and played an active role in the reconversion process that was completed on June 30, 1972.

Saigon: First Impressions[51]

It was October 12, 1970. As the Air Vietnam plane descended toward Saigon the panorama of flooded rice paddies told me that rain was a part of the Vietnam scene. Wilson Dizard and Peter Quasius, with whom I was scheduled to work, met me at the airport and escorted me to the Central Palace hotel. This would be my home until my name came up for a JUSPAO apartment nearly six months hence. My room was spare with essential furnishings, the most important of which was an air conditioner that worked. The weather reminded me of Panama, muggy but not unpleasantly hot. JUSPAO employees living at the Central Palace took their meals at Brinks, a U.S. military officers' club two blocks away. Brinks had been the scene of a Viet Cong terrorist attack on Christmas 1964 that killed two American officers, a constant reminder that it could happen again. At dinner my very first evening in Saigon I met several old acquaintances there.

The city's downtown section snuggled up into a crescent bend in the Saigon River, reminding me of New Orleans. Honda motorcycles swarmed along a broad avenue paralleling the river. Concrete barriers and barbed wire surrounded public buildings and armed guards stood

---

[50]. Conversation with Stephen Sestanovich (FSO Ret) who accompanied Zorthian on many weekend trips to visit the provincial psyops advisers.

[51] The remainder of this chapter draws extensively on letters to my family describing my day-to-day life and impressions of the Vietnamese people, the country, my official activities and especially the war. I have also drawn on oral histories of other USIA personnel assigned to Vietnam. The events described here (1970-1972) began just beyond the midway point of the ten-year American involvement in the Vietnam War (1964-1975) and ends before the collapse of the South Vietnamese government, in a sense analogous to entering a movie just beyond the midway point and leaving before it was over.

vigil at each gate. Saigon's downtown streets bustled with people. The military were everywhere evident—American, Vietnamese, Korean, Filipino, Australian—with no apparent friction between them and the local citizenry. I was immediately struck by the diminutive stature of the Vietnamese compared with Americans and Europeans. The men, small and wiry, appeared no more than five feet tall. Willowy girls and slender women in their *ao dai* (traditional dress) and black pajama pants, looked picturesque riding Hondas and bicycles or just walking down the street. There seemed to be a disproportionate number of women because of the war, but in a nation of 14 million that had a million under arms there were still more young males on the street than one would expect.

The many shops were filled with wares imported from Japan, Malaysia, Hong Kong, and produced locally. Outside, street vendors spread articles for sale all over the sidewalks, including numerous items that appeared to have been purchased from GI's or pilfered from PX stores or both. All went into supplying the local economy.

American GIs, clad in green fatigues, were well behaved. A 10 p.m. curfew gave them little opportunity to get into trouble. Watching them I was reminded of myself in China back in 1943-1944 with an evening pass to Kunming. I rather profited from my experience and hoped these young men would survive to profit from theirs too. The dungarees did not help the soldiers' appearance, but laundry facilities were scarce and dungarees were easy to keep clean. One involuntary GI, referring to these outfits, was quoted as saying "If the good Lord had meant me to be a soldier he would have given me wrinkled green skin."

Saigon was a warm, moist blanket, like a continuing mild Turkish bath but not nearly so unpleasant as I had been led to believe. The monsoon season, then tapering off, brought daily deluges in the late afternoons and early evenings. It was as though each day the rain gods sought to inundate the earth before they retreated and recouped for the next onslaught. The dry season, beginning in November, would bring some cool days; but as the season's end approached in April it would get beastly hot and make one pray for the cooling monsoon rains to return.

Welcome Aboard

Wilson Dizard, with whom I had worked during my NASA liaison assignment, was but the first of many encounters with colleagues from previous posts that I will refer to the course of this narrative. Such associations greatly facilitated my work in a difficult and trying environment, but it also reflected on both the collegiality of the Foreign Service and the relatively small size of USIA.

JUSPAO headquarters was located in the former Hotel Rex, half a block from the municipal government building. Ed Nickel met newcomers every Wednesday afternoon. As I entered his office with several other new arrivals, Maurie Lee, Ed's USIS deputy, greeted me warmly. We had served together in Japan in the mid-fifties when I was in Takamatsu and he was director of the Yokohama American Cultural Center. Ed introduced himself somewhat formally and then, seated between his two deputies, Maurie and a lieutenant colonel, he gave a little spiel on the organization and functioning of JUSPAO and asked if there were any questions. All the while his body language was telling us that we should get out as quickly as possible. I felt it to be somewhat artificial, but I had already heard that he had a reputation for keeping himself remote from the rank and file. As a result the lower echelon tended to rely on his deputies for guidance.

JUSPAO had several missions. In addition to its psyops function and coordinating information for foreign news, described above, it was also responsible for the traditional USIS cultural function. This was carried out through American cultural centers and Vietnamese-American (*Hoi Viet-My*) binational centers; but these were relatively insignificant in comparison to the psyops functions.

As Maurie Lee later described it, "It was our job to get out and convince the people through various programs to support their government (and this) was in many ways controversial... We were spread out all over the provinces of South Vietnam."[52] At the time JUSPAO employed some 550 people. These included 200 Americans, half USIS and half military, plus 350 Vietnamese. More than half of these were assigned to the regional and provincial branches where they worked in conjunction with the American military advisers and the Vietnamese Ministry of Information. Of those assigned to Saigon most worked in JUSPAO's media operations—press, broadcasting, motion pictures, television—and administration. A research section kept tabs on developments in North Vietnam, and an office of policy and plans, to which I was assigned, provided media and field officers with policy guidances on how to treat major issues.

---

[52] Oral history interview with Maurice E. Lee conducted by G. L. Schmidt. ADST Collection., Arlington, VA

Even so JUSPAO was small compared with USAID (U.S. Agency for International Development) that had over 2000 American officers in country. Of course JUSPAO, AID, and all other Embassy elements came under the direction of Ambassador Ellsworth Bunker, the President's personal representative in Vietnam.

On the Job

My assigned duty in Vietnam was to prepare policy guidances on the Vietnamese economy for use by JUSPAO operatives. As a general rule these guidances would state the background of a particular issue, outline new developments and then specify how they should be treated through our psychological operations. For example, when research revealed evidence of disastrous economic conditions in North Vietnam, that information was used in a radio broadcasts and leaflet drops to encourage NVN soldiers to defect or return home. However, my own work focused on providing economic information that JUSPAO personnel, working with Vietnamese government information officers, could use to drum up support for GVN (Government of Vietnam) programs. During my first several weeks in Saigon I prepared myself for the assignment by going through an immersion process on the Vietnamese economy and USAID's economic development program. I was still not convinced I was up to the task, but I was no less qualified than many others trying to do a job with inadequate preparation. I fell back on my journalism training and set about interviewing Embassy and AID economists and reviewing their numerous reports to Washington. Listening to the economists the picture seemed rather bright, although nearly everyone conceded it would take ten years for the country to get back on its economic feet. That was assuming, of course, that the war would grind to a halt during 1971. Public figures and journalists were predicting that it would. History proved otherwise.

My first guidance was on taxation. AID had a U.S Internal Revenue Service tax team in Saigon helping the GVN to improve its tax collection process. The first step was a nationwide tax survey, the first in Vietnamese history. As a prelude, the GVN information people were conducting a publicity campaign to prepare the public psychologically, and our psyops advisers were helping in the process. Working with Charlie Carpenter, an AID tax specialist with whom I had served in both Panama and Chile, I drafted a policy guidance that provided the necessary background information, outlined the goals and gave the political and economic rationale to stress in the media. It passed muster with the Embassy and was distributed to JUSPAO's media and field personnel. I could only guess at how it was used or how much good it did.

Labor Survey

It was January 1971. The U.S. Government had already begun steps to Vietnamize the war and draw down its military forces. This posed a difficult psychological problem for both countries in dealing with the thousands of Vietnamese workers on the U.S. payroll who would lose their jobs. I was given the task of surveying labor attitudes toward the U.S. withdrawal and how to deal with the public aspects. It was a real lulu. The only way to keep the discharged workers happy was to give them jobs that the GVN didn't have. For the workers themselves it was a dilemma. They did not want to lose their income from working for the U.S. government, but neither did they want the U.S. military to stay in their country forever. For us it was a case of being damned if we left and damned if we didn't. But there was no choice. We were leaving, period.

To get a feel for the problems that confronted Vietnamese employees of the United States as we withdrew our troops I visited a several cities and talked to leaders of labor unions whose members worked on the U.S. bases. Tom Miller[53], a USAID labor adviser I had known in Chile where he represented the American Institute for Free Labor Development (AIFLD), helped me line up representative contacts in Nhatrang, Camranh Bay, Qui Nhon, Danang and Hue, cities and provinces of greatest concern. Mr. Luong, a JUSPAO employee familiar with labor unions, accompanied me as interpreter. At each place we visited the decommissioned military bases and then talked with the local labor leaders.

---

[53] Miller was an ardent bird lover. One weekend he bought a large macaw and a bamboo cage for it at a Saigon street market. He set the cage with the macaw in the back of his jeep to take home, but when he arrived the macaw had chewed its way through the bamboo slats and "flown the coop." It no doubt returned to its vendor and was soon sold to another unsuspecting American. Such was the macaw's contribution to the Vietnamese economy.

At Nha Trang labor leaders manifested considerable concern about unemployment problems caused by the U.S. withdrawal. It was not a matter we could disregard.

Cam Ranh Bay, our next stop, was a combined USAF, Army and Navy base where the vast majority of U.S. troops and materiel support for the Vietnamese entered the country. The base itself, at once stark and beautiful, was one enormous sand dune located on a peninsula that juts out to sea and forms a huge, well-protected bay, reputedly the best harbor in Southeast Asia. The docks and surrounding area were jammed with tanks, trucks, earth moving equipment and cocooned aircraft being readied for shipment back to the United States.

The Cam Ranh labor leader seemed less concerned about unemployment than his Nha Trang counterparts because his base did not face immediate closure. I was struck by his naiveté in view of the American draw down under way but could not convince him that he had a problem on his hands. I suspect that his remaining tenure as union leader had a very short life.

Further up the coast at Qui Nhon the rapid phase out was creating tensions, and a shooting incident in which a U.S. soldier accidentally killed a 16-year old boy had touched off a series of anti-U.S. demonstrations, incidents that were bound to happen and be exploited as long as our troops remained.

In Danang, John Hogan, the regional psyops adviser for MR I (Eye Corps) and an old friend from my Caracas days, had a member of his staff reconfirm interviews for me with the Hue and Danang labor leaders. Those completed I went to Hoi An, an hour's drive south of Danang, to see a provincial psyops operation. The road was insecure at night because of VC activity, but safe during the day. Forrest Fischer, my Gemini V control officer in Buenos Aires back in 1966, was the psyops representative in charge.

Forrest's office and residence was in an attractive Vietnamese villa and was considerably more commodious than other psyops stations I saw in the course of my stay in Vietnam. Nevertheless, it was completely surrounded by a wall of sandbags, in essence a bunker. He had a Vietnamese staff of about ten people and worked with the GVN information and Chieu Hoi (open arms) officers in preparing pamphlets, leaflets, posters and broadcasts through which they sought to persuade the Viet Cong and North Vietnamese soldiers to defect to the GVN. He also accompanied U.S. military psyops officers on visits to hamlets to see how these materials were being used and what effect they were having.

Using Forrest's typewriter I worked a full day writing up my report on the labor interviews while they were still fresh in my mind. The next morning Forrest took me back to Danang and put me aboard an Air America Curtis C-46 for the return trip to Saigon.

A few weeks later I learned that Ambassador Bunker had read my memorandum of the conversations with Vietnamese labor leaders Apparently he was well impressed because he recommended that his Country Team members read it too. It was good to know my hard work was appreciated.

The Ambassador's reaction led to an invitation to present my findings at a psyops conference in Nha Trang where I indicated it would be better not to sugarcoat the bitter pill of job loss but to convey U.S. concerns for the workers' welfare. This was followed by a series of seminars for American and Vietnamese psyop personnel to assist them in mitigating the impact of the U.S. withdrawal on the workers. I do not kid myself that we were able to make any workers feel better about losing their jobs, but perhaps sympathizing with their plight helped relieve their sense of being abandoned by their American employer.

Despite my good feelings about the labor report, my encounter with the provincial psyops advisers at the Nha Trang conference troubled me. Nearly all of them were young officers assigned to their tasks right out of their normal military jobs. Most had had a maximum of 12 weeks training in psychological warfare. They arrived for a one-year tour of duty with no knowledge of the Vietnamese language and little feel for the country. They needed six months to get adjusted to their jobs, and during their remaining time in country they thought of little but getting out. The Vietnamese they were supposed to be advising knew this all too well. Consequently, unless the American officer had something material to offer such as a vehicle or a printing press or paper to print on, he had little influence with his counterpart. As we phased down our psyops program and forced the Vietnamese to rely on their own resources, our influence was reduced even further. It was a period of adjustment, no doubt all for the best.

Land to the Tiller

My most personally rewarding task in Vietnam was researching and preparing field guidance on the Land to the Tiller (LTT) program. This was a component of the GVN's land reform law that provided for the purchase of rental agricultural land from its owners and for transfer of titles to families that lived and worked on it, hence the name. The proprietors had no alternative to giving up ownership, but the GVN reimbursed them with cash and government bonds. This AID-funded program was designed to increase grain production, gain the farmers' allegiance to the South Vietnamese Government and put an end to the country's ancient system of tenant farming. Ultimately LTTT was designed to undercut the Viet Cong's appeal to Vietnamese villagers by providing them with the thing they most desired, ownership of the land.

My project required the development of an information plan to educate farmers and landowners about their rights and responsibilities under the Land to the Tiller law, including such things as grievance procedures and how to thwart your thieving landlord. Once my guidance was completed our psyops people would use it in the organization and oversight of a series of provincial seminars for rural officials. But first I had to educate myself, and that included research visits to the countryside in various parts of South Vietnam, a task this old country boy welcomed. In the process I learned a great deal about Vietnamese geography, history, culture and how the United States and the GVN were attempting to reorganize the society in the midst of the war, some of which follows.

A Visit to the Delta

Jerry Novick was regional psyops adviser for MR IV, based in Cantho in the Vietnam Delta. I had known him in Japan where he was regional public affairs officer in Kobe and my first supervisor during my Takamatsu assignment. He was proud of his operation in the Delta and invited me to come see what they were doing and how they were doing it. I accepted gladly and took a four-day familiarization trip to Cantho and IV Corps. The area incorporated the large, pancake-flat region at the southern tip of Vietnam. Geographically, it is only a few feet above sea level with alluvial soil 70 meters deep, all washed down by the Mekong River. Its rich, black soil was superb for growing rice, and that is what people did in the delta. Along the coasts they also grew bananas, garden vegetables and sugar cane. And they fished. There were great varieties of crab, shrimp, lobster and other sea life.

I flew down on an Air America Caribou[54], a twin-engined military transport with canvas jump seats and an open cargo door in the tail, and watched the rich green panorama unfold beneath us. Jerry met me, gave me a full morning's briefing, and sent me off in a helicopter to Rach Gia[55] (called Rock Jaw by the GIs), a fishing village on the Gulf of Thailand. The city was secure, but there had been some VC activity in the area. Jim Lovett, of USIS and the provincial psyops adviser, and his four military assistants filled me in on how they worked with GVN personnel in the conduct of propaganda missions around the province. There being no hotel, they put me up for the night in Lovett's office. The next morning I toured the town, shot up a roll of film and left in another chopper for Bac Lieu on the other side of the peninsula. The USIS adviser there had been medevaced out with malaria; but his military assistant, a young lieutenant from New Orleans, took me to call on several land reform officials, see a rice mill and visit three rice farms. I felt like I was back in Louisiana. I learned a lot about their problems and got a good feel for the people. Returning to Cantho, Jerry and I talked far into the night reviewing all that I had seen and done. Back in Saigon I felt much better informed about rural Vietnam, what the LTTT entailed and, incidentally, more familiar with JUSPAO's field operations.

Pleiku

In late November my LTTT project took me to Pleiku to witness a GVN-organized graduation ceremony for some 80 Montagnard village and hamlet chiefs who had completed a six-week's course in village administration. (Montagnard is French for highlanders, the indigenous peoples of Vietnam.) On this occasion President Nguyen Van Thieu was supposed to attend the graduation ceremony and announce the details of the Land to the Tiller law as it applied to the Montagnard tribespeople.

Pleiku is at 3000 feet altitude in a rolling, semi mountainous area. The weather is temperate, with warm days and cool nights, certainly

---

54. Operated by the CIA, Air America provided transportation for the civilian elements of the U.S. Government in Vietnam with older aircraft acquired from the U.S. military.

55. During the Vietnamese exodus of the late 1970s and early 80s Rach Gia was one of the principal embarkation ports, usually aboard rickety fishing vessels that took refugees to Thailand, Malaysia, Indonesia and other Southeast Asian countries. Uncounted thousands lost their lives at sea.

more pleasant than Saigon's hot, muggy climate. When the Viets first came down from China they pushed the local inhabitants (whom they call Moi or savages) back into the mountainous country and took over the lowlands for their own use. In effect, they treated the Montagnards much as we treated the Native Americans in fulfilling our own manifest destiny. When the French colonized Vietnam they found the Montagnards more friendly and trustworthy than the Viets. While they were in control they acted as a buffer between the two peoples. During the Vietnam War the Americans replaced the French in that role. Somewhat primitive, the Montagnards were semi-nomadic, used slash-and-burn agriculture, and moved their villages periodically to new farmlands. They used their property communally, but until that time the GVN had never recognized their right to own land. Marginal agriculture made for marginal sanitary and living conditions, so their numbers remained static and the area they inhabited underpopulated. In the spring of 1975 Pleiku would be the scene of a major North Vietnamese army breakthrough leading to the communist victory over South Vietnam.

But in November 1970 with no severe fighting going on the press corps got excited about the Pleiku event, perhaps because of President Thieu's intention to attend. JUSPAO laid on a plane to take the correspondents up, about 27 in all. I went along to get background for my policy guidance paper on the land reform program. As it turned out the president became involved in an announcement about the attempted rescue of U.S. POWs from a Hanoi prison camp[56]. Prime Minister Tran Thiem Khiem went instead.

When we arrived at the Pleiku site the Montagnards were lined up to welcome the dignitaries. They looked as though they had already been waiting for hours. At the appointed time the Prime Minister and Deputy U.S. Ambassador (and CIA Chief) William Colby arrived, and the graduating class went through the ceremonies—national hymn, speeches, oath taking. It was all a formality. The Montagnards and the Vietnamese couldn't understand each other's language, and there was no interpretation. Besides, much of what was said was drowned out by the

---

[56]. It failed. The POWs had been moved to another site. We knew nothing about it until the official announcement was made in Washington, and even then we didn't believe the first reports.

circling helicopter gunships that were giving the PM and us security protection. After the awarding of certificates, there was a celebration with rice wine kept in large stone jars under tents made of parachutes. The PM got the first sip of the bubbling brew through a communal straw, and the graduates polished it off. I declined the honor in favor of beer and sandwiches brought along for the correspondents.

Next came a visit to a Montagnard village. The officials, reporters and I all climbed into eight helicopters; and, after a short flight, we descended en masse upon the villagers waiting for us on both sides of a dirt pathway that led to the ceremonial site. The PM dutifully stopped a couple of times to shake hands with some of the local citizens and then proceeded to the platform where he sat and listened to more speeches, again with no interpretation and with helicopters circling overhead.

I took the opportunity to inspect the village. The houses were built on stilts, firewood stacked underneath. Pigs, chickens and children roamed the village grounds. This was a "model" village; and it had been swept clean for the occasion, but the people looked poor. We visited a school and several classrooms. The kids, undoubtedly bored, had been sitting there all morning waiting for us to arrive.

To wind up our visit the Self Defense Forces (SDF) showed us their stuff by warding off a simulated attack on the village. At a given signal several dozen local guardsmen dashed out to repel the "attackers," and the villagers took refuge in their respective bunkers. It was quite impressive. We were told the SDF had successfully fended off attacks by North Vietnamese Army troops and were proud of their achievement. Of course this whole exercise was intended as public relations for the GVN and had little benefit for the poor villagers. In other such cases following visits by Saigon officials the VC entered the areas at night massacring the population and burning the villages to the ground just to prove that they could. American press accounts of our visit that I saw described it with a healthy amount of journalistic cynicism.

The mission completed, our choppers descended and transferred us to our waiting planes. We were back in Saigon by 4:30 p.m. It was a most interesting day, but fruitless in terms of the LTTT because details of the law as applied to the Montagnards was never announced.

Awarding Land to the Tillers

In December 1970 and March 1971 I attended major LTTT ceremonies in Go Cong and Long Xuen, both in the Delta. The two ceremonies were similar, differing only in size. In Go Cong Prime Minister Khiem presided at the first ceremony in which farmers actually received titles to their land. In Long Xuyen President Nguyen van Thieu presided so it was given greater publicity.

I served as press escort for about 70 reporters attending the Long Xuyen ceremony. They were mostly Americans, but there were also Europeans and Vietnamese. We flew down in C-123 cargo planes. The ceremonies went off without a hitch. The Vietnamese officials in charge had turned themselves inside out to organize a good show for President Thieu, and all went smoothly. The president gave out land titles to the farmers, remuneration checks to expropriated landlords—20 per cent in cash and 80 percent in bonds—pinned medals on worthy land reform officials, and delivered a speech announcing a 5-year plan for rural development.

Ambassador Bunker and a goodly number of USAID and Embassy representatives attended. After the ceremony everybody went to a fair organized for the occasion. For almost an hour the reporters and I traipsed around the fair grounds following the president and Ambassador Bunker and admiring the well-displayed agricultural products. I had to admire Ambassador Bunker. He was in his seventies, six feet four inches, and erect as a beanpole. The sun was boiling hot, yet he wore a suit and appeared cool throughout. At noon we sat under trees and parachute umbrella tents and lunched on boiled egg, a Vietnamese style empanada[57], boiled unborn duck, beer, and a sweet I cannot describe.

Ho Chi Minh and Mao Zedong did things differently. They gathered all the citizenry together, executed the former landlords and installed the farmers in collectives controlled by the government.

LTTT Seminars

By now I had done enough research on LTTT. It was time for me to produce. By mid May 1971 I had completed my guidance on the LTTT program. It went out to JUSPAO psyops officers around the country with instructions to organize Land-to-the-Tiller information seminars in conjunction GVN Ministry of Information and land reform officials. These were carried out during the next two months and completed in

---

[57]. Spanish for a sandwich in which the bread, usually a bun, is baked around the meat.

Danang at the end of July. The LTTT program was certainly one of the GVN's most successful projects. Much credit for this goes to USAID that aided and abetted it from the start. When South Vietnam fell victim to North Vietnamese military conquest, Northern cadres sent down to affect land reform found that the job had already been done. They told reporters that they were impressed. Later Hanoi ordered massive land collectivization in the South, but the order could never be enforced and gradually faded. After 1989 such collectivization as did exist came unstuck.

Studying Vietnamese

The American buildup in Vietnam had been so massive and the tours of duty there so brief—18 months for Foreign Service personnel, a year for the military—that except for a very few specialists the U.S. Government gave little attention to training people in the Vietnamese language. French was useful in dealing with Vietnamese intellectuals because of the country's colonial history, but it was not widely spoken among the common people. I was surprised when I inquired to find that neither the Embassy nor JUSPAO offered classes in Vietnamese. One of our senior officers said, "Why bother with Vietnamese. You'll never learn enough to do you any good. Why not study French? It's more useful in the long run." Even so my overseas experience, especially in China and Japan, told me that learning the local language was a key to knowing the people and their culture, so I persisted. Finally, four months after I arrived, the Embassy announced a lunch hour Vietnamese class for beginners. I joined. There were six of us in the class. I found Vietnamese, a tonal and monosyllabic language, even more difficult than Chinese or Japanese. But through the lessons, a Vietnamese tutor and the tapes I used at home, I was able to master some useful phrases that I practiced at every opportunity to the surprise and delight of my Vietnamese acquaintances. These were exceptionally useful as icebreakers in interviews I conducted in the course of my work. Before leaving Vietnam I also improved my French with the help of a good tutor..

Friends and Relatives

With the huge numbers of American military and other U.S. Government personnel in Vietnam I was not surprised at encountering many former Foreign Service colleagues, but finding a college classmate and a first cousin, both from Louisiana, serving there was really unexpected. Bill Kohlmann and I had roomed together at Yale Graduate School. Upon completing his studies he had joined the CIA and at the time of my arrival had already been in Vietnam for four years, working as a specialist on An Quang Buddhism. He was a big help to me in trying to understand the intricacies of Vietnamese political and religious groups.

The other surprise was finding a first cousin, Captain Charles (Chuck) Davies, stationed at Long Binh, about an hour's drive from Saigon. Chuck had been in combat and was about to return home, lucky to be getting out in one piece. Before he left we enjoyed several weekends together visiting Saigon's Central Market and other picturesque sites.

An Apartment at Last

In mid-April, six months after I had arrived in Saigon JUSPAO provided me with a second floor apartment at 195-B Cong Ly, a four-story building where a number of other JUSPAO personnel were housed. An Embassy hospitality kit with essential housekeeping items plus several decorative Vietnamese objects made it livable. The apartment changed my hotel pattern of life. No more breakfast, lunch, and dinner at Brinks. I had my meals in the apartment and occasionally invited friends in for drinks and dinner. A capable Vietnamese maid took care of the housekeeping chores.

One morning I was awakened at five o'clock by the cheerful sound of a cricket's song to find that he had taken up residence with me. He stayed around for days. Vietnamese consider crickets to be good luck and write poetry about their magic qualities. Little boys catch them, put them in cages and sell them at street markets. I protected my cricket so he would see me safely through my tour in Vietnam.

Every night from my apartment I could hear the sound of outgoing artillery. I never knew whether the guns were being fired at some target or whether the noise was intended to scare off potential Viet Cong attackers. Once when I heard explosions in the distance and my windows rattle from the concussions I dashed up to roof, and on the horizon I saw spirals of smoke from burning ammunition and napalm dumps hit by the VC. I was in no imminent danger, but back home in the USA such events made scare headlines, a primary communist objectives.

Nixon's China Trip

Nixon's July 1971 announcement of his forthcoming visit to Mainland China caught us all by surprise and gave new perspectives to the conflict. For Vietnamese both North and South, the Nixon-Mao meeting presented the dilemma of an arrangement worked out by two big powers in which they would have no say. Following the February 1972 talks, Marshall Green, Assistant Secretary of State for East Asia and the Pacific, who had taken part in them, came to Vietnam to brief President Thieu on the details[58]. JUSPAO was deeply involved with statements and backgrounders for the media, policy guidances, talking papers, pamphlets, radio programs and endless queries. I learned the Shanghai communiqué backwards and forwards and inside out. The initial Vietnamese uneasiness that we might have sold them out diminished. China had the same problems with North Vietnam, so much so that Chou Enlai had to go to Hanoi to soothe anxious nerves.

The U.S. Drawdown

A month after the Nixon-Mao meeting I wrote home: "We are rapidly drawing down our forces. U.S. military bases that used to throb with motorized and helicopterized activity are now ghost towns or deserts. Dozens of air bases and army camps around the country have either been taken over by the Vietnamese Air Force or the ARVN (Vietnamese Army) or have been dismantled by the local citizenry in locust-like swarms of people who toted off every usable stick of wood or equipment. Tu Do Street in downtown Saigon which used to accommodate hundreds of GIs in its girlie bars every night has now reverted to being an ordinary Oriental street with only an occasional foreigner seen among the Vietnamese. The B-girls are suffering financially, of course, and many of them have found other work or gone to the countryside. The battlefield casualty rate among the Americans

---

[58]. See *War and Peace with China - First Hand Experiences in the Foreign Service of the United States*, by Marshall Green, John H. Holdridge, William N. Stokes, Dacor Press, Bethesda, Md., chapters 12-13. Of the Vietnam meeting the authors say that it was in a calm atmosphere and "went off without incident…"

has gone down drastically; but the Vietnamese casualty rate has gone up proportionately. It's all in the name of Vietnamization. How effective it will be in the long run I cannot even guess. But we cannot fight their war for them forever and I, for one, think it is high time we were getting out for good."

Escaping the Turmoil

Many USIS officers assigned to JUSPAO complained that the organization was overstaffed and that they lacked meaningful work. This never affected me. My assignment allowed me to follow my own schedule and to devote as much time as necessary to conduct and write up my research. With this freedom I tended to work intensively on a given task and, when it was completed, seek some diversion before beginning the next. Life there was no picnic. With the war going on, one was compelled to get out of the country or at least out of the war zone whenever possible. During my Saigon assignment I had three SMA (separate maintenance allowance) trips to the United States to visit my family. In addition I took side trips of several days each to Bangkok, Singapore and Katmandu. The latter was at the courtesy of Ambassador Bunker who regularly took Embassy staffers in his official plane whenever he visited his wife who was U.S. Ambassador to Nepal.

Within the country, my research took me to many parts of South Vietnam, from Danang and Hue in the north to Dalat and Pleiku in the Vietnamese highlands and Cantho and Rach Gia in Delta. as well as My Tho at the mouth of the Mekong. The widely varying cultures in each place gave me gave me a picture of a vibrant nation struggling to assert itself in the midst of turmoil. Within Saigon itself I found diversion visiting the picturesque Central Market and enjoying interaction with the salespeople and their multiple displays of fruits, vegetables and other products. At the Tet festival (equivalent of Chinese New Year) I had but to step outside JUSPAO to enjoy the millions of flowers assembled for the occasion and the gay atmosphere surrounding the throngs of families, lovers, and groups of pretty girls who seemed to have a good time just strolling around. Seeing the Vietnamese enthusiasm for the festival helped me understand why they were so angry with the Viet Cong for violating it in 1968 and 1969 with their Tet offensives. Each of these visits increased my respect for the Vietnamese people and their culture as well as my appreciation for the beauty of the country.

Men without Women

Some people have alluded to Hemingway's book of short stories, *Men Without Women*, in describing our situation in Vietnam without our families. The analogy was not quite correct. There was no lack of women. In fact there were too many whose husbands had gone off to war, gotten killed, or otherwise left their families without means of sustenance. It was only natural that these women would seek help where they could find it. Who could blame them if they looked upon American men there without their families as a viable solution? When married American men with live-in Vietnamese girlfriends took SMA leave, they were said to be leaving their loved ones to visit their families. But while Vietnamese women were good for their own men, the liaisons they formed with Americans were frequently unnatural for both sides. Most such alliances were temporary at best, but they often resulted in difficult emotional situations, not to mention thousands of fatherless Amerasian children who were never accepted into Vietnamese society. The war wreaked havoc on people's lives in more ways than in just blowing up their homes and bodies.

A Presidential "Election"

In October 1971 South Vietnam held a presidential election. At least that is what was originally intended; but as the date approached all viable candidates opposing President Thieu withdrew, leaving voters with no choice, not even for a protest vote. Rather than cancel the sham affair Thieu changed it to a presidential referendum, announcing that he would not be satisfied with a mere 50 per cent. He wanted 60 percent or better. On "referendum day" I took a swing around some of the polling booths. The voters were staying away in droves, some for fear of incidents but most because there was no contest. Nevertheless, Thieu's minions took their boss seriously and made certain that he "won" handily. The presidential inaugural ceremony, broadcast over TV, took place on October 31 on the square in front of the City Hall and the JUSPAO building. JUSPAO was closed with one exception. We kept our rest rooms open for use by the Thieu presidential party.

The noisy election campaign was a diversion from the reality of war. With American ground troops being withdrawn, ARVN (Army of the Republic of Vietnam) troops had taken over most of the responsibility for fighting the war. However the United States continued to provide air support.

JUSPAO Winds Down; USIS Winds Up

In August 1971 Bob Lincoln, a Yale graduate whom I had known in Washington, replaced Ed Nickel as director of JUSPAO. He came with instructions from Washington to convert JUSPAO into a USIS operation. Actually, with the Vietnamization program underway quite a few members of JUSPAO were leaving and not being replaced. For five years JUSPAO had served as a surrogate Ministry of Information. Now, for better or for worse, the Vietnamese were doing the job themselves. It was time to revert to straight USIS work.

I was considered "essential" so I would stay until the end of my prescribed tour. When I arrived ten months earlier my section had consisted of ten officers. Now we were down to three. Lincoln appointed Frank Scotton, who had been involved in the Vietnam psyops program since 1965, to succeed Wilson Dizard as head of policy and plans. I was designated planning officer. The third member, John Dixon, would soon depart; and I would next encounter him in 1988 in Peshawar, Pakistan, dealing refugees fleeing the war in Afghanistan.

Initially Lincoln took a go-slow approach, giving me responsibility for drafting the conversion plan. After hashing out two drafts with the assembled chiefs of division and JUSPAO's top management we submitted our plan to Ambassador Bunker who approved it and gave us the green light for transforming JUSPAO into a USIS operation. When completed our staff was less than a fourth the size it had been when I arrived in October 1970.

JUSPAO was winding down, but USIS was winding up. We were getting rid of the big psyops organization that had been assembled for support of the war, but at the same time we were reorganizing what was left to carry out a rather large scale USIS operation.

We set June 30, 1972 as our target date for the conversion. Lincoln asked me to draft a USIS Country Program Memorandum (CPM) that would formulate our objectives and priorities. As a preliminary exercise, Deputy PAO Brian Battey (who had replaced Maurie Lee) and I carried out a series of consultations with the chiefs of our cultural and information divisions and representatives in the four regions, gathering their ideas for the new organization. The CPM required an evaluation of our operation for 1972, an outline of plans for 1973, and projections for

1974. As I went through the drafting exercise there were times when I thought I was writing fiction. Certainly my crystal ball was never muddier. I kept asking myself whether the Country Plan would have a country?

In early June we moved JUSPAO from the Hotel Rex to the American Cultural Center building, a space about the third the size of our former quarters. The Cultural Center was relocated in the Vietnamese American Association (VAA).

June 30, 1972, marked the end of JUSPAO. At midnight it went out of existence and we became USIS Vietnam. Someone should have organized a party and blew taps, but no one did. JUSPAO passed into history unmourned and unlamented. Perhaps someone with a feel for history, JUSPAO's history, will tell the full story, warts and all. If so they should feel free to draw on this modest account.

Lecturing

In an earlier chapter I wrote of speaking to Vietnamese audiences on the U.S. scientific achievements under NASA's space program. Even though I enjoyed giving these lectures it seemed to me that since the people I was addressing were going through a life and death struggle to defend their democracy, I might better speak on the American democratic experience. Thus when Forrest Fischer, then director of the USIS cultural centers in Hue and in Danang, invited me to speak to a class on American government he was teaching at Hue University, I jumped at the chance. I chose "The Formation of American Foreign Policy" as my topic and put together an hour's lecture that I used several times at the VAA in Saigon and at Hue University. The lecture was well received in both places. The students were interested in what I had to say and asked sharp questions. The most interesting came in Hue where a student asked: "Is the CIA legally authorized to organize foreign armies as it has been doing in Laos?" Under the wartime circumstances I was somewhat baffled as to how a U.S. government official like myself should answer that without lying through his teeth. I weaseled out of it by responding that as a military organization the CIA was a first class intelligence agency. That got me off the hook but did not really answer the question. I was not sure whether even a Congressional investigation could answer it.

The War Goes On

On Easter Sunday 1972 the communists began their long anticipated offensive against the demilitarized zone (DMZ) in the north. It coincided with the visit by some high level Russian military brass to Hanoi and preceded a Moscow visit by President Nixon the following month. The timing indicated that the Russians wanted a North Vietnamese victory behind them when they confronted the American president. It was no wonder that many Vietnamese saw themselves as pawns in the game of international power politics. Meanwhile, under the Vietnamization program, U.S. troops continued to go home. Cynics said all we were doing was changing the color of the corpses.

Peace talks had begun in Paris but Nixon continued to threaten to blow the North Vietnamese off the map if they didn't withdraw from the South. Nevertheless, the continuing drawdown of American troops sent a different message, and the NVNs kept up their offensive.

In a letter home I wrote: "Mr. Nixon talks tough, he acts tough; but this is a Vietnamese war, a Vietnamese quarrel among themselves. And even if we do force a solution down their throats, as soon as we get out of here they'll be at it again. That's why I have come to the conclusion that the sooner we withdraw the better off both we and they will be."

With a war going on it seemed fruitless to carry on our normal peacetime USIS activities such as lectures, exhibits, concerts and similar programs. Yet we felt it necessary to plan for when there was no war, if that day ever came to Vietnam.

By mid May as the opposing armies were preparing to fight for Hue in Quang Tri province, the South Vietnamese Government closed all the universities and called up 17 year olds and people 39 to 43 years old for military duty. Young women were told to study nursing. Casualties were high on both sides, and every day we heard of someone who had lost a son or a relative. It was a dirty, ugly business.

American reportage was often unbalanced and seriously colored U.S. domestic views of the war's progress. Later that year Barney Seibert of the UPI told Bill Gausmann (our resident expert on North Vietnam) and me about the last days of the Battle of Quang Tri. Sixty foreign correspondents—mostly Americans—were in nearby Hue when the North Vietnamese Army (NVA) took the town. When the South Vietnamese Army (ARVN) took it back there was only one—Barney. The Southerners won the battle without the use of air power and with fewer men than the NVA. It was a bloody fight and both sides lost heavily.

As the NVN offensive continued, USIS posts in different parts of the world, citing conflicting news agency reports, began bombarding USIA Washington with questions about the real situation in Vietnam. The Agency asked us to provide them a backgrounder with details. Lincoln passed the job on to me, and I prepared an 8-page talking paper on the "Facts on the Current North Vietnamese Invasion." USIA sent it to all posts around the world. The only acknowledgement I got was a note scribbled at the top by my boss saying "Congratulations, Harry."

As we entered June the war continued to plod its bloody path, but things seemed to have bogged down completely for the NVN offensive. The SVN Army began to show its mettle and blunted the NVA at practically every point. President Thieu was saying the war would be resolved on the battlefield, an all too prescient remark.

Refugees and Casualties

In mid-June a fierce battle at An Loc, some 60 miles northeast of Saigon, produced a flood of civilian refugees trying to escape the fighting. I was in the process of drafting a psyop policy paper on the plight of refugees and what the GVN and the United States were doing to help them, so I visited a refugee camp to gather impressions.

It was a 45-minute drive from Saigon. About 5,000 people had arrived there several days earlier. They were given temporary shelter in U.S. Army tents, about 50 persons in each tent. Many were suffering from shellshock, but they were so happy to be alive and out of the An Loc hellhole that they weren't complaining—yet. Most had walked a large part of the way and rode the rest in army trucks. Some walked through the jungle to escape a town that the communists had taken over, always fearing they might get caught and shot. At the time there were some 800,000 like them around the country.

The camp was as well ordered as one could expect with that many people clustered together in an open field with no sign of sanitary facilities. They were mostly women, children and old men. All able-bodied young men were either in ARVN or had been captured by the North Vietnamese and impressed into work details. The refugees arrived with just the clothes on their backs. The GVN had gone all out to provide them with food. Each person checking in got a rice ration. Children under two got milk rations.

Dozens of civilian groups were pitching in with clothing, bedding, food and other necessities. High school and university students and many other volunteers were working at this camp and others on weekends, cutting hair, digging latrines and whatever they could to make life more bearable for these innocent victims of the North-South war. The refugees stayed in these temporary shelters until they could get located with relatives, friends, or in a more permanent camp.

Visit to a Field Hospital

A week later, as a sequel to my visit to the refugee camp I visited an ARVN field hospital for soldiers wounded at the battle of An Loc. It was even more tragic than the refugee camp. Hundreds of young men lay in their bunks with bloody bandages covering leg and arm stumps and other injured parts of their bodies. A few moaned in pain, physical and mental, but most seemed to suffer in quiet resignation. Before going I had asked one of our military advisors what kind of gifts I might take. The answer was reading material—magazines and books—in Vietnamese if possible but English would do, especially if illustrated.

"How about some old Playboy magazines?" I asked.

"Great," he said, "they'll love them."

He was absolutely right. I entered one of the hospital tents with an armload of the magazines, and when I held one of them up several soldiers shouted "Playboy!" in unison. At that the entire ward came alive with arms reaching out for copies. Within a minute my whole supply was gone. Men are the same everywhere. There's nothing like a pretty girl, even if it's just a picture, to cheer them up.

Sadly, in a post Vietnam War visit to a Ho Chi Min City Buddhist temple I encountered a number of legless war veterans begging for whatever help they could get. Some had undoubtedly met their fate at the battle of An Loc.

Leaving Saigon

Two months before the official end of my Vietnam tour of duty—July 14, 1972—I received "loose pack" travel orders, meaning I was to leave my personal effects in Saigon for future shipment to wherever I was assigned. Shortly afterward I was offered the choice of Information Officer in Lima or Press Attaché in Tokyo. After six years as Information Officer in Panama and Santiago, Lima would just be more of the same. I needed a change. I chose Tokyo. Subsequently, however, USIA informed me that USIS Tokyo had filled the position from within its existing staff, leaving me with no ongoing appointment. I was relegated to the invidious ranks of Washington unassigned, meaning I would go there await an appropriate job opening.

The Embassy gave me an official "check-out sheet" that looked like a book—eight pages of items to check off and eighteen pages of instructions, thus confirming the common Saigon saying that the only thing more complicated than checking in was checking out.

I had very little to pack except personal items acquired in Vietnam. I donated my excess clothes to the refugees. Everything else, from kitchen utensils to the sheets I slept on was Embassy owned. Bill Gausmann took over my apartment and all its equipment. He is even took over Ms. Thoa, my maid, and her little boy. She was pleased to have a new employer and Gausmann was lucky to get her. All I had to do was make a paper transfer to him and walk out the front door with my suitcase.

On July 10 my successor, Bill Ayers, arrived and I was free to go. The contrast between my departure from Saigon and from my previous foreign posts was drastic. It was more like leaving Washington. Frank Scotton gave us a "hello and farewell" dinner at a Chinese restaurant, and that was that. Since I had annual leave coming (if you don't take it you lose it) and there was no particular reason to hurry home. I had arranged for Margaret to meet me in London for two weeks of sightseeing around the British Isles.

It was our first visit to England so everything was new. We got acquainted with London, saw some of its famed theatrical productions and then spent two delightful weeks touring England and seeking out our ancestral roots, mine in northern England's Lake Country, Margaret's in Yorkshire.

Home Leave

Back at USIA Washington there was still no word on my next assignment. I took my family to Lake Charles for the month's home leave due me after 18 months in Saigon. While there Otis Hays, country desk officer for Vietnam, called to say USIS Saigon was desperately in need of someone to coordinate policy meetings with the Embassy and prepare reports to Washington. Bob Lincoln insisted on having someone familiar with the Vietnam program. A man with previous

Vietnamese service was scheduled to go but would not be available for two months. Would I be interested in handling it on a temporary basis?

My prospects for several possible assignments had already gone by the boards. "Doesn't the Agency have something more permanent for me yet?" I asked.

"I just spoke with personnel, and they still don't have anything in sight for you."

"Well, I'll make you a bargain. If you can get a commitment out of personnel that they'll have a decent job for me when I return, I'll go back to Vietnam for two months and do Mr. Lincoln's job for him."

"It's a deal," Otis said.

Margaret was not happy about my returning to Saigon. I was not overly enthusiastic; but like so many of my predecessors I had caught the Vietnam virus and was vitally interested in everything happening there. Another short stint in that beleaguered country would do me no harm and might be worth the effort if it resulted in a satisfactory assignment afterwards.

Return to Saigon

On September 10, 1972, I left Washington on Pan American Airways for my fifth trip to Saigon, only this time I went via New Delhi. As the saying went, I was "flying rupees." The U.S. Government paid Pan American for my ticket (as it did for many others) from a rupee account accumulated through the sale of agricultural products under Public Law 480, and PanAm used the rupees for its expenses in India. The catch was that travelers had to spend at least 24 hours in that country. I used my time in New Delhi to visit the Taj Majal. Back in 1943 when I was a soldier on my way to China our C-47 transport had stopped in Agra to refuel. When we took off our pilot did a turn around the Taj to give us a look. I vowed to come back at my first opportunity. This was it. My dreams of seeing the Taj in the moonlight were not fulfilled, but it was still thrilling to witness the gleaming white marble with all its colored marble inlays in midst of a monsoon downpour.

During the next two months I wrote seemingly endless reports to inform our superiors and the bureaucrats back in Washington about what was going on, but I fear my undying prose more likely ended up in that great Washington paper maw, glanced at by a few and quickly forgotten.

One very minor incident in my second tour reflected the times. I described it in a letter home.

"October 23, 1972 - Henry Kissinger has come and gone again. Except for the hustle and bustle caused by dozens of security guards and police who surrounded the Embassy during his entire stay we would not have known he was here. He left today saying only that the talks had been "productive." Sunday morning I stopped by the Embassy to read some cables. As I entered the compound gate I got swept aside by an onrush of guards dashing toward their respective automobiles, jeeps, and motorcycles. Behind them came Mr. Kissinger and Ambassador Bunker chatting amiably, all very relaxed. It was an amusing contrast. Mr. Kissinger flew over to Phnom Penh for lunch with Lon Nol, came back that afternoon, had another meeting with President Thieu, then left."

During this period much of our attention focused on the U.S. Presidential contest between George McGovern and President Nixon and on their respective promises for getting us out of Vietnam. McGovern proposed a "quick surgical cut" that would leave the patient bleeding to death before he could recover his forces. Mr. Nixon offered an extended withdrawal that promoted parasitical tendencies that were already a major weakness of the South Vietnamese society. On November 7 the American voters chose Nixon, not because they liked his plans so much but because they trusted McGovern's even less.

The Vietnamese were happy to see Nixon win. They thought he was on their side. Thieu concluded the American election had given him and Nixon a mandate to set even tougher terms for peace at the Paris peace talks. My own attitude was the quicker we got out of there the better off both we and the Vietnamese would be.

When I left Saigon on November 16, 1972, it was still two and a half years before the Government of South Vietnam would fall to the communists. Departing Vietnam at that time reminded me of leaving China back in 1945 at the end of World War II. There was a great deal more to come that might prove even more dramatic than anything that had happened during my two years in that country. Even so, I was certain I could watch developments just as well from Washington as I could from Saigon.

Before leaving for Vietnam in October 1970 the author posed for this photo with his family at their Washington residence. Mrs. Kendall and their three daughters remained in the United States during his two years in Saigon.

On a field tour of the South Vietnam delta the author visited Provincial Psyops Advisor James Lovett (right) in Rach Gia. JUSPAO provided USIS advisers like Lovett for each of South Vietnam's four regions and 26 provinces. The other photo shows Lovett with his team of military psyops officers.

IX A Vietnam Retrospective

Those who cannot remember the past are condemned to repeat it.
George Santayana

The Enigma

In 1974 Robert A. Scalapino, professor of political science at the University of California, Berkeley, was lecturing in Vietnam on the U.S. involvement in the war. When he had finished his presentation a very thoughtful Vietnamese officer stood up and said, "Now, Professor, when the United States forces came into Vietnam in 1964-1965, you came without our knowing you were coming, and it took us a long time to adjust to it. Now you are leaving us and you're doing it without our knowing it, and we don't know why. We have difficulty understanding what United States policy is all about."

Professor Scalapino pondered the officer's statement a few moments and said, "I cannot respond to that comment."[59]

Many of us who served in the American Embassy in Saigon during the Vietnam conflict and performed our assigned duties to the best of our abilities shared the Vietnamese officer's bafflement about United States policy in his benighted country. We followed the lead of our superiors, often with personal doubts about the wisdom of the policies we were espousing. Among ourselves we frequently debated individual decisions, but as officers committed to support the foreign policy of the United States we did our duty, always with the hope that our leaders in Washington would find some way to end the bloody conflict with honor to the United States and the least possible damage to the Vietnamese people.

Even though I was beginning to have some doubts about our Vietnam policy when I went to Saigon, I was still convinced that the United States was doing what had to be done to put an end to communist aggression. I came away with the feeling that there had been some serious errors in our Vietnam policy that led us into that tragic morass.

---

59. Conversation with Scalapino.

As I see it there were two basic mistakes. One was the decision to go into Vietnam to prevent what was conceived to be monolithic communism—as represented by the China and the Soviet Union—from taking over South Vietnam and all of Southeast Asia. As we realized later communism was no more monolithic than capitalism. In fact, the Sino-Soviet alliance fell apart in 1959-1960 well before we became so deeply involved in Vietnam. Furthermore, the Chinese and Vietnamese have been at each other's throats for more than a thousand years, and the Vietnamese have thrown the Chinese out on various occasions. Although the Mao Zedong government may have supported Ho Chi Minh's aspirations for national unification under a communist government, there could have been little expectation that the two countries would remain staunch allies over the long term. This was vividly demonstrated in 1979 when the Chinese, seeking to "teach Vietnam a lesson" over their treatment of Cambodia, were taught a lesson themselves by military defeat at the hands of superior Vietnamese forces.

The other basic error was in trying to tell the South Vietnam how to run its government. In doing so we manipulated Ngo Dinh Diem and all of his successors. We imposed decisions upon the South Vietnamese leaders that they could not or would not carry out. In some cases it was because they lacked the will or the means or both. In many cases it was because they disagreed with their American advisors. The murder of Ngo Dinh Diem was in part our own fault even though our people didn't pull the trigger. Although we did not like Diem and his aggressive suppression of Vietnamese Buddhism, it was the responsibility of the Vietnamese people, not the United States, to remove him from power. We encouraged the Vietnamese generals to pull a coup to unseat Diem without any real concept of who could lead the country in his absence. The crude manner in which the coup was executed plunged us even more deeply into the morass[60]. After Diem we imposed on Vietnam a series of bumbling military leaders we thought would follow our orders. Some of them tried, but in taking their orders from Washington they alienated any support they may have had from the Vietnamese people.

---

[60]. Robert S. McNamara, *In Retrospect - The Tragedy and Lessons of Vietnam*, New York - Times Books, 1995. In chapter 3 McNamara gives a blow-by-blow account of the coup to unseat Diem

Robert McNamara, former secretary of defense under Presidents Kennedy and Johnson, has admitted[61] that he and many of our top leaders in Washington made serious mistakes in judgment. It was not that they lacked the necessary knowledge and information, or even that our high-level decision process was inadequately organized. Key people within the Johnson administration opposed military intervention in Vietnam. These included State's George Ball, Ambassador John Kenneth Galbraith and some senators, particularly William Fulbright. We had more than enough experts on China[62] and the Soviet Union. While there were fewer on Vietnam, the advice of these specialists was pushed aside and totally ignored in favor of preconceived notions based on our World War II experience; hardly applicable to a small country engaged in a civil war. McNamara took a military approach to this highly political war and relied more heavily on advice from his military leaders in the field than on the political counsel of acknowledged Vietnam and Sino-Soviet experts.

Missed Opportunities

There were also missed opportunities for peace in Vietnam. One can only speculate on what the history of that part of the world might have been had President Truman agreed to meet with Ho Chi Minh as he requested in the immediate aftermath of World War II. There is no doubt about Ho Chi Minh's communist convictions. These were amply demonstrated by his conversion of North Vietnam into a communist society. Nevertheless, Ho's primary motivating forces were nationalism, the universal Vietnamese desire for independence from France and, after the 1954 Geneva Convention that divided Vietnam, national unification. President Roosevelt had staunchly opposed allowing the French to reassume its colonial role in Indochina[63].

---

[61]. McNamara, op. cit., describes in great detail the decision making process in the Kennedy and Johnson administrations which led to the U.S. involvement in Vietnam, acknowledging where he and other U.S. leaders were at fault.

[62]. The Department of State's expertise on China had been seriously decimated by Senator Joseph McCarthy's attacks on their loyalty, but there were numerous China scholars in American universities available for consultation had the White House and the Department of Defense chosen to listen to them.

[63]. Archimedes Patti, *Why Vietnam: Prelude to America's Albatross*, Berkeley, University of California Press, 1980, 612 pp.

The Truman administration, faced with a recalcitrant Charles DeGaulle and the necessity for bringing France into the reconstruction of post war Europe, acceded to the French President's vain hopes of restoring French colonial rule in Indochina. Eisenhower and John Foster Dulles went along with this decision, and the United States supported French colonialism until the Vietnamese soundly defeated it in the battle of Dien Bien Phu. The 1954 Geneva conference divided Vietnam into the communist North and noncommunist South, and thereafter the United States became the patron of South Vietnam. At this conference, the Eisenhower administration, to obtain an agreement on partitioning the country, agreed to hold a nationwide election on reunification. South Vietnam President Ngo Din Diem was all too aware that the election would favor Ho Chi Min's Viet Minh Party, and with the backing of the United States, he never allowed this election to take place.

In an interesting episode at that Geneva Conference, China's Premier Chou En-Lai extended his hand to Secretary of State John Foster Dulles in a gesture of friendship. Dulles walked on past and left Chou standing there. Here was an opportunity for the opposing leaders to talk to each other to try to achieve some understanding, but Dulles seems to have refused on the basis that he considered the communist Chou En-Lai to be evil. Be that as it may, leaders of countries as powerful as the United States and China have the responsibility to make every effort to resolve national differences. On this occasion Mr. Dulles' personal prejudice caused him to abjure that obligation.

In the Kennedy administration, as acknowledged by McNamara, the United States failed to follow through on a recommendation by President DeGaulle for a neutral Vietnam out of the belief that such action would permit the communists to take over. This, they believed, would make the "dominoes" fall and lead to communist controlled government throughout Southeast Asia[64].

In Vietnam, as in China, the United States based its policies on a sense of morality that condemned not only communism as evil, but also the people victimized by the system. As we now see, many of these people were desperately seeking to get out from under the communist yoke.

---

[64]. McNamara, p. 113

The basic errors committed by our top governmental leaders were propagated a thousand fold in lesser decisions by the Washington bureaucracy and by the American military and civilian leaders in Vietnam seeking to uphold U.S. policy..

In effect, we found ourselves trying to run a government of a country where we not only did not understand the language; we also did not understand the culture, the people or their history. Yet we were fighting their war for them. We were conducting a horribly expensive program in terms of money and lives and effort based on tragic misperceptions. Even so, there is no doubt that our leaders followed these policies out of conviction that they were doing exactly what needed to be done. To borrow a phrase from former Senator Sam Nunn (D. Ga.), they were always wrong but never in doubt. It took massive demonstrations by the American people and a presidential campaign focused largely on the Vietnam War to persuade Washington that we should withdraw. By winning the election Nixon was given that responsibility. The methods he chose—a questionable treaty with the North Vietnamese and a phased withdrawal of American forces—did not save us from national humiliation when South Vietnam fell to communist forces in April 1975.

Ambassador Bunker

Whatever those of us working at the American Embassy in Saigon may have felt about the U.S. involvement in Vietnam, I think I can safely say that all, without exception, felt the deepest respect for our Ambassador, Ellsworth Bunker. This grand old man of the Foreign Service had already served as ambassador to Argentina, India, Nepal, and the Organization of American States. In 1967 when President Lyndon Johnson asked Bunker to replace Henry Cabot Lodge as U.S. Ambassador to the Republic of South Vietnam he was 73, well beyond the age of retirement.[65] In 1971 President Nixon asked him to remain in

---

[65] Bunker accepted the appointment on the condition that he maintain direct contact with the President without going through the Department of State. The request was granted and he submitted private reports to Presidents Johnson and Nixon throughout his tenure in Saigon. See *The Bunker Papers. Reports to the President from Vietnam, 1967-1973*, edited by Douglas Pike, 3 vols, Institute of East Asian Studies, Berkeley, 1990. I was instrumental in getting the Department of State to declassify them from top secret under the provisions of the Freedom of Information Act.

Saigon, which he did until 1973. Bunker exemplified the best traditions of the Service by responding to his country's call to carry out an extremely difficult task under unsavory conditions. It was not for lack of trying that he was unable to resolve the situation during his ambassadorship.

Who We Were

Over the years USIA sent nearly a quarter of its Foreign Service personnel to Vietnam. The standard tour was 18 months, barely enough to get acquainted with the country, let alone attain expertise in Vietnam's highly complicated political and military situation. Many were assigned to positions ill suited to their personal training and background, felt underworked and resented having been sent where they were not really needed.

Vietnam occupied top priority worldwide in USIA's scheme of things, so all the Saigon and provincial positions had to be filled. The 25 per cent differential pay was attractive for some, but given a choice most would have declined the honor of a Vietnam assignment. Nevertheless, on joining the Foreign Service officers accept USIA and State's worldwide availability policy and have the choice of going where assigned or resigning. Some chose the resignation route.

Working from a distance as I did in Latin America during the sixties (1964-1970), despite the intense anti-Vietnam War atmosphere I encountered in Panama and Chile, I entertained few doubts about our government's policy in Vietnam until I actually arrived on the scene, and even then my questioning focused on how best to get the job done and get out of Vietnam as quickly as possible. To that end I devoted myself eagerly to the tasks described in the foregoing chapter.

USIS officers serving as provincial psyops advisers (PPA) in the 26 provinces had experiences quite different from mine. Forrest Fischer, who served as PPA in Hoi An south of Danang, said that "being in MR-1 and in a place like Hoi An, I was closer (than you) to the killing fields… I had more of an opportunity to observe the suffering of the people, the soporific fatalism of the ARVN, the single-minded arrogance of the U.S. military officers, the opportunism of Vietnamese officialdom, and worst of all, the blindness to reality of our own leaders, both military and civilian… In my view, our disastrous policy in Vietnam was born of paranoia over communism that infected our nation in the 1950s. A warped fear of communism at home led to the

House Un-American Activities Committee and the Joe McCarthy excesses."

The quality of the USIS personnel in Vietnam was uniformly high, but few of them had any special knowledge of Vietnam. Less than half a dozen could speak the language, and not many more than that had been in Vietnam long enough to fully grasp the problems that confronted us. One of these was Frank Scotton, who had been in Vietnam since 1965. He and Everet Bumgardner[66], there since 1960, had been involved in organizing armed propaganda teams and working in the countryside. When I arrived in 1970 Frank was psyops adviser for the city of Saigon. In September 1971 he was appointed head of JUSPAO's planning staff where we worked together until my departure in 1972. Later, he and Ev Bumgardner worked with me on Vietnam affairs out of USIA's Office of East Asia and Pacific in Washington, D.C.

JUSPAO's other Vietnam expert was Douglas Pike, a specialist in international communications who went to Vietnam in 1960. Doug made a study of the National Liberation Front (Viet Cong) as a social organization and their use of informal channels, outside the mass media, as a means of communicating ideas to the peasantry who were their principal support. He took a year's leave at the Massachusetts Institute of Technology (MIT) and wrote a definitive book, *Viet Cong: The Organization and Techniques of the National Liberation Front of South Vietnam*[67] that has been translated into 18 languages. Subsequently USIA sent him on a round-the-world lecture tour to explain the United States role in Vietnam[68] and he served as a special consultant on Vietnam to the Departments of State and Defense.

---

[66]. Bumgardner was a close associate of John Paul Vann and an important source of information for Neil Sheehan's Pulitzer Prize winning book *A Bright and Shining Lie - John Paul Vann and America in Vietnam*, New York, Vintage Books, 1989. He was a briefing officer in the Foreign Service Institute's Vietnam Training Center in 1970 when I attended it in preparation for my Saigon assignment. He later succeeded Otis Hays as USIA's Vietnam desk officer. See next chapter.

[67]. The MIT Press, Cambridge and London, 1966.

[68]. See chapter on Chile and oral history "Interview with Douglas Pike, February 1989, conducted by John Hutchison, "ADST Collection, Arlington, VA.

Most of JUSPAO's military officers had undergone minimal training in psychological operations. Those I knew best performed well, but they tended to regard their work from a purely military point of view, i.e. defeating the enemy, as opposed to USIS officers who think more in diplomatic terms of conveying the rationale of American foreign policy to foreign audiences. A three-week Vietnam training program at the Foreign Service Institute, such as I went through, was prescribed for all Embassy officers assigned to Vietnam. It acquainted me with some of the problems we would encounter, but by no means made me an expert. USIS and military psyops officers were intermingled in Saigon and in the countryside in the four military regions. Thus, two inadequately trained groups of American officers were assigned the role of advising the Vietnamese how to conduct the psychological warfare aspects of their internal political and military struggle.

Our Vietnamese employees on the professional level were well educated, competent, and a pleasure to work with. Some had been long-term USIS employees; many others were taken on to fill the multiple needs of JUSPAO. Although I had no personal knowledge of infiltration by Viet Cong agents, I do not doubt that there were several. Some may have acted out of personal conviction, others out of threats of violence to themselves or their families. It was a wartime situation and such activity was to be expected.

Transition to USIS

I was grateful to be part of the team that transformed JUSPAO into a standard USIS operation. Although my 18-month tour came to an end shortly thereafter, from what I observed during my subsequent two months' temporary duty in Saigon and my two-year Washington assignment as area policy officer, the mechanisms we developed worked well under Bob Lincoln and his successor public affairs officers. I like to think that during my two years in Vietnam I made a useful contribution to the total U.S. effort. However, given the massive social changes that occurred following South Vietnam's defeat by Hanoi it would be virtually impossible to assess any lasting effect of the informational program carried by JUSPAO and USIS.

It is not possible to discount the horrible wounds inflicted on Vietnamese society by American military action; but if we can set this issue aside for a moment, I think the principal achievement of the United States action in South Vietnam from 1964 to 1975 was in persuading the Vietnamese that they should modernize their economic and social system. The Vietnamese are a very intelligent people, and they quickly learned to appreciate the innovations introduced by both the American government and private enterprise during the brief life of the Republic of South Vietnam. Many of their most capable people traveled back and forth to the United States under our governmental and private programs. They were introduced to a wide variety of economic, technical, educational, military and cultural activities. The disastrous changes that the communist victors imposed on the South Vietnamese most certainly strengthened their memory of the benefits to be derived from a modern technological society under a capitalist system. Judging from Vietnam's headlong rush to establish its own market economy during the 1990s the Vietnamese who remained did not forget what they had learned while the Americans were there.

Post-Retirement

After retiring from the Foreign Service at the end of 1979 I continued my interests in Vietnam and Indochina. In 1981 I co-authored a book with a Vietnamese refugee (see last chapter). In 1982 I conducted a small research project on Vietnamese attitudes toward the Soviet presence that the Institute of East Asian Studies published in *Asian Survey*[69]. I also worked with Douglas Pike in his Indochina Studies Program and with Berkeley's Vietnamese Student Association and assisted in the resettlement of several former JUSPAO/USIS Vietnamese employees in the United States.

In 1992 I returned to Vietnam for a two-week visit at the time the country was just beginning to convert to a market economy. Everywhere I went I was received with warmth and friendliness. The hustle and bustle I encountered in both Hanoi and Saigon, but especially the latter, convinced me that Vietnam would not be long in taking its place among the economic "tigers" of Southeast Asia. I welcomed President Clinton's normalization of U.S.-Vietnam diplomatic relations that I felt was too long in coming. In an ironic statement about the futility of the Vietnam War, Clinton appointed former Vietnam POW Pete Peterson as the first U.S. ambassador to Hanoi.

---

[69]. "Vietnamese Perceptions of the Soviet Presence," *Asian Survey* (Berkeley, University of California Press), Vol. XXII, No 9, September 1983, pp 1052-1061.

In sum, I feel very sad about America's Vietnam experience. On the contrary, I feel good about my own personal experience in that country. I look forward to the day when the wounds inflicted on both our societies by the Vietnam War have thoroughly healed.

X USIA Washington - East Asia Policy Officer

The transition from Saigon to Washington was relatively painless. Margaret and the children were well established in our home in Wood Acres, and a new job awaited me at USIA headquarters. I would now be commuting by bus instead of by Boeing 747.

Otis Hays had kept his promise to find me a decent job in recompense for taking on the extra two months in Saigon. He and Stan Moss, my former classmate at the University of North Carolina and then USIA's chief of Foreign Service personnel, had arranged for me to take over a newly created position as media development officer for East Asia and the Pacific (IEA), proof that the "old boy" network was alive and well. Given my Vietnam experience, it was a good job for me and I was right for the position. USIS posts abroad, especially in East Asia, urgently needed greater Washington support in helping them explain the American position in Vietnam and the ongoing Paris peace negotiations. I was well prepared to become their man in Washington.

The East Asia Area Office (IEA)[70]

USIA, like the Department of State, had area offices for each of the world's major geographic regions. Thus, besides the office for East Asia and the Pacific, there were area offices for West Europe, East Europe and the Soviet Union, the American Republics, Africa, and the Near East and South Asia. An Agency assistant director who had a deputy and one or more assistants with area wide responsibilities headed each area office. Country desk officers coordinated Agency support to USIS establishments in their respective posts and policy matters regarding each country with State Department counterparts. Field operatives looked upon desk officers as "our man in Washington." Directors of USIA's area, media and cultural exchange divisions reported to the Agency director who was in turn responsible to the President of the United States.[71] At that time James Keogh, a former Time-Life

---

[70]. Each USIA element has its acronym preceded by "I" for Information.

[71] In 1999 by an Act of Congress USIA was merged with The Department of State, thus eliminating this link.

correspondent and speechwriter for President Nixon was the director of the U.S. Information Agency.

Kent Crane, a political appointee and protégé of Vice President Spiro Agnew, was area director for East Asia when I joined the staff. He had served with the CIA in Indonesia and had worked on Agnew's team during the 1968 presidential campaign. Maurice (Maurie) Lee, who had been deputy director of JUSPAO, was Kent's deputy. Except for the secretarial staff most of us in the area office personnel were career FSOs, but since Crane was new to the Agency the director chose a veteran FSO—Lee—to "show him the ropes."[72]. Officers with area-wide responsibilities were Ivan (Ike) Izenberg for policy, myself for media development, and Lorin Jurvis for administration. The desk officers were Robert Kays, Japan and Korea; Theodore (Ted) Liu, China and Taiwan; Frank Albert, Southeast Asia, Australia and New Zealand; and Everett (Ev) Bumgardner, Indochina (Otis Hays left shortly after I arrived).

Delores (Dee) Brabham, my secretary and assistant, was the office mother hen, mainstay and corporate memory. She knew everyone in the Area and was always ready to lend a helping hand to visitors and office personnel alike. She had been there years before I arrived on the scene and remained years afterward, moving up to the position of administrative officer.

Many personnel changes took place during the course of my two-and-a-half years in Washington. Of significance to this narrative were the appointment of William Payeff and Clifton Forster[73] to succeed Kent Crane and Maurie Lee as area and deputy area directors for East Asia. Frank Scotton[74] came back from Vietnam to work with Ev

---

[72] Oral history "Interview with Maurice E. Lee conducted by G. L. Schmidt," ADST Collection, Arlington, VA.

[73]. Payeff had been deputy assistant director for Near East and South Asia; his previous service in Asia included Cambodia, Vietnam, Hong Kong and Taiwan. Forster had been public affairs in Tel Aviv; he had also served in The Philippines, Japan and Burma. Crane resigned from USIA; Maurie Lee became Country PAO in Manila.

[74]. Scotton had been my superior in Saigon. Now, by a curious bureaucratic twist, I found myself supervising him. We both took it with a grain of salt.

Bumgardner on Indochina and handle the newly acquired (from South Asia) Burma desk.

Policy Officer Plus

The year 1973 was a busy one for me. In February I took over as East Asia Policy Officer, succeeding Izenberg who left to become PAO in Hong Kong. My responsibilities included supervising the work of our five country desk officers and coordinating East Asia policy with the Department of State and other USIA elements. It was at State that I encountered Arthur Hummel again. He had been deputy PAO in Tokyo during my 1955-1957 Takamatsu assignment. Now he was deputy assistant secretary of state for East Asia under Marshall Green and, subsequently, Philip Habib[75], two of America's most distinguished diplomats. I developed a deep respect for the manner in which Art and his superiors managed American East Asia policy in a time of crisis. Later Hummel would become America's first post-World War II ambassador to China.

During much of my first year at IEA I was "acting" this, that or the other. I served as acting area deputy director in June when Maurie Lee went to Manila as country PAO and acting area director during Kent Crane's many travels in Asia and during the interregnum following his resignation. When the Payeff-Forster team took over in November I broke them in to their new jobs and returned to being area policy officer until my next overseas assignment came up in July 1975. It was good to be working with Cliff again. We had enjoyed excellent rapport when we

---

[75]. Habib (1920-1992) had been U.S. Ambassador to South Korea and Kissinger's deputy at the Paris peace talks on Vietnam. After his stint as assistant secretary of state he became Ambassador at Large under President Reagan for whom he carried out numerous special diplomatic missions. A superb negotiator, he had the unique ability of getting to the heart of the matter at hand without offending his opposite number. I got to know Phil (as he was universally known) quite well after he retired to Belmont (near San Francisco) and I to Berkeley. He was a UC Berkeley graduate (PhD 1952 Agricultural Economics—Forestry). He continued active in foreign affairs until his death. Phil had a special fondness for Foreign Service Officers, remembered everyone by his/her first name, and was very much loved and admired by them. For an account of his diplomatic activities in the Near East, see John Boykin, *Cursed is the Peacemaker, The American Diplomat Versus the Israeli General, Beirut 1982*, Belmont, CA. Applegate Press 2002.

worked together in Japan during the mid fifties. The sense of mutual confidence again prevailed both on and off the job.

Kent Crane

Kent Crane stimulated strong feelings, both pro and con, among his associates. Some said the best thing about him was his secretary Cathy[76], an attractive and highly efficient lady who kept things moving during Kent's frequent absences on official—and personal—business. He was a strong-willed man with extensive Washington connections. For his first conference of East Asia Public Affairs Officers Kent arranged for his field officers to meet with Senators Hubert Humphrey and Henry Jackson and House Speaker Gerald Ford, among others. As a participant in those meetings I was impressed.

Despite his continual exposure to our veteran field officers and USIA's philosophy of free and open communication with overseas audiences, Kent frequently disagreed with the Agency's basic approaches to public diplomacy. Perhaps he was tainted by his earlier CIA experience; but in any case, with his self-described "flamboyant" character he tended to create more enemies than friends within the Agency bureaucracy. I was not a party to Kent's interpersonal relationships with USIA Director Keogh, but it was obvious that there was little mutual respect between the two men. As director for East Asia, which included Vietnam, his area was getting the lion's share of USIA's meager resources; and there were many opportunities for disagreement. Kent often bypassed his boss by going directly to the Vice President's office to get decisions he was unable to get through Agency channels. It was a badly kept secret that Keogh tolerated him only because of his White House connections. The matter was resolved in October 1973 when Vice President Spiro Agnew resigned under fire. Having lost the protection of his mentor, Kent left USIA shortly thereafter.

In fairness to Kent, I should say that he was always considerate in his treatment of me as a subordinate. He did complain once that I did not consult him enough. The problem was that he was frequently away and, if there, he would be on the phone interminably. Decisions could not be postponed. If he was not available I made them myself. We were

---

76. Cathy later became Mrs. Crane following Kent's divorce from his first wife.

neighbors of a sort, living within a few blocks of each other. Kent entertained well, and Margaret and I were often guests at his house, usually in the company of other Foreign Service officers in Washington on consultation. Upon his resignation Kent wrote me a generous letter of appreciation calling me "prominent among the real professionals in the public affairs field."

Developing Programs

Putting the best possible face on an impossible situation in Vietnam was our major problem in East Asia and, together with Ev Bumgardner and Frank Scotton who carried the ball for USIA in numerous interagency meetings. I spent interminable hours at this task.

During and after the Paris cease-fire talks that Hanoi used as a ploy for time, the USIA mandate called for explaining the negotiations and their outcome to other Asian countries. Our most effective instrument had proved to be a program using "authoritative spokesmen." Daily cables from field posts pleaded for such personalities. Our job was to find them, not easy under the circumstances.

The most authoritative people were those directly or indirectly involved in the negotiations, but they could not be spared from their tasks. Furthermore, Secretary Kissinger conducted the talks in secret and maintained a personal monopoly on information about them. Officials outside his inner circle were forced to depend on the media for information and that was heavily laden with speculation. They hesitated to speak out.

Among non-government officials, Asia scholars were the most acceptable. They were generally well versed in their subject and could speak freely; but many scholars were staunchly opposed to the U.S. position in Vietnam. USIS officers frequently brief visiting speakers on local attitudes concerning specific topics, but they never tell speakers what they can or cannot say to an audience. Any effort to do so would be decried as censorship or worse. Hence, we tended to rely on people we knew would not embarrass us on Vietnam or other sensitive topics. People working in our speakers bureau developed a sixth sense about who NOT to invite. Writing down names was a no-no. One officer brought public wrath upon his division by keeping a list of such individuals in his desk drawer. It was discovered and widely denounced as a "blacklist." Kent Crane once canceled a speaking tour of a highly reputable scholar for what he believed to be inappropriate comments about our U.S.-China policy. Years after I left the Agency, that gentleman was still complaining bitterly to me about the action in which I had played no part.

There was no shortage of academic lecturers, but our budget was too small to afford sending more than a handful of them to Asia to carry out field program requirements. We filled in the gap by sending out "talking head" videotapes gleaned from the Sunday TV talk shows or from PBS (Public Broadcasting System) programs such as the McNeil-Lehrer Report. I found myself devoting my evenings and weekends to monitoring television to pick out programs that best supported the official U.S. position. Once selected, our TV branch obtained the necessary broadcast clearances, then duplicated and shipped the tapes to our field posts. There, USIS public affairs officers either placed them with local TV stations or held invitational showings for selected audiences. In the next chapter I will relate how we regionalized this operation in Tokyo by videotaping visiting authorities on U.S. foreign policy. Subsequently USIA developed its own "WorldNet" TV network to feed policy oriented programs (eg. the President's annual State of the Union speech or public statements by the Secretary of State) via satellite to its posts around the world for direct or delayed telecast by local TV stations and networks.

At the Office

"What did you do at the office today, Daddy?" my children often asked. Much of a Washington bureaucrat's daily work seems humdrum and comes together only in terms of the big picture, but in fact it was often exciting as it related to major international developments. Bees producing honey would be a fair comparison. The work of a single individual takes on meaning only when it is seen as part of the whole, but unless each one does his part the job is less than complete.

These were times before e-mail and faxes. Correspondence from the field came by cable to the Agency's Operations Center where they were reproduced and distributed to addressees. On any given morning, when I arrived at USIA, I would be confronted with a stack of cables that had come in from field posts overnight. (Time differences being what they were, folks in Asia worked while we slept and vice versa.) The appropriate desk officer would handle cables slugged for action by our East Asia division. Information copies of requests for media program support enabled the desk officers to monitor them and insure that appropriate action was taken. Still others would be advice on political, economic and cultural developments that had to be considered in planning future programs. Having gone over the cables and acted on them or assigned action as necessary, I would have phone calls to make or answer, meetings to attend at State or USIA, visitors to brief, and background or policy guidance papers to write. Nearly always some emergency situation would arise demanding that I drop everything and turn my attention to "putting out the fire." Then, almost before I was aware of it, the day had come to an end and there was still a stack of unread documents. The temptation to say "to hell with it" was great; but I frequently slipped unclassified documents into my briefcase on the bare possibility that I might have a quiet evening at home to catch up on them. After making sure any classified documents were locked away, I would grab my hat—if it was wintertime—and dash out to catch the last express bus home. Tomorrow, another day, was likely to be identical. Is there any wonder Foreign Service Officers have strong preferences for field assignments over those in Washington?

On the Home Front

Returning to the United States after eight years abroad required considerable cultural adaptation. I renewed my skills as general handyman and gardener while Margaret served as housekeeper, cook and chauffeur for our children. The OPEC (Organization of Petroleum Exporting Countries) oil embargo brought on an energy crisis, and we waited in long lines to purchase a few gallons of gasoline. We took our chances with everyone else on overcrowded buses and anguished at the slow progress of Washington's subway system, still two years away from completion.

Vietnam, the energy crisis and the growing Watergate scandal kept the political pot boiling, but not everything was hard work. In the summer of 1973 we escaped the cares of Washington with a two-week family vacation to visit my mother and other relatives in Lake Charles. In our second summer we drove to California to visit Betsy and Nancy in college.

Washington had many amenities. We reveled in the cultural offerings at the John F. Kennedy Center for the Performing Arts, at the Arena Stage, and at the superb Smithsonian museums of art, history and science. As much as anything we relished Washington's outdoor life— the beauty of the Virginia and Maryland countryside and especially hiking and biking along the banks of the Chesapeake and Ohio (C&O) Canal paralleling the Potomac River. No less enjoyable were the many pleasant evenings and weekends we spent with friends from our alma maters and former Foreign Service posts.

Although Washington winters could be gloomy, spring transformed the city's rather gray urban setting to a lush green wooded area and a flower lover's paradise. First come the Japanese magnolias and then the cherry blossoms and multi-colored azaleas followed by the white and pink dogwoods, always making the rejuvenation process a delight to watch.

A Field Trip

Throughout my first year and a half at IEA I filled in for other members of our staff while they went to Asia on field trips. First Crane went, then Lee, then Crane again; then after Payeff and Forster had taken over they went on separate orientation trips. While each was away I took on additional duties. These trips are a legitimate part of the Washington area office jobs. USIS field officers need to talk face-to-face with their Washington representatives at least once a year to resolve the many operational, personnel and policy problems that arise. Likewise, to properly represent field requirements at headquarters, the Washington officer needs the gut feeling for the problems he can get only through on-the-spot observations.

As USIA's policy officer for East Asia one of my jobs was reviewing the yearly country plans submitted by each of the posts under our jurisdiction. These documents, prepared by the country public affairs officers, analyze the political and psychological situation confronting the United States in each country and identify the public diplomacy resources needed to cope with the given circumstances. The plans specify objectives to be accomplished—or at least pursued—within the anticipated budget, not infrequently diminished from the previous year. Examples of support a post needed would be speakers on U.S. defense, economic and cultural relations with the host country; a translation program on American history textbooks for use by the ministry of education in its schools, or a continuing series of articles on U.S. scientific and technological achievements for placement with local newspapers or periodicals.

In 1974 USIA incorporated numerous changes in guidelines to the field for preparing 1975 country plans. They had no more than hit the desks of the PAOs than cabled questions began pouring in. Since I was overdue for a field trip, I proposed to Payeff and Forster that I make a swing around the area and devote my visits to briefing our USIS posts on the kinds of support they could expect from Washington. The visits would also enable me to better represent field needs and achieve unity of direction between USIA and our East Asian posts.

Bill and Cliff agreed, and once again I headed for Asia "riding rupees" around the world. The six-week trip (May 8-June 13) took me to eleven East Asian countries, in this order: Japan, South Korea, Taiwan, The Philippines, Hong Kong, Vietnam, Thailand, Singapore, Indonesia, Laos, Burma and back through New Delhi to Washington, D.C., including several rest stops along the way. In between posts, at airports and in flight, I wrote copious notes to myself for a report to the area director. Had I not done so, at the end of the trip everything would have been a blur. Unfortunately, those notes have long since disappeared and the report, if it still exists, is buried in USIA's historical files. The following account—drawn from my letters home, also written on the run—reconstructs the major events of that trip.

Japan

Tokyo was a good place to start. Alan Carter, the PAO at the time, was in the process of transforming the six American Cultural Center[77] libraries into what he called the "Infomat." Essentially, Carter was converting the American Cultural Centers' traditional open library system into reference libraries dependent on computers and specialized publications for carefully defined USIS target audiences. Some, including myself, thought the "Infomat" objectives too narrowly defined. In the process he dropped "cultural" from the Centers' title, calling them simply "American Centers." The innovative system was also an economy move that eliminated the purchase of books and publications not specifically attuned to country objectives. While Carter jazzed up the Infomats with supergraphics that caught the public eye, the changes made the center libraries less useful for Japanese university students who had traditionally constituted a large portion of the USIS library patrons.

---

[77]. The number of centers in Japan had been reduced from 14 at the time I was there in the mid 1950s to six located in Japan's most important urban centers—Tokyo, Sapporo, Nagoya, Kyoto, Osaka, and Fukuoka.

As a former center director, I was one of those who seriously objected to the procedure. The move was very controversial, but Alan Carter was a highly persuasive personality. He argued forcefully that the Agency's constantly diminishing budgets compelled USIS to draw upon new communications technology as a means for achieving its objectives. Carter won out[78] but only after an extended debate within the Agency that antagonized many field officers.

Carter also introduced the use of the computerized Distribution and Records System (DRS) that identified target audiences by individual and institution and kept records of their participation in each USIS program, eg. attended what lecture, received what publication, was invited to an Embassy reception. Examples of target audiences would be journalists, high-level government officials and university professors specializing in American studies. The DRS system was inevitably criticized for failing to identify some individuals who should have been brought into it, but it did establish a method in the often-haphazard conduct of public affairs and was eventually adopted by USIA for all of its posts overseas. As technology progressed the DRS has given way to more efficient systems.

Other posts in the area, faced with problems similar to USIS Japan's, wanted more information. So in addition to reviewing the Japan country plan with Carter and his staff, I visited the libraries in Tokyo, Kyoto and Osaka and briefed myself on the "Infomat" operation. It is fortunate that I did. At each of my other stops cultural and public affairs officers voiced some of my own reservations; and I found myself answering numerous probing questions about the Infomat approach. Eventually other USIS posts took Carter's ideas that seemed relevant and adapted them to their particular requirements.

Korea

This was my first visit to Korea. PAO Clyde Hess had organized a working buffet dinner at his home and invited his American staff and ten of his top local employees. After dinner we all sat in a circle and the Korean staff members threw hard policy questions at me. Until that

---

[78]. For more details see Green, *American Propaganda Abroad*, New York, Hippocrene Books, 1988, ch 9 "Nuts and Bolts of American Public Diplomacy." Also see oral history "Interview with David Hitchcock conducted by G. Lewis Schmidt, November 17, 1992." ADST Collection, Arlington, VA.

moment I had thought Koreans would be very much like the Japanese. I couldn't have been more wrong. Whereas a Japanese group of that nature would have asked only a few polite questions in a deferential manner, these Koreans asked tough questions and pulled no punches in doing so. I had been billed as a policy officer. They wanted answers to policy questions that confronted them daily in their dealings with the Korean public: Questions about the purpose of U.S. military forces in South Korea, about the U.S. role in Vietnam where Korean forces were also stationed, about U.S. relations with their old enemy Japan, and, of course, about Watergate. At the end of a two-hour session I was wrung out and felt that I had more than earned my day's pay. I had also ceased thinking of Koreans as Japanese who speak a different language. These, I told myself, are a tough minded people and worthy allies of the United States.

Bob Kays, formerly on the Japan-Korea desk in Washington, was then deputy PAO in Seoul. He, Clyde and I spent the next day (a Friday) going over their country plan. On Saturday Bob took me to the Korean National Museum and then to the DMZ (Demilitarized Zone) on the border between North and South Korea. At Panmunjom we got a military briefing on the continuing inability of the two Koreas and the Great Powers to resolve their differences about that divided country. With obvious relish, the briefer told us how the North Koreans had sawed off sections of the American side's chairs so they would have to look up to their opposites across the table. In my photo album I have a picture of myself looking through binoculars into North Korea. I had no idea that more than 25 years later Korea would still be a divided country and Secretary of State Madeline Albright[79] would also be looking through binoculars into North Korea.

Taiwan

Sunday, May 19, 1974, was to have been a rest day for me. But that's not the way it was. I arrived from Seoul late Saturday evening planning to sleep late the next morning and then visit the National Palace

---

[79] Subsequently Ms. Albright visited Pyongyang for talks with Kim Jong Il about a potential visit by President Clinton but nothing came of it. As of mid-2002 a deteriorating economy in North Korea has stimulated renewed negotiations between the two Koreas.

Museum and catch up on my letter writing. Harry Britton, the deputy PAO (Bob Clark was Country PAO) met me at the airport with a schedule that programmed me for breakfast, all afternoon, and a working dinner with the USIS staff from which I returned at near midnight.

I did get to see the museum and it was a real eye opener for me. I had heard and read about the fabulous collection of Chinese art treasures the Chiang Kai Shek government had taken to Taiwan when it evacuated from Beijing; but, as I wrote my wife, it has to be seen to be believed.

The Philippines

Arriving in Manila on Tuesday afternoon I plunged right into consultations. PAO Maurie Lee had gone to Washington to see his son graduate from college; but that evening his wife Ann and Paul Phillips, the deputy PAO, teamed up to give me a welcoming party at the Lee residence attended by the whole USIS staff—wives and husbands.

The next two days were filled with appointments, including an extended visit to the USIA's regional printing plant that serviced USIS posts throughout East Asia with publications in both English and Asian languages. USIS Saigon was the biggest customer by far. I got briefed so well I wrote three pages of notes while waiting to get on a Quantas plane headed for Hong Kong.

My notes included impressions of Manila: "Hot. Very friendly people. Everybody speaks English but look as though they should speak Spanish or Malaysian. Much unemployment as well as underemployment. Long lines at the visa section of the American Consulate, all wanting to emigrate to the United States. One of the world's great waterfront boulevards, formerly called Dewey, now President Roxas. Many remnants of American colonialism such as the Embassy itself, once the U.S. High Commissioner's residence[80]. A

---

80. Cliff Forster, who spent his early years in Manila where his father worked for the Red Cross, provided this note: During the period when the Philippines were officially considered an American colony, U.S. Governors General resided in Malacanan. "Colonialism" ended in 1935 when, under the Tydings McDuffie Act, the Philippines became a commonwealth with independence promised in 1946. The residence on Dewey Boulevard was completed shortly after the creation of the commonwealth. When that occurred Frank Murphy, the last Governor General, became the first resident High Commissioner and moved into what is now the Embassy; and Manuel Quezon,

sprawling city, seemingly without end. Numerous Japanese tourists buying tourist junk and copies of currency used in the Philippines during the Japanese occupation, 1941-1945. 'The yen is mightier than the sword', say the Filipinos."

Few people escape the physical punishment that country hopping in Asia imposes on itinerant Washington officials. I was not so favored. The stress of travel, long working hours with insufficient rest and a changing diet took its toll on me in Manila. Something hit me in the gut, and I developed a severe case of the trots. Fortunately I had some lomotil pills that the nurse at USIA had given me as a precaution, and the worst passed in time for me to remain on schedule.

Hong Kong

Ike Izenberg was preoccupied with changes being made in USIS library practices as a result of Alan Carter's initiatives. Since his Hong Kong offices were in the American Consulate General and not open to the public, Ike conducted much of his programming at the USIS library located in a readily accessible building in Hong Kong's business district. His chief librarian, Ms. Sukchun Auyeung[81], supervised the programs that also served to increase library patronage. The system was working well, so after much discussion Ike decided he would make no changes. "If it ain't broke don't fix it," he said.

Saigon

Marshall Brement[82], a State Department FSO, had succeeded Bob Lincoln as Public Affairs Officer in Vietnam, but he was away so I dealt with his deputy, Jim Culpepper, and with Pat Ayers, then in my old job

---

the first president of the commonwealth, moved into Malacanan. After the defeat of Japan in the Second World War, the United States kept its promise and granted independence to the Philippines on July 4, 1946.

[81]. Following the Sino-British decision that Hong Kong should revert to China in 1997, Auyeung immigrated to California where she is now chief librarian at Gavilan College in Gilroy.

[82]. Brement was a State FSO detailed to USIA and was studying Russian, hoping for an assignment in Moscow. Alan Carter succeeded Brement and was there in April 1975 at the time of the communist takeover.

as policy officer. Pat Ayers was part of a USIS husband and wife team. Her husband, Bill Ayers was information officer. I had arrived on a weekend and the first two days were restful, the second two hectic. I had a good long visit with Bill Kohlmann, my Yale classmate, and we went to a Chinese opera and Vietnamese nightclub together. Monday and Tuesday were filled with reviewing the post's country plan with which I was intimately familiar from my previous incarnation, interviews, briefings, attending a press seminar at the VAA (Vietnamese-American Association), and writing thank you letters to the posts I had already visited. Each day seemed to end up at a dinner with visiting newspapermen and journalism professors taking part in the press seminar. One of them was Professor John Merrill of LSU who had conducted similar programs for me in Panama in 1967 and in Santiago in 1968. Actually, it was old home week greeting many Vietnamese friends, including my former French and Vietnamese instructors. Most of the USIS Foreign Service Nationals would later show up in the United States as refugees following the fall of Saigon to the North Vietnamese army.

Singapore

There was no direct flight from Saigon to Singapore so I went to Bangkok and waited three hours for a Singapore Airlines flight, using the time profitably by writing up my Saigon notes while sitting in the Bangkok departure lounge. Singapore PAO Bob Nichols picked me up at the airport when I arrived at 4:30 in the afternoon and took me to his residence, a lovely place with large spacious rooms, high ceilings for tropical comfort and a huge garden.[83] I was an overnight houseguest, and we talked until nearly midnight. The next morning Bob and I paid a courtesy call on his ambassador, and then he and his staff briefed me on the operation of USIS Singapore's "Resource Center," the Nichols version of Alan Carter's Infomat. That afternoon I went on to Jakarta. It was a busy day.

---

[83] Later when I sought assignment to the PAO job in Singapore I found myself one of 18 on a list and wound up in Bangkok instead.

Indonesia

It was a Thursday well into the third week of my trip. USIS hospitality had ranged from the overwhelming to near neglect. In some places our people had programmed my every minute. In Jakarta, everything seemed left to chance, to be arranged on the spur of the moment. For a change it was refreshing. Acting PAO Bob Mount met me at the airport, and we spent the rest of the afternoon and evening discussing the USIS program and the problems of operating under an authoritarian government based on political coercion in a multi-cultural island country with numerous ethnic groups. The next day I talked to whoever was available at the moment, including Ambassador David Newsom.[84] Mount had told me that on Newsom's arrival in Jakarta two months earlier he told his staff they need not wear jackets to the office. I appeared in the Ambassador's office with tie but sans jacket, only to find that he was wearing a jacket. I apologized saying I was following his orders. "Oh," he said, that's perfectly all right. I only wear this one for distinguished Washington visitors."

On Saturday, USIS turned me over to a driver and an Indonesian press assistant named Atmakusumat, Atma for short. USIS hired Atma after his newspaper was closed following that year's January riots. He turned out to be a good guide and traveling companion and took me through some interesting countryside to Bogor,[85] a resort town about 50 miles from Jakarta. There we saw the former Dutch Governor General's palace where President Sukarno also lived before being deposed. It was situated in the midst of beautiful tropical gardens that reminded me of Summit gardens in the Panama Canal Zone. Thanks to Atma I left Indonesia knowing considerably more about the country than when I arrived. In a letter home I remarked, "The Indonesians are a warm and outgoing people with a ready smile that makes you feel welcome. I would be very happy to be stationed there."

---

[84]. A graduate of U.C. Berkeley (BA 1938), Newsom began his career as a newspaper reporter and had served with USIA in the Near East. Among the American ambassadors I have known I would rank Newsom in the same category as Phil Habib and Ellsworth Bunker.

[85]. The Government of Indonesia uses Bogor as a site for international conferences. The APEC (Asia Pacific Economic Cooperation) heads of state meeting of 1994 was held there.

Bangkok, Vientiane, Rangoon

Laos was my next port of call. To get there I first had to go to Bangkok. At the time Bangkok was to Southeast Asia as Atlanta is to the Southern United States. You couldn't get anywhere in the region without going through the Bangkok airport. I needed a rest so, remembering my first visit to Bangkok from Saigon in 1971, I stayed overnight and most of the next day at the lovely Oriental Hotel on the banks of the Chao Phya. From my window I could watch boats plying up and down the river. Later in the day I took the hour's flight to Vientiane and went through my now familiar exercise. In every country I saw people I had worked with in some previous incarnation. For that reason the hospitality was usually generous and the lag time minimum in reviewing the USIS country operational plans before they were sent on to Washington. It was hard work and fun at the same time.

After Vientiane I returned to Bangkok where I visited and admired the AUA Language Center without the faintest idea that four years later I would become its director.

In Rangoon, the last official visit on my itinerary, the rigor of my arduous travels caught up with me. My old lumbosacral pains returned with such a vengeance I could hardly move.

The next leg of my trip was to have been on Burma Airlines to Katmandu. I was looking forward to visiting PAO Kent Obee, Margaret's cousin whom I had persuaded to join USIS when he was fresh out of Georgetown. There I could relax before the long trip back to Washington. Burmese labor problems intervened. The day after I arrived in Rangoon airport workers announced an indefinite strike beginning at midnight. Burma Airlines canceled its flight to Katmandu. The only flight out was on KLM to Karachi an hour before the strike deadline. I was staying with Arnold Hanson, the PAO. He was not optimistic.

"You are welcome to stay as long as you like," Arnie said, "but I cannot guarantee when this strike will be over."

I reflected briefly. There were several items still on my Rangoon agenda, but we had already done the essential review of Arnie's operational plan. Before leaving Washington I had made a commitment to my daughter Nancy to be home in time for her high school graduation. It would be wiser to move on, back pain or no back pain.

Fortunately the KLM flight was on time and nearly empty. I stretched out and asked the airline hostess to wake me at Karachi.

There, at an airport hotel, a masseuse slathered my aching back with olive oil and gave me one of the best massages I have ever experienced. Since I was "riding rupees" I still had to spend 24 hours in New Delhi. From there I called Kent to say that I deeply regretted having to cancel my visit to Katmandu. Pan American Airways got me home in time to see Nancy graduate from Walt Whitman high school.

After such a long trip one wonders whether it has been worth the effort. My Officer Evaluation Report for 1974, written by Cliff Forster, comments: (His) "on-site review contributed significantly to (country plan preparations), and it is noteworthy that other Agency elements, including the Office of Policy and Plans, cited East Asia's plans as among the best received this year." Nuff said.

Maintaining Credibility: Watergate

At USIA I resumed my normal office duties. My intense exposure to USIS operations in Asia left me considerably enlightened about their needs, and I set about working out details with our media and other support elements. The first hand knowledge I had gathered served me well during my remaining year as East Asia policy officer. During that year two issues eclipsed all others: Watergate and Vietnam.

As important as Vietnam was, explaining Watergate and its effect on the American Presidency took equal precedence. The ongoing political turmoil over the Watergate scandal dominated the Washington scene. In October 1973 Nixon had named Congressman Gerald Ford as his vice president to replace Spiro Agnew. By the summer of 1974, facing almost certain impeachment, Nixon chose resignation instead, leaving Ford in charge of the White House. USIA's media, under the guidance of Director James Keogh, saw to it that Nixon's downfall was described with dignity and accuracy for a bewildered world.[86]

Vietnam Finis

Contradictory media and Embassy reports from Vietnam gave us a continuing headache in formulating USIA's information output. The Embassy's official reports were often at variance not only by independent news sources but also by back channel reports not cleared by the Saigon embassy. Who to believe? For VOA and other USIA news

---

[86]. Fitzhugh Green, *American Propaganda Abroad*, p.39

media credibility was essential. Huge audiences around the world depended on the Voice of America for objective news about what was going on in Vietnam. We could not remain silent. As an official U.S. government information agency, we played it as cautiously as possible, using news reports only after they had been confirmed by two or more sources. Somehow things worked out and people still believed what they heard on VOA.

The last few months of the U.S. presence in Vietnam were painful. Our Embassy in Saigon tried to put a good face on the South Vietnamese efforts to stem communist aggression, all the while urging greater Washington support for the Thieu government. President Ford made a half-hearted effort, but Congress turned a deaf ear to his pleas.

Finally, on April 30, 1975, our agonizing over how to report the war in Vietnam resolved itself with the fall of Saigon to the communists.

Assignment Tokyo

During this period our East Asia area office was grappling with the problem of how to bring more U.S. expertise to bear in our overseas activities, particularly in terms of American participants for our speaker programs. The Agency's budget for funding travel to and from Asia for these individuals was insufficient to get more than a small percentage of the people we needed out to the field. Our posts were prepared to pay lecture fees and local expenses out of their own budgets if they could just get the right people. We knew there was considerable American talent traveling back and forth to Asia under non-governmental auspices. However, all too often the Agency or the posts learned about them too late to take advantage of their presence.

After some discussion we began to see a solution in the establishment of a regional programs office (RPO) in Asia to keep tabs on travel by potential lecturers and somehow arrange for them to take part in our USIS programs. Tokyo was the logical place. It was centrally located and had the greatest amount of traffic in terms of potential speaker talent. Bill Payeff and Cliff Forster asked me to draw up a project paper for the establishment of an office there.

I put considerable thought and effort into the project proposal. Then, on the basis of my having drawn up a job description they offered me the position. I was hesitant at first. I was not too happy with the idea of living in Tokyo. Leon Picon [87], an old friend and former cultural affairs officer in Japan, had been feeding me horror stories about life in that smog-ridden metropolis. He had served there during the period of rapid industrialization (1955-1966) and his tales made Tokyo sound like what Mexico City has become in more recent years. On further consultation I learned that an anti-smog campaign was underway in Tokyo and conditions were improving. That, plus the knowledge that no other suitable position would open up in Asia within at least a year persuaded me to take the job. My family was pleased. We treasured the memories of our first Japan assignment and looked forward to returning. We would leave the first week in July 1975. I began a refresher course in Japanese immediately.

In preparation for the East Asia RPO job I needed to determine the kind of professional talent I could draw upon. I selected several universities with established Asian studies programs; then, armed with a list of past participants in USIS speaker programs I visited Columbia, Harvard, the University of Michigan, the University of Chicago, and U.C. Berkeley. In meetings with scholars at each campus I explained that USIS posts would not only provide visiting lecturers with honoraria, per diem and in-country travel costs, they would also assist them in meeting their professional counterparts. Everyone I talked with was receptive to my proposal and promised to spread the word. These included Robert A. Scalapino, then dean of the Department of Political Science at U.C. Berkeley. It was a fortuitous meeting. We would be closely associated in years to come.

A Graduation and A Wedding

With some careful juggling of dates I was able to time my departure to Japan to attend both my daughter Betsy's graduation from Mills College in Oakland and, a month later, her marriage to David Rains Wallace, an environmental writer. Then, following a brief visit with my mother in Louisiana, Margaret and I left for Tokyo. Nancy and Judy, our two younger daughters, would join us in early August.

---

[87]. Leon Picon, Oral History Interview, ADST Collection, Arlington, VA.

Washington Assignments in Perspective

Career Foreign Service Officers look upon periodic Washington assignments as a necessary evil, mandated by law to insure that personnel who serve this country abroad maintain contact with American realities and do not become a client of the host country. As a distinguished public affairs officer put it, "One of the most difficult decisions a Foreign Service Officer can make (even though he or she may not be aware of the choice) is how to give the highest priority to the interests of the United States while maintaining harmonious or stable relations with the host country."[88]

Whatever the difficulties, and there are many, for the FSO the best jobs are always overseas, almost no matter where. In Washington, whether with State, USIA or AID, you are a small cog in a big wheel, hardly noticeable in a city overrun with high profile politicians, where chiefs of state come and go almost daily with barely a ripple. Overseas you are somebody. You have status. You work with the chosen few, and you have a strong, self-fulfilling sense of making a difference in the global picture. Abroad, local citizens see you as representing the country the whole world looks up to. For your fellow members of the elite-minded diplomatic corps, who pay attention to such matters, you are a representative of the world superpower. On the personal level, the American Embassy establishment provides you with social status, protects and looks after you from the moment you arrive until the moment you leave. In short, it's a good life. You will never get rich, but then so long as you are in the Foreign Service you will enjoy the excitement of foreign travel at U.S. Government expense; and you will never want for the necessities of life, including those that satisfy the ego.

I was no exception to these attitudes concerning my second Washington assignment. Even though coordinating our Asian area's policy and material support kept me in continual touch with our field posts, I still felt there was something lacking. The missing element was the all-important daily contact with the foreign audiences we were trying to influence. For me and other FSOs that is the one that has always made Foreign Service so attractive.

---

[88]. Bernard Lavin, Oral History Interview, December 14, 1988. ADST Collection, Arlington, VA. Lavin served as USIA personnel officer at height of demands for staffing JUSPAO, 1967-1970, but he was not responsible for sending me there.

Although we enjoyed living in Washington, as I have tried to show in this chapter, we looked forward eagerly to our next overseas assignment. Therefore it was a keen sense of anticipation and of returning to the field of action that Margaret and I headed for our second tour of duty in Japan.

XI Tokyo - Regional Programs Officer

Return to Japan

On July 10, 1975, Margaret and I arrived in Tokyo to begin our second tour of duty in Japan. It had been 20 years since we first landed in Yokohama for a two-year assignment in Takamatsu. We looked forward eagerly to renewing old acquaintances and getting to know the new Japan.

During our 18-year absence Japan had transformed itself from a defeated military aggressor barely able to feed its own people into a world economic power. It had not done so alone. The United States had made numerous American scientific and technological advances available to the Japanese to help its former enemy regain self-sufficiency. During the Korean War America had invested heavily in the country's economic growth and opened American markets to Japanese exports. Once established in the American market the Japanese began expanding their economic vitality to other Asian countries, particularly South Korea, Taiwan, Hong Kong and Singapore, contributing to their growth as Newly Industrializing Economies. The nation that had failed in its effort to establish a "Greater East Asia Co-Prosperity Sphere" through military conquest was now well along the road to achieving that goal through peaceable, economic means.

On the minus side, while still portraying itself as a small, resource-poor island nation, Japan had begun to build an enormous trade surplus with the United States. Much of Japan's economic growth had been achieved at the expense of the environment. Though steps were being taken to reduce Tokyo's air pollution, smog still hung heavily in the air. Mount Fujii, once a feature attraction of the Tokyo landscape, could rarely be seen from the city. Through their overseas investments Japanese corporations (zaibatsu) were happily responding to their neighboring countries' cry to "Send us some of your pollution!"

The Embassy Compound

Japan's new prosperity was everywhere evident as we traveled from the Haneda International Airport (Narita would open nearly three years later) to the American Embassy compound in the Roppongi-Akasaka area of downtown Tokyo. There, with the help of the Embassy's general services section, we quickly settled into a three-bedroom apartment on the third floor of Grew House. It had the basic furnishings. A "welcome kit" served our essential needs pending the arrival of our effects. We had reservations about living in an "American ghetto" rather than in the Japanese community where we could mingle more freely with local citizens, but we had little choice in the matter. The U.S. Government-owned apartments came rent free to Embassy employees. If we chose to live elsewhere we would get no rental allowance. The Tokyo housing market was and still is extremely tight and inordinately expensive.

The Embassy compound was situated on highly valuable property the U.S. had acquired during the Occupation. It consisted of three six-story apartment buildings named in honor of Joseph Grew, U.S. Ambassador to Japan from 1933 to 1941, Admiral Perry who had opened Japan to international trade in 1854 and Townsend Harris, the first U.S. Consul to Japan. There were also a recreation building, a swimming pool and a commissary that provided basic necessities for Embassy employees. In the 1980s larger, more modern units that retained the same names replaced the three original apartment buildings.

I described our new living situation in a letter to my mother: "We live in a compound with most of my office colleagues. We see them not only at the office but also nights, weekends, and in between. Margaret shops at the commissary in the basement of our apartment building, and once a month we go to a U.S. military commissary in Yokohama (Yokosuka Naval Base) to purchase supplies not available here. The commuting tables have turned. Judy goes to school by train and subway, an hour and a half each way. I walk to work—15 minutes."

Establishing the Regional Programs Office

USIS was located in a U.S. Embassy annex in the Toronamon section of downtown Tokyo. The annex, known as the Mantetsu Building, had once belonged to the Manchurian Railway Company and had been taken over by Occupation forces as headquarters for CIE\SCAP[89]. The Embassy Chancery, just a block away and adjacent to the Ambassador's residence, was an elegant structure, but by the mid-1970s it no longer met the needs of the burgeoning American Embassy

---

[89]. Civil Information and Education/Supreme Command Allied Powers

staff. Many elements were temporarily housed in rental units scattered around the city.

By the time I arrived in 1975 the U.S. Government had sold the Mantetsu building for a handsome price and was using the money to build a new Embassy on the site of the outdated one. When completed, all Embassy personnel would be under one roof. Here was one instance when the U.S. taxpayer got a break. The transaction produced a tidy profit that was made available for other projects. We were able to continue using the Mantetsu building until the new Embassy was completed in November 1976. Afterwards, the Japanese purchaser converted the Mantetsu site into a large office-building complex.

James D. Hodgson, former secretary of labor in President Nixon's cabinet, was then U.S. Ambassador to Japan. William Doran Miller[90] was Minister-Counselor of the Embassy for Public Affairs, having succeeded Alan Carter when the latter was transferred to Saigon. Earlier, Miller had expressed apprehension about whether a regional programs office might work at cross purposes with his Japan program staff. It was a legitimate concern, but Bill Payeff, USIA Assistant Director for East Asia, reassured Miller that I was a team player, would integrate well with his organization and may even be able to supplement the efforts of USIS Tokyo.

I reported to work at USIS on July 11, the day after our arrival. Two Japanese secretaries greeted me when I announced myself in Miller's outer office. They did not introduce themselves, but one of them gave me more than just a casual glance.

I was not kept waiting. The secretary seated next to the PAO's office said Mr. Miller was expecting me. "*Dozo. O hairi kudasai.* Please go right in," she said.

It was the same office in which I had met Acting PAO Lew Schmidt twenty years previously when I arrived for my Takamatsu assignment. Only the occupant had changed.

Miller said he had heard good reports on me but wanted to hear my concept of how the new Regional Programs Office would function. I explained that I expected to recruit speakers and performing artists who might either be living or traveling in the area and make them available to

---

[90]. Miller's previous USIS field experience had been in the Mid East and South Asia. Before coming to Tokyo he had been PAO in New Delhi.

other East Asian posts for programming. USIA had given me a budget to cover speaker travel. I would compile an inventory of resident talent and be on the lookout for people or groups coming to the area that might fit into the area's USIS country programs. In this I hoped to enlist the assistance of our other Asian posts. Area Director Bill Payeff had sent a message explaining this to all East Asian posts.

I told Miller I would not concern myself about Japan because they already had a strong speakers program and a staff to handle them. To this Miller agreed noting that other posts were always asking him to send them his speakers; but while he and his staff would like to help out their first responsibility was Japan, and they had been unable to respond adequately. He hoped I could relieve them of this burden.

I was sure we could develop a mutually satisfactory working arrangement and offered to have the USIS Tokyo draw on the people I identified. I also said I wanted to work with the audiovisual center in producing videotapes for regional use by East Asian posts.

Miller concurred and reassured me that the Embassy would make its communications facilities available for my use. He generously offered whatever advice and support I needed, especially while getting established. In anticipation of my arrival USIS Tokyo had set aside an office for me, and he had arranged for a Japanese member of his staff to work as my assistant. With that he stepped to the door and beckoned to a lady in his outer office who entered immediately. I recognized her as one who had looked me over carefully on my arrival.

"Ms. Misa Otake," Miller said, this is Mr. Kendall."

Then to me, "Ms. Otake will be serving as your secretary and administrative assistant."

"I am very pleased to meet you," she said with a courteous bow. "I hope you'll forgive me for looking at you so intently when you came in awhile ago."

Miller explained that Ms. Otake had been with USIS for nearly 20 years, that she knew all the ropes and counseled me to rely on her.

Fortune smiled on me when Bill Miller assigned Misa Otake to be my assistant. Misa, as she liked to be called, was a refined woman of medium build in her mid-forties. She had a graceful manner and an easy smile. She spoke English with confidence and only a tinge of Japanese accent. As I learned later, she had worked with the Occupation forces in Okinawa before joining USIS. She was highly respected and much loved by Japanese and Americans alike. I also learned that she had looked

242

carefully into my background before accepting Miller's offer to work in the Regional Programs Office.

Thanks to Misa my office was ready for me to begin work, but there was one change I needed to make. I had brought my own paintings, one of them an original print by a Singaporean artist I had acquired on my first trip to that city. I substituted it for what I thought a rather mediocre American reproduction. After I hung my print the USIS exhibits officer, one of the remaining few Carter adherents, insisted I take it down. Alan Carter, he said, had established the rule that only American art should hang in USIS offices. I refused to budge, saying Southeast Asia was in my bailiwick and an appreciation of their art would enhance U.S. cultural exchanges with that area. Bill Miller did not contradict me, and my print remained. Word got around that I had won a battle that many in USIS Tokyo had been fighting for several years. The incident made me a minor hero.

Misa introduced me to everyone that mattered on the USIS Tokyo staff and filled me in on their jobs and personalities, thereby getting me off on the right foot. I would be working most closely with the Japan programs division, then headed by Irwin Kern. His office handled visiting speakers and scheduled them for lecture tours around Japan, principally to the six American Centers. I would also coordinate my efforts with the cultural affairs staff, then headed by John McDonald who looked after visiting Fulbright professors and performing art groups.

Family Matters

Our French poodle "Charlie" arrived two days after we did, extremely happy to be with his family again. Shortly afterwards Nancy and Judy arrived. We enrolled Judy in the tenth grade at the American School in Japan (ASIJ). It had a magnificent plant, a reputation for strong scholastic discipline and a curriculum that included Japanese. At the nearby International Christian University Nancy encountered a student group from several University of California campuses preparing for a two-and-a-half week tour of Japan. As a UC Santa Cruz student herself, she was welcomed into the group. With them she visited shrines and temples and ancient cities, became thoroughly immersed in Japanese culture, and wound up determined to return for her junior year. Nancy was born during our assignment in Takamatsu, and before she left the four of us visited there, renewed old friendships and luxuriated in reminisces from bygone days. Summer over, Nancy returned to UC Santa Cruz for her sophomore year and Judy entered ASIJ. Our household effects arrived and Margaret busied herself with transforming our bare-essentials apartment into a home. I was already immersed in my RPO job.

Speakers and Clients

Visiting American speakers were and still are the single most useful program medium available to USIS field posts. These specialists give a personal touch in conveying American concepts to foreign audiences in a give and take fashion. Furthermore, their status as private U.S. citizens, free to criticize U.S. actions as they see fit, gives them enhanced credibility; and their contacts provide long lasting professional networking for both sides. Posts scheduled visiting American speakers in a variety of ways based on the individual's qualifications and how well he or she might be known. Most frequently USIS scheduled them for presentations at American cultural centers with audiences invited according to the speaker's area of specialization. Quite often posts also arranged for visiting professors to address local university audiences on their own campuses or to meet privately with their professional colleagues. Media interviews scheduled by USIS helped expand the impact of a speaker's visit. Many PAOs and CAOs used the occasion of a speaker's presence to invite individuals they wished to cultivate to their homes for informal dinners and private discussions. In my previous posts I had not only programmed speakers in these ways myself, but I had also been scheduled similarly during my tour of Latin America with the Gemini spacecraft and the Apollo 11 moon rock.

My first move was to develop an inventory of potential talent already in the area, eg., Fulbright professors. Our field posts cooperated readily as did the USIA Speakers Bureau in Washington, alerting me whenever they learned of potential talent coming to East Asia. This allowed me to verify their availability and qualifications for our programs and to determine individual posts' interest in using them.

Posts based their choices on how a given speaker might support a particular country plan objective. My previous position as area policy officer and visits to East Asia posts enabled me to anticipate needs and responses. Speaker performance evaluations helped me determine whether I should schedule further programs for that individual and allowed me to alert posts already on his schedule about strengths and weaknesses. There was nothing secret about the evaluations, and I customarily showed them to the individual on request.

With my travel budget I could send speakers and artists wherever they were needed within the East Asian area. The posts paid the speakers a modest honorarium and covered their in-country travel and per diem costs. These were important for our guest speakers and essential to enlisting their participation in USIS programs; but for the individuals involved the most valuable aspects were the ready-made professional contacts and travel that the programs provided. It was a win-win program for both sides.

My first RPO speaker was a vigorous young environmental engineer who was in Japan studying Asian methods of waste disposal, not usually considered a prime concern of USIA. Nevertheless, our posts were hungry for good speakers; and, as an American expert in a field of increasing concern to many cities in Asia, he would reach new and important audiences. I offered him, expecting to get one or two responses; but practically every post asked for him. He was a smash hit, hiking around the garbage dumps of Southeast Asia, suggesting to the local authorities how to better manage their waste disposal problems. He made lasting impressions wherever he went.

Also among my early offerings were two Fulbright professors in Tokyo—John Hancock (architecture, University of Washington) at Tokyo University, and Edward Beauchamp (education, University of Hawaii) at International Christian University. Their subjects fit well into USIS cultural programming for professional audiences, and the two made several RPO lecture tours around the area. They and their wives became our good friends during their time in Japan.

Among those who traveled under RPO auspices during my tenure were many well known academic personalities: Professors Robert A. Scalapino of the University of California at Berkeley; Ezra Vogel of Harvard; Lucian Pye of MIT; Donald Zagoria of Columbia University and Hunter College; Stanley Spector of Washington University, St. Louis; and especially Charles Anderson, professor emeritus in American literature from Johns Hopkins University.

Weston (Westy) Fenhagen, PAO in Kuala Lumpur, alerted me about Charles Anderson who was then a visiting scholar at Kyoto University. Anderson's literary field was a subject of continuing interest in USIS cultural programming and he became an enthusiastic participant in our programs. His warm personality and delightful sense of humor won him admiration everywhere. He brought American literary figures to life for his audiences, always leaving them asking for more. Every post wanted him, from Australia to Korea and then on into India and Europe. He became the single most popular lecturer on our USIS circuit.

Regional Audiovisual Center (RAVC)

The Regional Audiovisual Center was an outgrowth of a USIS Japan program that produced Japanese language films for their audiences and added Japanese soundtracks to Agency-produced films. As videotapes came into general use RAVC began servicing other East Asian posts on a limited basis, filling a need not covered by USIA's world wide service. Kurt Wenzel,[91] with whom I had worked in Saigon, headed up the RAVC with the assistance of Bernard Singer, the regional motion picture engineer, and a staff of highly competent Japanese technicians.

Many highly qualified spokesmen on U.S. East Asia policy came to Japan on very short notice with little or no time available for public programming. Kurt and I worked closely with the visitors' Embassy control officers to fit half-hour videotaped interviews into their schedules, thus serving the needs of USIS Japan and other East Asian posts.

When I arrived in Tokyo Kurt was producing videotapes in rented Japanese TV studios that had to be booked a week in advance. Because this was both inconvenient and costly he was able to persuade the Agency to fund a fully equipped studio in the Embassy basement where we could schedule interviews on very short notice. We gave the programs a newsworthy touch by using Japan-based American journalists as interviewers. The journalists welcomed the arrangement. In addition to their fees, they got exclusive interviews and good leads for news coverage.

Interviewees who faced our cameras represented a wide range of specializations. They included American officials from the various branches of government, scholars, writers, performing artists, and professional people. We taped the programs, informed the regional

---

91. Wenzel had been a German POW captured by the U.S. forces in the World War II North African campaign. He spent the duration of the war in a Texas internment camp and stayed on to become an American citizen. He was a wizard with films and turned his talents to video as that medium grew.

posts of the videotapes' availability and filled the requests as they came in. For the Japan program we either used interpreters or voiced the interviews over in Japanese. For other posts we sent the tapes out in English, the lingua franca in the region.

During my association with RAVC only one videotaped program gave us policy problems. Produced by USIS Seoul, it was a discussion by three American political scientists on President Carter's proposal to withdraw American troops from South Korea. One of the professors supported the withdrawal; the other two vigorously opposed it. Since it was a highly controversial subject under heated debate in Washington, we asked for the Agency's approval before distribution. After an agonizing waiting period we were instructed to shelve the tape. Although the pros and cons of the matter were being discussed heatedly in the public news media, it was thought unwise for USIS to show the tape pending a firm White House decision. When President Carter withdrew his proposal the matter became a dead issue.

Hitting the Road

My duties required that I make periodic visits to the area's USIS posts to explain RPO services, get a better understanding of their program needs and interview potential speakers. By September of 1975 I had already received invitations from half the posts. Misa was working out extremely well. She prepared the speaker itineraries and handled all their travel arrangements. She could easily run the office in my absence. It became obvious I should hit the road without further delay.

My area[92] was vast. It extended from Korea down to Australia and New Zealand, including Burma and all of Southeast Asia except Indochina where we had no diplomatic relations. (The Vietnam War had just ended.) I made my first trip in mid-September, visiting Manila, Taipei, Hong Kong and Okinawa[93]; and in November I visited Korea. It

---

92. After the establishment of the Regional Programs Office in Tokyo other areas picked up on the idea, establishing one in London and another in New Delhi. We worked out cooperative arrangements for utilizing speaker talent.

93. There was no USIS post in Okinawa. I wanted to see the Expo-75 Oceanographic Exposition organized by the Japanese government to commemorate the reversion of Okinawa from U.S. to Japanese control. Back in Washington I had invested considerable time and energy helping to organize the American exhibit for which USIA was responsible. Margaret joined me in Naha, Okinawa's capital city. The Expo was a

was a useful exercise. Later I would have to expand the number of posts covered in one trip. Over the next two years I would visit all of the USIS posts in East Asia and the Pacific at least once but several of them more often.

I had learned the hard way from my previous swings around Latin America and Asia that rest on such trips was essential. I normally scheduled myself for two days at each post, leaving my weekends free whenever possible. My procedure was simple. After a meeting with the country PAO who briefed me on his major country objectives and needs I would then work on the details with his program staff. Often there were working lunches and dinners. On many occasions my hosts used these as opportunities for me to meet candidates for the RPO speaker program, thus building up my inventory of available talents. After the first several visits a pattern had been set, and there is no need to repeat the details. But some related recollections may be of interest.

For the East Asia area office back in Washington, the Regional Programs Office was an experiment. After my first few visits Bill Payeff asked some of the country PAOs to let him know how it was working out. Maurie Lee, in Manila wrote, inter alia, "We (have been) able to benefit by (Kendall's) inputs on possible speakers in a number of categories and in direct support of several of our program projects... His helpful manner and knowledge on a wide spectrum of USIS affairs continue to be noticed by USIS officers at this post and we look forward to a cordial and fruitful relationship in the coming year."

Apparently I was doing something right, because in November Bill Miller wrote, in part: "Mr. Kendall has fitted in very well and is working smoothly with our post program officers... He has built on our contacts without detracting from them. He has opened up new leads for speakers of talent... He has also taken off from us the burden of recruiting speakers and answering communications for other posts... He has been able to mesh his activities with our programs like a true USIS professional."

In February 1976 I took an extended, month-long trip to my "East Asia domain," as Margaret called it. It included an area-wide Cultural

---

scientific success but a public failure. The island is very much out of the way; and the site, 20 miles from Naha with inadequate transportation, discouraged even Okinawan visitors. The public stayed away in droves.

Affairs Officer (CAO) conference in Penang—organized by USIA Washington—followed by visits to Kuala Lumpur, Singapore, Bangkok, Rangoon, Katmandu and New Delhi, Hong Kong and Taipei in that order. The New Delhi portion allowed us to pay for my travel with Indian rupees.

I was on the agenda of the Penang conference to discuss the RPO speaker program. (The timing indicated someone wanted to get out of mid-winter Washington.) It was a good meeting that left time for swimming and relaxation at the Rasa Sayang Hotel's magnificent beach. But what surprised and pleased me most was the unanimous chorus of praise from CAOs around the area for the work my office was doing in providing them with speaker talent.

After the Penang conference and a meeting with USIS in Kuala Lumpur I took an all-day train ride to Singapore, mostly because I wanted to see what the countryside looked like. As I wrote to Margaret and Judy: "I have *Shogun*[94] to read and a window seat in a first class car with a bar and a dining section. This is no Shinkansen (Japanese bullet train) but it should be an interesting ride." It was, but every time I looked out the window all I saw was rubber trees and more rubber trees.

In Singapore PAO Gerry Stryker[95] had scheduled two full days of appointments for me. They included an official lunch at a huge dim sum restaurant where, to our surprise and fascination, 500 Russian tourists from a Soviet cruise ship joined us. They were a somber group and did not at all seem to enjoy the exotic food. Other memories of Singapore were a spectacular view of more than a hundred seagoing ships in the city state's expansive harbor as seen from my 20th floor hotel room; and eating boiled crabs at a popular family restaurant with a Singaporean journalist who had been our house guest in Washington.

Bangkok was uneventful. The post took literally my request to limit social activities, and I was able to finish *Shogun*. Rangoon, always full of surprises—and disappointments—had not changed since my last visit two years earlier. In fact, it had not changed since the British left in 1946. When I checked in at the airport for departure to Katmandu I

---

[94]. A novel by James Clavell, Atheneum, New York, 1975, 802 pp.

[95]. Stryker was a bilingual China specialist. The long hiatus in U.S.-China diplomatic relations had relegated him and many other FSOs in his field to being China watchers from the periphery in such posts as Singapore, Hong Kong, and Taiwan.

learned that Ne Win, the dictator, had pre-empted the Burma Airlines plane scheduled for the Nepal run. No one knew when he would return. I cooled my heels at the airport for six hours; and then, because Katmandu had no night landing facilities, I spent an unscheduled night in Calcutta. As a result I had to cut my carefully planned weekend visit with Kent and Ruth Obee in Nepal—in recompense for the one missed two years earlier—from two days to one. Despite Burma Airlines I was able to make amends to the Obees and had a short but enjoyable stay.

"Next time bring Margaret with you," Ruth said. "Better yet, send her here so we can have a long visit, say three weeks."

"I'll try," I promised. (Shortly after I returned to Tokyo Margaret accepted the kind invitation.)

In New Delhi I worked up a system for exchanging speaker talent with USIS India and for paying their international air travel out of the U.S. Treasury's rupee account. The flight back to Hong Kong took most of a day; time enough to complete my trip report to Bill Payeff.

Hong Kong was a relief after India. In South Asia nothing seemed to work right. In Hong Kong everything did. With CAO Merve Haworth[96], an old friend from our Takamatsu tour (1955-1957), I got a lot of work done and we relived some of the "good old days" over excellent Chinese food. I also built up my relations with the Asia Pacific Council of American Chambers of Commerce (APCAC) by attending their annual meeting in Hong Kong. In Tokyo I had cultivated relations with the group as a fruitful source for speaker talent on trade and economic themes. Several of their members knowledgeable in U.S.-Asian trade concerns accepted USIS invitations to speak to specialized audiences on problem-solving techniques.

Taipei was an anticlimax. I did some USIS work but also stocked up on pirated[97] editions of American best sellers. The hardbacks sold for less than U.S. paperbacks.

---

[96]. Merve spoke both Japanese and Chinese fluently. With the exception of a single tour of duty in Washington, he spent his entire Foreign Service career in Osaka, Taipei, and Hong Kong. He married late, to Susan Ch'en of Taipei; and the couple adopted a boy and a girl, both of Chinese American ancestry, but no relation. In Hong Kong Susan turned her hobby of collecting Chinese antiques into a thriving business that she carries on alone after Merve's death in 1992.

[97]. Taiwan now observes international copyright laws governing intellectual property rights; but pirated books, compact discs, video and audiotapes as well as computer

Back in Tokyo it took me three weeks to catch up on the work backlog and even longer to cope with the new work I had created for myself.

Meanwhile, at Home

During my month-long absence Margaret immersed herself in American community cultural activities, studied Japanese, took pottery classes in Kita-Kamakura with her good friend Kimi Burleson[98] and tried to keep tabs on Judy. This was no easy task. Besides going to high school, Judy had many distractions: modeling for Japanese advertising agencies that liked to use young American women for clothing ads; ski trips to the Japanese Alps; and an unending social whirl which used up all her weekends. It was safe, easy and cheap to get around in metropolitan Tokyo, and Judy and her friends took full advantage of it—to the detriment of their schoolwork. But life in Japan was an adventure and an education in itself.

That summer of 1976 our daughter Betsy and her husband came to Japan for a visit. It was David's first time in Japan and Betsy's first time back since 1957. We took them to Shimoda on the Izu peninsula (where Admiral Perry's "Black Ships" landed in 1854) and enjoyed the beach and hiking trails overlooking the rocky Pacific coast. Afterwards, with Judy as escort-interpreter, Betsy and David toured Kyoto's temples and shrines that Betsy had studied about at Mills. David, the naturalist, wanted to see a national park so they paid a visit to the Josin-Etsu Highland National Park in the Japanese Alps that resulted in an essay.[99]

In September Nancy came to Japan for a year's study that included three months of living with a Japanese family in Kyoto. Subsequently, she studied Japanese sumie (black ink brush painting) in Kita Kamakura and lived happily with a retired history professor and his wife, neither of whom spoke English. By the time her "Junior Year in Japan" was up she was adept in Japanese and the ways of Japan. She stayed on with us for

software continue to be marketed widely in Mainland China.

98. Wife of Hugh Burleson, USIS Tokyo research officer.

99. "Japan's Wild Nature," in *The Untamed Garden and other Personal Essays*, by David Rains Wallace, Ohio State University Press, 1986; McMillan Collier Editions, 1988.

the remainder of our Japan assignment, studying at Tokyo's Sophia University.

On the Road Again

My February trip took me to only the top half of my "East Asian domain." Now USIS posts in the bottom half were urging me to come. For my part I wanted to discuss program matters with them and meet with potential speakers. The dog days of August were at their worst in Japan; but "down under" it was winter. I embarked—not without trepidation—on another month-long trip with two to three days at each stop.

This one took me to first to Manila and then to Papua New Guinea; New Zealand; Australia (Sydney, Canberra, Melbourne and Perth); Indonesia (Jakarta, Surabaya and Bali where Margaret met me for a week's vacation); Singapore; Malaysia; Hong Kong and return to Tokyo. I scheduled two to three days at each stop.

While I repeated my litany at each post, I also did a lot of listening, adapted my speaker offerings to their specific requirements and added more speaker talent to my inventory. It was so long with so many stops—14 cities—before it was over I had begun to feel like the world was made up of airplanes, airports and hotels. When I returned it took me another month to pull all the details together.

An Imperial Garden Party

Japan sparkles in the autumn sun, especially after a month of dreary rain. On those days Tokyo becomes a sea of black umbrellas, and the best recreation is a comfortable chair and a good book. But the end of the rain brings frosty nights, turning city's maples a fiery red. When that happens the maples are even more beautiful than the cherry trees in the spring.

Such was the last week of October 1976. On the final Friday of that month Emperor Hirohito held his annual garden party. It was a morning affair. Margaret and I joined Hugh and Kimie Burleson and some 1500 other people to celebrate the occasion. Diplomats and politicians turned out in morning coats and striped trousers. Japanese women wore their formal kimonos; Western women wore long dresses. The temperature under a brilliant sun was an ideal 65 degrees. Working out of tents on the spacious grounds, the palace staff served drinks and savory morsels until an official passed word that the royal family would be coming through. Then, quietly, almost imperceptibly, small groups spread out along the garden paths. All bowed respectfully as the Emperor and Empress passed slowly by, followed by the Crown Prince (now Emperor) Akihito and his wife, stopping here and there to exchange a few words. As they approached us Hugh, fluent in Japanese, greeted them and drew a warm smile from the Empress. Intrigued by this Japanese-speaking American, she stopped to chat for a few moments. What was said was unimportant, but we did feel honored by the gesture. By eleven o'clock the party was over. Margaret and Kimie left for Kita-Kamakura for their weekly pottery class. Hugh and I went back to work.

An Award and a Promotion

At the end of two years in Tokyo I was faced with a decision whether to go on home leave in the summer of 1977 and return for another two years or stay on for a three-year tour as I had in Spain, Panama and Chile. My former colleagues back in Washington had been very favorably impressed by the results of my work with the Regional Programs Office and the praise my colleagues had given it during the East Asian cultural conference in Penang. Unbeknownst to me, they had recommended me for a meritorious service award. The citation, approved and signed by the USIA director commended me for "launching the IEA Regional Programs Office in Tokyo and achieving in a period of time far ahead of expectations a viable, valuable resource tool for East Asia USIS posts."

Bill Payeff sent me the award certificate with a congratulatory letter saying, inter alia, "You have accomplished a great deal in a very short time and this award is both an expression of appreciation for your accomplishments and a sincere tribute to your professional competence."

The award carried no monetary benefits per se, but it led to my promotion to FSIO-2 effective March 13, 1977. If one can believe it, I was as grateful for the recognition of my work as I was for the promotion. Until then I had even considered returning to Washington to allow Judy to complete high school at the same school where her sisters had graduated. But the promotion gave me a significant increase in income as well as making me eligible for a more responsible job in the Foreign Service. Since retirement pay is based on the "high three"—i.e. average top pay for three years, remaining with the Agency until mandatory retirement three years hence would guarantee a long-term increase in my post-retirement income.

At the time the Agency was combining the position of chief of the Japan program division and field supervisor. It was an FSIO-2 level job. The individual the Agency had selected to fill it would not be available until the summer of 1978. It was offered to me for the year, and I opted to take it for that period and then move on to another assignment. As RPO I had been working closely with the Japan program division. It was a good operation full of opportunities for creative programming. During my previous Japan incarnation I had been a cultural center director and loved the centers and the kind of work they did. Furthermore the job would give me a chance to travel around Japan, and a year would give me time to look for another overseas assignment.

In the spring of 1977 I took my last long field trip as RPO to consult with our posts in Taipei, Hong Kong, Kuala Lumpur, Bangkok, New Delhi and Katmandu, lining up programs and acquiring new speaker talent. It was much the same as the earlier trips except for the details that I will not repeat here.

The Regional Programs Office workload seemed to increase geometrically. After the first year it had become more than Misa and I could handle alone; and we had to hire a secretary who worked under Misa's supervision. RPO communications on speaker programs with other East Asia posts began occupying an inordinate share of USIS Tokyo's cable traffic, so much so that Bill Miller asked me to limit our output. RAVC reached its near capacity of videotape production, and still our USIS clients around Asia were requesting more. Word about the RPO's speaker circuit had gotten around, and now potential speakers were calling me instead of the other way around.

In effect, we had clearly accomplished our objective of providing East Asia's USIS[100] posts with an abundance of resource people and materials for their programs by drawing on talent available within the region. The Regional Programs Office was a going concern. When my successor, Eugene Schaeffer, arrived in early July I was able to turn it

---

[100]. Under President Jimmy Carter and the Agency's new director, John Reinhart, USIA's name was changed to International Communications Agency (ICA) with the resulting confusion with CIA. An effort at damage control by calling it USICA did not help. President Reagan restored the name U.S. Information Agency. I use the acronyms USIA and USIS throughout.

over to him with a strong sense of achievement, though tinged with sadness for having to end a very satisfying experience.

Japan Programs Officer

That summer in 1977 the annual Foreign Service "musical chairs" exercise brought my old colleague Cliff Forster to Tokyo to succeed Bill Miller as Country PAO with the official title of Minister Counselor for Public Affairs. Bob Kays, another good friend with whom I had worked in Washington, moved from deputy PAO in Seoul to deputy PAO in Tokyo. I would work with them as chief of the Japan program division and field supervisor. On a personal basis Margaret and I were delighted to be reunited with the Forster and Kays families.

In July I moved from the Regional Programs Office to USIS Japan's "front office"—a suite on the opposite (south) side of the building. My suite mates were Cliff, Bob, an American executive secretary plus two Japanese secretaries who occupied a reception area. One of them, Sumie Yamauchi[101] handled my secretarial work among other duties. I am much indebted to Sumie for all her help, her unflagging interest in my family, her sunny disposition and always greeting me with a cheerful smile.

Ambassador Mike Mansfield

For me, 1977 was a good time to work in the American Embassy in Tokyo. Shortly after taking office in January of that year President Jimmy Carter had appointed former Senate Majority Leader Mike Mansfield as the United States Ambassador to Japan, replacing James Hodgson. Ambassador Mansfield had long been known as a friend of Asia and a strong advocate of the U.S.-Japan alliance. His mature age and political seniority automatically drew the respect of the Japanese. Those of us in the Embassy felt honored to have such a distinguished person as our leader. Ambassador Mansfield knew how important USIS could be in helping him to de-escalate the tensions surrounding the economic issues that were just beginning to build up over the trade imbalance. There was much rhetoric on both sides, and the Ambassador

---

101. Sumie, like her good friend Misa, had been with USIS many years. Her first boss was Cliff Forster when he was Regional PAO in Kobe in the mid fifties. I note this to reemphasize that while the American "bosses" come and go the Foreign Service Nationals (FSNs) provide the continuity so essential to USIS operations abroad.

went to every prefecture in an effort to calm it down. USIS officers accompanied him on all these trips. During my tenure he took part in a number of trade conferences with the Keidanren (Japan Industrial Organization) that I helped organize, and he never failed to draw a large and appreciative audience. His remarks, always pithy and to the point, were frequently quoted by the Japanese news media. After I left Japan Simul International, a prominent Japanese firm, published a volume of Mansfield's speeches translated into Japanese. The book became a best seller.

Ambassador Mansfield's press conferences were always on the record, and at the end of each session he would say, "Well, boys, tap 'er light." Since he smoked a pipe Americans thought he was referring to the tobacco, but when several Japanese journalists and a New York Times correspondent asked Cliff Forster exactly what the expression meant, Cliff asked the Ambassador himself to explain.

"Well, Cliff," the Ambassador said, "when I was a young fellow, I used to work in the copper mines in eastern Montana. As you pound that stick of dynamite into the shaft walls, you'd holler 'tap 'er light' down the line. Tap 'er light is what we've got to do here in Japan. We've got to keep these economic issues from becoming political issues by tapping 'er light. We don't want to tap her too strong. Let's see if we can't do it without raising the decibel count."[102]

The New Job

My new job description assigned me the task of managing the USIS program division in the design, development and execution of programs in support of the USIS country plan. Although the plan was quite detailed, in essence it described the methods and tools that USIS would rely upon to explain U.S. economic policies, foreign policy and political processes to the Japanese public and to promote Japanese appreciation of American creativity and excellence in the arts and humanities.

As country program officer my duties would include supervising the six American Centers, providing them with program support and coordinating their activities with those of USIS Tokyo. Besides providing the Centers with support from Tokyo, we wanted to

---

[102] Oral history interview with Clifton Forster, May 29, 1990, conducted by G. Lewis Schmidt. ADST Collection, Arlington, VA.

encourage each of them to develop cooperative programs with local Japanese institutions that would promote closer U.S.-Japanese relations at a minimum cost to us. Finally I would be helping the Centers to broaden the base of our their audience, especially among university students destined to play leadership roles in Japanese society.

This was a tall order, even if I achieved only a small part of it; but we had a large and competent staff of both American and Japanese personnel and ample resources to draw upon. Cliff, Bob and I discussed in considerable detail how I should approach my job. Once satisfied we were all on the same wavelength, I set about it with enthusiasm.

My supervisory responsibilities focused primarily on the speaker program division, headed by Ray McGunigle, and the six American Centers. These were the survivors of the original 14 American Cultural Centers during my previous Japan assignment. They were located in Japan's major metropolitan areas: Tokyo, Sapporo (on the northern island of Hokkaido), Nagoya, Kyoto, Osaka, and Fukuoka (on the southern island of Kyushu). I was also responsible for the American Center library services headed by Alice Lage and worked closely with Kurt Wenzel of the Regional Audio Visual Center in developing videotapes for the Japan program.

The Program Division

Ray McGunigle had replaced Irwin Kern as head of the programs division that was responsible for lining up speakers for the six American Centers. Ray was an energetic and imaginative officer who knew how to make the best use of available talent and resources. As former American Center director himself (Nagoya), he understood Center needs and served them well. He had two American assistants, five Japanese employees who handled logistics, travel and administrative details, plus two interpreter-translators. Few of our speakers could handle Japanese, and the only way we could be confident of reaching our audiences was by using interpreters. These people were highly skilled and a key to our success. When not working as interpreters they translated articles for *Trends*, our Japanese language magazine, which Bob Kays supervised.

The program division managed a fascinating parade of personalities around whom we built the substance of our programs. During the year I headed the division we handled over 100 individual American speakers. This included briefing them thoroughly before putting them on the rostrum, tailoring the program and itinerary for optimum effectiveness, and then debriefing each one at the end of his or her stay. A few names will help establish the level of the program. They include Richard Holbrook (later U.N. Ambassador under President Clinton), Economists Sidney Weintraub of the University of Texas and Lawrence Kraus of Brookings; political scientists Ezra Vogel of Harvard, Jean Kirkpatrick of Johns Hopkins School of Advanced International Studies (later U.N. Ambassador under President Reagan) and her husband Evron Kirkpatrick, head of the American Political Science Association; sculptor Helen Frankenthaler; novelist E. L. Doctorow, plus dozens of Fulbright professors in a variety of disciplines.

Although the program division did excellent work, I was concerned that we were not drawing sufficiently upon the resources and ideas that other USIS elements could provide. My solution, not very original, was to establish a program review committee that met weekly to discuss upcoming events and coordinate input from the various USIS elements. I used the meetings as a managerial tool to keep myself informed, get the word out to all parties concerned, process staff ideas into the development of programs and to air staff complaints. With this committee I could leave the operational details to McGunigle and his team and concentrate on policy. Everyone cooperated and the system worked splendidly.

In the speaker business it was often feast or famine. The feast season came during vacation times in the United States when university professors came to Japan on research projects and offered their services as lecturers. Then came periods of famine when we had to scrounge. We never actually solved the problem but we did alleviate the situation by recruiting the Embassy's political and economic officers to fill in the gaps. Ambassador Mansfield's special assistant, Dr. Martin Weinstein, came to our assistance frequently to lecture on political and security issues in U.S.-Japan relations. He was a professor of government specializing in Japan and could lecture in Japanese. His predecessor, Michael Armacost (later Ambassador to Japan) had been a regular speaker on the USIS Japan circuits. I also brought in members of the American business community to speak on U.S.-Japan trade and economic relations.

Cultural Programs

Japanese audiences had an almost insatiable appetite for American cultural programs. Big name American performing groups regularly toured Japan on a commercial basis under the sponsorship of Japanese newspapers and/or television networks. These included groups such as the New York Symphony, the Martha Graham dance troupe, Alvin Ailey Dance Theater and popular orchestras such as Gladys and the Pips plus numerous individual artists who came on their own or under commercial sponsorship. Major Japanese department stores frequently exhibited the works of well-known American creative artists such as Helen Frankenthaler in their spacious salons. USIS was involved in these programs from the beginning to the end.

Cultural Affairs Officer John F. McDonald, bilingual in Japanese, and his staff were deeply engaged in facilitating the visits of these artists, particularly in the early stages of the negotiations. While the Japanese sponsors covered the major expenses of bringing the groups to Japan and publicizing their appearances, the Embassy and one or more of our American Centers frequently acted as co-sponsors of reputable groups. Once advance arrangements were completed, our principal responsibilities were to insure a smooth relationship between the American visitors and their Japanese sponsors, take part in the inaugural ceremonies, and attend receptions held for the visiting artists.

The cultural affairs officers also participated in a very active exchange programs—e.g. Fulbright[103], American Field Service, Eisenhower Fellowships—and maintained contact with Japan's many educational and cultural institutions.

The American Centers

My real love was the American Center programs. I made it my first order of business to visit all six centers and meet individually with the directors and each of the Japanese employees. During the year I was on this job five of the six centers were taken over by new directors, so I spent a great deal of time helping them to get started in their new jobs and become involved in the planning process as well as the execution stage of USIS programming. The new directors, like their predecessors, had all gone through two years of language training, were competent in written and spoken Japanese and integrated themselves well into their communities.

---

[103] The Japan-United States Educational Commission, which administers the Fulbright program, continues to run a very active program of educational exchanges between Japan and the United States.

In fact, I must confess to having been envious of their ability with the Japanese language. I had begun my own two-year assignment in Takamatsu without knowing the first word of Japanese. While I learned a lot on the job and felt I had achieved a reasonable success as a center director, not knowing Japanese was a real handicap. Since that time however the Foreign Service Institute had significantly improved its language training program and USIA had made competence in Japanese mandatory for center directors.

Each Center had a staff of eight to ten skilled Foreign Service Nationals who were the director's mainstay in conducting day-to-day operations. A "chief advisor" headed up the local staff, served as the director's principal contact with Japanese organizations, and frequently acted as interpreter for speaker programs. Other staff members included program assistants, an administrative assistant, librarians, a film/video technician and a driver who met visiting speakers (and me) at the railway station or airport and saw them off again.

A multi-purpose room served as the focal point for Center programming—lectures, group meetings, film showings, exhibits, and even small concerts, though larger ones would be scheduled at other premises. The library, or Infomat, was the heart of non-program activities. Professors, university students, researchers, the media and commercial organizations seeking economic and technical information about the United States used these services extensively.

Shinkansen Cowboy

I have no record of how often I visited each center during that year, but I spent so much time traveling I began calling myself a Shinkansen (bullet train) cowboy. I timed many of my visits to coincide with speaker programs we had organized. For example, when novelist E.L. Doctorow or political scientist Donald Emmerson toured Japan under our auspices, I accompanied them so I could observe how the Centers handled their programs and, in the process, serve as escort for the visitors.

Former PAO Alan Carter, convinced that the American Centers were overreaching themselves with their public library and community center approach, had made drastic changes in their operational style. As noted in the previous chapter, large libraries were pruned down to "Infomats," eliminating books that did not specifically serve USIS program objectives. Center program activities supporting these objectives were held primarily on Center premises and rarely outside the Center. Intended or not, this had the effect of making the centers overly dependent on USIS Tokyo and the putting a cap on Center initiatives for developing programs in cooperation with local Japanese organizations.

Cliff Forster, Bob Kays and I were of the strong opinion that individual Center directors should seize every opportunity to work with Japanese institutions in developing co-sponsored programs that supported our country objectives whether or not they were held on the Center premises. We also felt that the directors should expand their operations to include audiences beyond those listed in their Distribution Record System (DRS), particularly to university students and organizations outside Center cities.

I spent many hours discussing this subject with members of the Program Division and with the Center directors and their staffs. By the end of the year I could report to my superiors that the Program Division and the individual centers had moved more and more in the direction of co-sponsored programs, both in and outside their Centers. I also noted that the involvement of Japanese organizations had given greater credence to our programs and had reduced costs to USIS at a higher level of programming at less expense, as evidenced by a surplus of program funds.

Library Services

Alice Lage, our chief librarian, was a cat lover. A single woman, intensely dedicated to her work, she could always be distracted by mention of her cats. She had two, but a calico cat named "Alligator" was her favorite. I found Alice a tremendous source of professional knowledge and energy in the conduct of the six Center libraries. Not being a librarian myself or understanding much about library science mechanics, I depended on her and she never let me down. Her operation involved ordering, receiving, cataloging and shipping books to each of the libraries. She visited them all regularly, kept them up to date, and dispensed freely with motherly advice to "her librarians." Occasionally, in the intensity of her work, she would by-pass the Center directors and go right to the Center librarians. The directors would complain to me, but they all respected her and these minor tiffs were soon smoothed over. As I wrote to my successor: "Libraries and librarians are an integral part of our program operation. As the single most expensive aspect of that operation they are under constant scrutiny by USIA Washington and should also be under yours." I last saw Alice in Beijing in 1980.[104] I had just retired from the Foreign Service. She was in China for a librarians' meeting. We were both attending the Peking opera to see "Monkey King" and entirely by chance drew adjacent seats on the second row.

Meanwhile, at Home

The shift in jobs and my increased responsibility for official entertainment justified a larger apartment on the sixth floor of Grew House. About once a week we hosted one or more of our visiting speakers for drinks and dinner together with other Embassy/USIS couples. Margaret did most of the cooking, but she brought in our regular three-days-a-week Japanese maid to help out with the preparations and cleanup. The purpose, of course, was to show our guests a little home hospitality in appreciation for their contribution to our Japan program. While they were also working dinners at which we talked about topics and audiences they would be addressing—or had already addressed—we also very much enjoyed the social experience with a number of distinguished personalities.

The change in jobs did not end my travels. But now, instead of being on the road a month at a time it was usually a couple of days. Margaret accompanied me on a number of occasions to inspect the local potteries and other artistic activities. Our daughters Nancy and Judy took full advantage of our extended stay to improve their proficiency in Japanese. They gained acting experience with the Tokyo International Players (a theatrical group) and earned pocket money teaching English to interested Japanese. Judy carried her English teaching over to TV where she played a role in NHK's nationally televised English for Tomorrow. She received a number of flattering marriage proposals— which she ignored—and I encountered many of her fans in my travels around Japan. Margaret, for her part, derived satisfaction from tutoring Japanese Fulbrighters in English preparatory to their departure for the United States.

That Christmas-New Year season we indulged ourselves in a 10-day vacation trip to Taiwan and Manila, exposing our daughters to yet other

---

104. Alice died of cancer in 1996.

facets of Asian culture. For me it was a much-needed rest before the onsurge of another season of intense program activity. In May, Margaret, Nancy and I watched proudly as Judy received her high school diploma from ASIJ. We were uncertain whether she had learned more in the classroom or from her numerous extracurricular activities around Tokyo, but in the fall, ready or not, she would begin a new phase of her life in college.

Search for a New Assignment

Several years previously USIA had initiated a practice of periodically announcing foreseeable openings in Foreign Service position. The "Open Assignments" list, as it was called, carried the grade level, language requirements, availability date and current occupant. Officers scheduled for transfers were invited to bid on positions for which they were qualified in three geographical areas in order of preference, giving a rationale for each.

In another development, a group of Foreign Service Officers brought a class action suit against the Department of State and USIA seeking to increase the mandatory retirement age from 60 to 65. They argued that Civil Service employees working overseas with the Department of Defense under circumstances similar to their own could work until 65; why not Foreign Service Officers? A U.S. Court of Appeals found in favor of the Foreign Service employees. Those of us in the Service were heartened that we would no longer be considered obsolete at age 60. State and USIA took the case to the Supreme Court, but the Appeals Court ruling in favor of retirement at 65 held until the higher court handed down a decision.[105]

With the one-year cap on my Tokyo job and mandatory retirement approaching, I was intensely interested in the Appeals Court decision. When an Open Assignments list came out in October 1977, I went over it carefully and submitted a list of 10 positions in Europe (where I really wanted to go), Asia and Latin America. When another list came out in January, I submitted other bids. Ben Fordney, Chief of Foreign Service

---

[105]. In 1979 the Supreme Court ruled that the 60-year retirement age had been established by Congress and was therefore the law of the land. Its effect on me is discussed in the next chapter.

personnel, duly acknowledged them all saying I would get my chances along with everyone else.

The official announcement of my next assignment did not come until May 6, less than two months before I was to depart Tokyo. The post I drew had not been on my list. I would go to Bangkok as director of the American University Association Language Center, succeeding Milton Leavitt. In the next chapter I tell how it came about.

At a big embassy like the one in Japan, FSOs come and go all the time, so my departure was nothing out of the ordinary. Even so, my working colleagues showed their appreciation for my efforts with jovial farewell parties. Sidney Hamolsky, who was to take over the Japan Program Officer position, would not arrive until after I had departed. I left him a memo: "On Being Chief, Program Division." In it I said, "Running the Program Division is sort of like operating a computer. Once you learn which buttons to push it will do marvels, but always heed Ambassador Mansfield's admonition to 'tap 'er light'."

At Panmunjom the author and Robert Kays (hidden) of USIS Seoul look across the DMZ into North Korea.

In Tokyo because of high housing costs the American Embassy provides living quarters for its personnel. Here, left right are Margaret, Judy, Nancy and Harry Kendall on the grounds of the Embassy compound.

Novelist E. L. Doctorow, center, was one of many distinguished American intellectuals who spoke to Japanese audiences under USIS sponsorship during Kendall's tenure as Japan Programs Officer. With him are the author, at his left, and Tokyo program officers James Jensen and Shirley Scher.

Japan's annual English speaking contests are widely popular among students. Here the author presents award to a winner in the national contest.

XII Bangkok - Director AUA[106] Language Center

The phone rang at 3:00 a.m. Tokyo time. I answered it drowsily, wondering what crisis had arisen to warrant a call at this ungodly hour. Mort Smith, USIA area director for East Asia, was on the line. For him it was 2:00 o'clock in the afternoon. "Sorry for the time difference," he said, "but we need you in Bangkok as soon as possible and I want to get your OK so we can write the orders."

"Doing what?"

"As director of the AUA, the binational center."

"Gee, Mort, that sounds fine, but you know I had asked for a European assignment this go round."

"Yes, I know, but we've got an urgent situation there. Milton Leavitt, the present director is retiring, and that position is much too important to leave uncovered for long. It's our biggest binational center anywhere, and you're the only qualified person we have available for the assignment. Besides, it's a dammed good job, and better than anything I can find for you in Europe. I know you'll love it."

I reflected sleepily on what he had said. It was April 1978. I had been in Tokyo for three years and was due for home leave and transfer in July. In fact, I had given USIA a list of preferred assignments, but Bangkok was not among them. I had been in Bangkok on several occasions in the course of my travels around East Asia. I also knew Milt Leavitt, but at no time had I focused on the operation of the AUA Language Center. Even so, I was familiar with our binational centers in Latin America. They played an important role in fostering good inter-American cultural relations, but junior officers usually staffed them. I was a senior officer with 27 years service in USIA behind me. More than 20 years earlier I had been director of a small binational center in rural Japan that had since been closed. For the past year I had been

---

[106]. Acronym for American University Alumni Language Center. An earlier version of this chapter is included in a volume commemorating the 72nd anniversary of the American University Alumni Association of Thailand, edited by Adul Pinsuvana, in Thai and English, Bangkok, 1996. The publication marked the end, in 1995, of USIS support to the binational institution.

supervising six USIS cultural centers in Japan. Why was I suddenly being asked to serve as director of another binational center?

I asked Mort to give me a day or two to think it over. He agreed but asked me to make a decision as soon as possible. The post was pressing him for a commitment. It was evident Washington had already submitted my nomination to the post and gotten approval. Mort said he wanted me to get my home leave and be in Bangkok by the first of August.

I didn't get much more sleep that night. Margaret and I talked it over. She, too, had been counting on a European assignment to wind up our Foreign Service career. She had been the Leavitt's houseguest in Bangkok en route to and from Katmandu two years earlier, but didn't much care for the tropics. Nevertheless, she had always been a good sport about adjusting to my diplomatic assignments. Nancy and Judy, two of our three daughters who were living with us at the time, would be in college in the United States. Our eldest daughter, Betsy, was married and living in Oakland, California. So if we accepted the Bangkok assignment it would be just Margaret and myself and our standard French poodle, Charlie, an essential member of our family.

I discussed the pros and cons of the assignment with my longtime friend Cliff Forster, director of USIS in Tokyo. He was familiar with the AUA operation and spoke enthusiastically about its standing in the Bangkok community, its English teaching program, and its wide range of cultural activities. "Being director of AUA is one of the few good jobs left in USIA," he said.

I wired Mort Smith that I was pleased and honored to accept.

Margaret and I returned to the United States in June and went through the mandatory but routine consultation in Washington, D.C., where I learned a bit more about the AUA and what would be expected of me. I also met Morton Abramowitz, the newly appointed ambassador to Thailand who was going through his pre-departure briefings at the State Department. After an abbreviated home leave, visits with our respective families in Louisiana and North Carolina and with Betsy and David we headed back across the Pacific to Bangkok, stopping in Tokyo to pick up our French poodle.

Arrival

Pan American's round-the-world flight 001 touched down at Don Muang Airport at thirty minutes past midnight on August 10, 1978.

Nelson Stephens, the USIS Cultural Affairs Officer, and Julia Burks, head of the AUA's English teaching program, were there to greet us. Julia, a slender attractive woman with slightly graying hair, had served as acting director of the AUA pending my arrival. She was the widow of a Foreign Service Officer and had joined USIA as an English teaching specialist after her husband's death. In a noticeably Texas accent Julia told me she was really glad to see me because she had more than enough to do with her English teaching program without trying to run the Center too. I gathered that boredom would not be part of my new job.

We retrieved Charlie from customs, and as we drove toward Bangkok I expressed concern whether the management of the Erawan Hotel where we were to stay would accept our poodle as a guest. Charlie got the word and put on his best behavior, greeting everyone as we entered the hotel lobby. He so charmed the staff that the manager said he could stay in our hotel suite until we found permanent quarters. We were vastly relieved and appreciative that Charlie's merits should be so recognized.

As we parted Julia let me know that the AUA Chairman, Phra Bisal Sukhumvit[107], expected to see me the first thing in the morning, and that my assigned car and driver, Khun[108] Boonsong, would pick me up. As an afterthought she said the AUA began work at 7:00 a.m., but as the boss I could come in when I was ready. Given the late hour I said I'd be in around 8:00.

At the AUA

Phra Bisal's secretary, Khun Uraiwan Limpiakorn, greeted me with a warm smile. Julia had told me she also served as the director's secretary and would be working for me. Her demeanor was reassuring. "Khun Phra has been expecting you," she said, escorting me into the chairman's office.

Phra Bisal was a slightly built man, in apparent good health though somewhat frail. His sparkling smile belied his 79 years. He welcomed me

---

107. "Phra" is a title of Thai aristocracy. Thais are normally addressed by their first names. In the Thai language the ending "l" has an "n" sound. Thus, Phra Bisal's name is pronounced "Phra Bisan."

108. "Khun" is the equivalent of Mr., Mrs., or Ms.

to Bangkok and said Jim McGinley, the American Embassy's Country Public Affairs Officer, had told him about me. As a USIS officer assigned to the AUA, I would be responsible to him as well as to the chairman.

Khun Uraiwan served us tea as we began our conversation. Phra Bisal spoke of his background and the history of the AUA. He was a 1922 graduate of MIT and had been a close friend of King Bumiphol's father, Prince Majidol, who was studying medicine at Harvard at that time. In fact the king was born in Boston. After returning to Bangkok Phra Bisal had helped organize Thai graduates of American universities into the American University Alumni Association of Thailand (AUAA). During World War II he was active in the Thai underground resistance to Japanese occupation and collaborated closely with the American forces.

In the immediate postwar years many Thai students wanting to study in the United States found their English inadequate. In 1952 the AUAA, with the help of a land grant from the Royal Thai Government, established the AUA Language Center to teach English and help students prepare for admission to American universities. Phra Bisal was named chairman and remained in that position for many years. Later the Center, known simply as the AUA, also began teaching Thai to new arrivals from the United States and other countries.

In 1967 USIA lent its support to the AUA by appointing a Foreign Service Officer, Milton Leavitt, as its executive director. Subsequently, then PAO Lew Schmidt proposed that the USIS library and the AUA join forces. Merging the two would give the Center's students greater access to English language materials and the USIS library a larger audience for its books. Phra Bisal and the Association's board of directors agreed to accept under conditions that guaranteed Thai control of the Center. They were receptive to the many cultural programs USIS had to offer but did not want the AUA to be used for dissemination of political propaganda. USIA Washington agreed to this and gave the center a grant to construct a new building for the library that was officially inaugurated in October 1968. According to Leavitt, "It was immediately successful. The Board Chairman and the Board of Directors saw that they had done the right thing."[109]

---

[109] Milton Leavitt, Oral History Interview, ADST Collection, Arlington, VA. Leavitt served two tours as AUA director—1967-1970 and again 1974-1978.

AUA Organization

Phra Bisal, as official head and chairman of the AUA, was responsible to the Royal Thai government for supervision of the Center's activities carried out by a staff of some 75 Thai employees and the 100 teachers of English for the AUA's 8,000 adult students.

At the time of my arrival USIS was contributing the services of two senior officers, Julia Burks and myself. I served as the executive director, responsible for both administrative and program activities, maintaining liaison with USIS and representing the AUA at public functions. I could count on a loyal and faithful Thai staff to assist me and to steer me clear of many pitfalls as I worked myself into the job.

Julia provided professional direction for the Center's extensive English teaching program. She and her small staff selected and trained its teachers, all native speakers of English drawn primarily from the resident American community. She also selected teaching materials, worked out class schedules, and supervised classroom instruction. This position was especially important because tuition fees paid the Center's operating expenses, including staff and teacher salaries.

Besides two Foreign Service Officers, USIS Bangkok provided AUA with a locally hired director of cultural affairs who handled both USIS and AUA originated cultural programs. The USIS library came with a staff of Thai librarians, English language books, magazines, video and audiotapes that served the needs of students and researchers from Bangkok universities. Thai university professors regularly assigned reading materials in the AUA/USIS library to their students, many of whom went on to study at American institutions and develop strong ties with the United States. Don Hausrath, a regional USIS librarian based in Bangkok, helped keep the AUA library at the forefront in modern library technology. In fact, the AUA librarians were regularly called upon to conduct courses for Thai librarians from around the country.

Since its founding in 1952 the AUA had served as the United States' most important cultural link with our strongest ally in Southeast Asia. Ambassadors came and went, some of them barely noticed by the Thai public; but the AUA was an institution that every educated Thai recognized and cherished. Over the years a multitude of Thai students had experienced their first contact with Americans and American culture while learning English in the AUA's classrooms. AUA programs drew intellectual audiences for a wide variety of economic, political, social and cultural themes, including Thai and American views on contentious

273

problems in Thai-American relations. Its theatrical group performed many of the best-known American dramas. The AUA was, in fact, an American oriented institute in the heart of Bangkok and had developed a reputation for being Bangkok's foremost cultural center. It would be my responsibility to help maintain that high standing. I must admit to being somewhat awestruck as Phra Bisal outlined the AUA's many activities.

Meeting the AUA Staff

Having filled me in on AUA's background Phra Bisal took me on a tour of the center's facilities and to meet some of the staff. As we walked down the long, external corridors of the three-story building, we passed classroom after classroom filled with students reciting English language phrases in unison with their American teachers. Bangkok's torrid climate required open doors and windows to permit maximum air circulation, but this also gave full vent for the students' enthusiastic and somewhat noisy recitations.

The session in Phra Bisal's air-conditioned office left me unprepared for the oppressive mid morning heat, and I naively asked whether it would be possible to air condition the classrooms.

"Too expensive," the Chairman replied laconically. "If we did that we'd have to double or triple the tuition to a level the students could not afford. Besides, they are accustomed to this weather. And you'll get used to it too."

"Ummmmm," I said to myself, "Is that possible?"

In the registrar's office Phra Bisal introduced me to Mrs. Pat (Khunying[110] Patanadis Kachachiva) and members of her staff. "This is where the money comes in," he said. "Without Mrs. Pat we couldn't run this operation." Mrs. Pat, I learned later, was a member of minor royalty and, next to the chairman, the most respected person in the AUA. She ran an efficient operation but also ruled her ample staff with an iron hand.

Next-door was the administrative and finance office. "And this is the man who spends the money Mrs. Pat takes in," the chairman said laughingly as he introduced me to Khun Sujint Taebanpakul. A diminutive, balding man with a ready smile welcomed me with a *"wai"*

---

[110]. A feminine title of minor royalty. In English she was always called "Mrs. Pat."

(hands placed palm to palm and held before the chest or up to the chin for more respect) and a double handshake. He, in turn, introduced me to his assistants. I did not realize it at the moment, but twice a month until my departure at the end of the following year they would be bringing me some 200 payroll checks for the AUA staff and its teachers, each to be signed by me.

We met other members of the staff in such rapid succession that it took me several days to get them all sorted out. As Phra Bisal escorted me around the Center I found myself being particularly impressed by the spontaneity and respect, even reverence, with which each individual rendered a *"wai"* to the chairman. It was quite apparent that they both respected and loved the old gentleman. And as my own esteem for him climbed I secretly hoped some of that respect would rub off on me. I would try my best to earn it.

In the English teaching section Julia Burks took me over, introducing me to each of her staff members and some of the teachers who happened to be present. They all seemed glad that Julia would now be relieved of administrative duties so she could devote her energies to the English teaching program. That done, Julia took me to a second floor office where we were greeted by a tall, lean, sharp faced American in his late forties. He was Dr. Marvin Brown, resident linguist and head of the Thai teaching program.

Marve, as he was called, welcomed me somewhat formally. As we talked I detected a shyness that belied his background as a scholar and teacher. He held graduate degrees in linguistics from the University of Colorado and from the University of California at Berkeley. Not long after finishing his university work he had gone to Bangkok, fell in love with the place and joined the AUA staff. He had developed the Center's Thai language textbooks and supervised the development of much of its English teaching materials and techniques. One of his regular duties was helping Julia train the AUA's English teachers, most of whom had no previous English teaching experience. His success could be measured by the popularity of the AUA's English teaching classes with Thai students and Thai classes with foreigners. Nevertheless, he remained an intensely private person.

I would meet many more AUA personnel and supporters later, but first I needed to check in with PAO Jim McGinley and the USIS administrative section in a different section of the city so I could get on the payroll.

At USIS McGinley[111] briefed me on the role I would be expected to play as a U.S. Government official at the AUA. Basically he reaffirmed what I had already heard, that the AUA was carrying out an extremely important function in building good U.S.-Thailand relations and that the Ambassador put great stock in its work. He asked me to give AUA my very best and promised me his full support. I was impressed and reassured by the high esteem in which he held Phra Bisal Sukhumvit and the whole AUA establishment. I reported back to Margaret at the hotel that this was going to be challenging and enjoyable assignment.

The AUA Patriarchy

On September 7, a month after our arrival, Phra Bisal gave us our official introduction to the Thai community at a reception held in the AUA library. There were more than 200 names on guest list that I have kept to this day, and I believe most of them attended. It is worthy of note that the first name on the list was Khunying Chintana Yossundara who subsequently succeeded Phra Bisal. The gala occasion served to impress me all the more with the importance of the role I had undertaken. The people I met there had all been a vital part of the AUA in the past, and I would be turning to them for support throughout my stay in Bangkok.

Meanwhile, relying on Julia's expert guidance, I had plunged immediately into AUA's daily administrative and program routine. During the initial weeks I spent several hours each day with individual section chiefs learning about their operations and the problems I would have to confront. The overall picture that emerged was of a well established—almost patriarchal—organization headed by Phra Bisal Sukhumvit. As an incoming executive trying to assume control, I would be accepted so long as I had the blessings of the patriarch. I made it my first order of business to work out all policy matters with Khun Phra.

Several months later Margaret and I attended Phra Bisal's 80th birthday celebration. He was still active and had just published his memoirs on work with the Free Thai (opposing the Japanese occupation) during World War II. Nine Buddhist monks from nine

---

[111]. McGinley was transferred to USIA Washington in 1979 and later served as Country PAO in India. Robert L. Chatten who had previously served in Latin America succeeded him.

different temples chanted for an hour, wishing him even longer life and happiness.

Studying Thai

One of my first acts was to enroll in the AUA's Thai classes. Studying languages was no new experience for me. In the past I had studied Chinese, Spanish, French, German, Japanese and Vietnamese. I cannot say I had really mastered any except Spanish, but I had learned enough of the others to get along socially and handle most of my daily needs without an interpreter. Marve Brown, his assistant Khun Wipa, and the six Thai teachers were very helpful; and I soon found myself able to order basic Thai foods in a restaurant or to hail a taxi and get to my destination. After several months' study Marve presented me with a "diploma" for having completed three of the AUA's Thai Language texts. He flattered me with the remark that I was unique among AUA directors to have achieved this. Later, my ego was somewhat deflated when I learned that my successor, Larry Daks, spoke fluent Thai, learned as a Peace Corps volunteer in Thailand years earlier.

After a valiant but futile effort, Margaret recognized that she would have little success in trying to learn a tonal language. She opted instead to join the ranks of AUA's English teachers. She had taught school before our marriage and had done some English tutoring on previous assignments. But recognizing that Thai students had special needs all their own, she took Julia's and Marve Brown's class for beginning AUA teachers and was immediately assigned to teach two, later three one-hour classes daily. She enjoyed the interaction with the students and their eagerness to learn English. Besides teaching she also gave me some useful feedback from other English teachers.

Administrative Duties

Years of tropical sun and rain had taken its toll on the AUA's decor. With USIS Bangkok's assistance we obtained the services of a USIA decorator and gave the building a bright new beige and brown face. Not long after that was completed, an architect member of the Alumni Association noted that the original AUA building, to which a wing had been attached on each end, was sinking faster than the two wings. Shorter pilings had been used on the central section; and as a result it was sinking faster in Bangkok's soft, loam soil than the two wings, pulling the outer buildings down with it. It would be necessary to cut the buildings apart to prevent structural damage. This work was still underway when I left at the end of 1979.

While these and other administrative details occupied much of my time, I really derived greater enjoyment from cultural programming to which I had devoted most of my Foreign Service career. Working with the cultural staff we used the AUA's excellent facilities to put on film and musical programs, plays, exhibits, and lectures in both English and Thai. We could nearly always count on sizeable audiences drawn from both the Thai and international communities. We felt particularly good when members of the Thai Royal Family came for these programs, as they did on several occasions during my tenure. Some of my special treasures are photos of myself with the Royal Princess Sirindhorn at the opening of an exhibit where she officiated and another of me receiving a special citation from her on behalf of the AUA for its cultural work and community services.

Community Services

We also provided many special community services such as seminars for Thai high school teachers of English, and briefings for American Field Service (AFS[112]) students preparing to depart for the United States. I felt particularly good about arranging for the AFS to have its office at the Center. Another special service the AUA provided was the TOEFL (Test of English as a Foreign Language) exam for applicants for entrance to American universities.

On September 23, 1978, Princess Chulabhorn, third daughter of King Bumihpol, came to take the TOEFL exam so she could get admitted to Harvard. As noted above her grandfather, King Majidol, had studied medicine at Harvard and her father was born in Boston. Naturally there was much excitement among the staff. We offered her a private test but she declined, saying she would take it with the others. When she arrived, driving her own car, she was preceded by one police car and followed by two others. She got out of her car, locked it, handed

---

[112]. An organization that conducts high school student exchanges between the United States and foreign countries. The students reside with private families and study in the host country's high schools. Thailand regularly sent a large group (25-30) to the U.S. and hosted a similar number of American students.

the key to her maid-in-waiting, and proceeded to the waiting room set aside for her. Since she had come 45 minutes early I kept her company until test time. She was in her final year as an organic chemistry major and spoke English very well. After the test was over she said it was not difficult. In the end, though, her father, the king, decided she should study at Bangkok's Chulalongkorn University rather than in the United States as his first daughter had—and married an American. It was obvious he did not wish to lose another daughter to the Americans.

Ten years later, in May 1988, Princess Chulabhorn came to Berkeley to give a lecture on agricultural chemistry. It was a very accomplished academic presentation. Afterwards we had a chance to chat and I asked if she recalled taking the TOEFL at the AUA. She said, "I do indeed. It was a very interesting occasion."

The AUA's Thai lecture program provided a forum for many of Thailand's more notable citizens. Among them were people with whom I would have occasion to work during my subsequent career at Berkeley. The list reads like a Thai Who's Who in academic and diplomatic circles. They included former Foreign Minister Dr. Thanat Khoman, Ambassador Sarasin Viraphol and Professor Kramol Thongthammachart (who was to become prime minister in 1992) and many more. Two of the more interesting and picturesque personalities who appeared on our stage and were guests at our home were Khun Mechai[113], then head of Thailand's highly successful family planning program, and Ms. Prateep Ungsongtham, head of the Klong Toey Community Development School and Magsaysay Award winner for public service in 1978. I was happy to be at least partially instrumental in getting Ms. Prateep an invitation by the Department of State to visit the United States.

In December 1978, several months after our arrival I described my work in a Christmas letter to family and friends:

"This is a sleeper. As jobs go in USIS, binational center directors are not too high on the totem pole; and most of these assignments go to young aspirants to cultural attaché positions. The Bangkok binational center director supervises more than 150 employees, American and Thai, and manages an annual budget surpassing a million dollars. The center is equivalent to a medium sized university with a yearly

---

[113]. He so popularized use of the condom that the Thai word for condom is *"Mechai."*

enrollment of nearly 17,000 students, 8,000 at any given time. Our classes begin at 7:00 a.m. and run continuously until 9:00 p.m. We have a library of 23,000 volumes with 40,000 members who may be anything from high school students to supreme court justices. Any given day will see AUA programs ranging from seminars on human rights, to classical and pop music concerts with paid attendance. All this activity places heavy demand on the director's time and Margaret is getting used to my returning home at 8:00 or 9:00 p.m. after a 7:00 a.m. departure for Thai language class. Even so it is an extremely gratifying job. The AUA is not only an English teaching institution, it is a major center of cultural activity in Bangkok."

Through no influence of my own the AUA director was an individual of considerable prestige in the community. Since the institution was founded in 1952, hundreds of thousands of young Thais had studied English at the AUA. Many went on to American universities and returned to play important roles in their nation's political, economic, and cultural life. AUA's contributory role was almost always recognized; and the incumbent director, rightly or wrongly, derived the benefit of his predecessors' good works. I would be less than candid if I did not acknowledge that I thoroughly enjoyed the role. Years later, whenever I met a Thai I needed only to mention my former connection with the AUA to establish immediate rapport.

One minor and quite amusing incident illustrates the ordinary public's esteem for the AUA. Margaret and I and a couple of friends were driving along Pechburi road in Bangkok one night looking for a certain movie theater. Somehow I got lost and found myself going the wrong way down a one-way street. A young policeman stopped me and asked for my driver's license. He wasn't impressed by my American Embassy credentials or by the diplomatic plates on my bright red Pacer.

"Okay," he said, "there will be a fine on this. Who are you? Where do you work?"

I gave him my name and told him I was the director of the AUA.

"Oh, the AUA director," he exclaimed. "I studied English there. That's a fine school. You just turn right around and go this way. Your movie theater is about five blocks down from here."

Life Outside AUA - The Erawan and other Adventures

Finding permanent quarters was more difficult and time consuming than we had been led to expect. It was a time of great influx of foreign entrepreneurs, especially Japanese, whose living allowances far surpassed ours. It took us three months to find a modest, two-bedroom apartment that met our needs, located on Soi (lane) 15, just off Sukhumvit Road[114]. Before moving we were fortunate in being able to obtain the services of a cook/housekeeper who made it possible for us to meet our obligations for official entertainment. Khun Somboon turned out to be a gourmet cook with Thai dishes and has become a lifelong friend. Subsequently she came to the United States to study and is now happily married to an American and living in Portland, Oregon.

While house hunting we enjoyed life at the Erawan, sleeping under the same roof as visiting personalities like Viet Nam's Pham Van Dong and China's Deng Xiaoping. In fact, when Deng Xiaoping came the management moved us and gave him our suite. Charlie charmed all the hotel personnel, but he was not the slightest bit impressed with the VIP parade. His biggest thrills came in his twice-daily walks along Rajdamri Road with Margaret or me.

The old Erawan was the Thai Government's official guesthouse. It had a backyard swimming pool and dining terrace where one could enjoy meals in quiet, peaceable surroundings. One of my choice memories is savoring breakfasts of juicy, red papaya on the pool's edge in Bangkok's soft, warm morning air. Even more memorable was the Vishnu shrine on the corner where multitudes of Thai faithful came to pray and leave offerings. The story we heard was that during the construction of the Erawan Hotel many workmen had suffered unexplained, even fatal accidents. Finally, in desperation, the construction crews refused to work any further until a shrine was built honoring Vishnu, the "Preserver." After the shrine was completed the workmen resumed construction; and miraculously, no further accidents occurred. This story and others like it added a mysterious fascination to the shrine. I very soon made it a practice every evening before retiring to take Charlie for a walk and then relax briefly in the shrine's enclosure, spellbound by the music, the dancing girls, and the wafting fragrances of orchid offerings and burning incense sticks. The old Erawan has since been torn down and rebuilt into a more modern though much less

---

[114]. A major thoroughfare named for AUA Chairman Phra Bisal Sukhumvit, minister of public works at the time the road was built.

charming hotel, but the shrine remains and continues to attract hundreds of faithful to solicit the aid of its magical powers every day.

While work at the AUA was intensive, on weekends Margaret and I found time for swimming at the Royal Bangkok Sports Club or for excursions to Pattaya where several USIS officers maintained cottages on the beach. Marv Brown and his lovely Thai wife Kwan took us on one of our more unforgettable outings to a fishing village some 25 kilometers south of Bangkok at the convergence of two rivers on the Gulf of Thailand. I cannot remember the name of the place, but we both have vivid memories of observing an ever-moving drama of boats and barges from a balcony overlooking a broad expanse of water while consuming delicious crab claws, delicate fish, mussels, and shrimp all steeped in tasty Thai spices.

Nancy and Judy joined us for Christmas 1978, and we used that occasion to show them around Phuket, Chiangmai, and, of course, the beaches at Pattaya. Judy enjoyed the visit so much she took leave from her studies at Mills College at the end of the spring session and returned to Bangkok. She immediately began studying Thai and was soon correcting my tones. She also joined the AUA English-teaching faculty, taught several classes daily and remained with us until we left Bangkok at the end of 1979. One of her more memorable acts was to persuade her parents to invite all the AUA's English teachers and some of the staff to our home for a dinner party commemorating her 20th birthday. As an attractive young woman she animated the hearts of AUA's younger generation and received several marriage proposals, which she declined in favor of completing her studies at Mills.

AUA Branches

The AUA operated three branch language centers with an American contract employee supervising each. They were located at Chiangmai in the north, Thailand's second largest city; at Khonkaen in the northeast, strategically important for its nearness to Laos and Burma, and at Songkhla in the south near the Malaysian border. The branches were closely associated with USIS and the consulates in their respective cities, an operation mutually beneficial to both parties. The branches served AUA and USIS as an important point of contact with provincial audiences, particularly in the academic field. The USIS library premises gave AUA attractive classroom space and the students constituted an audience for the libraries. I made it a point to visit the branches regularly to demonstrate interest, and in doing so I became better acquainted with the very different Thailand that exists outside Bangkok.

Refugees

My visits to Songkla and Khonkaen also educated me on the problems of Vietnamese and Laotian refugees. In early 1978 when the communist government of Vietnam launched its program to nationalize all private enterprise it touched off the biggest refugee exodus since the fall of Saigon in 1975. The majority of those leaving the country were Sino-Vietnamese and large numbers wound up in Thai refugee camps[115].

Ambassador Morton Abramowitz played a leading role in coordinating both official and unofficial management of the refugee problem and made the American Embassy in Bangkok the focal point of these activities. He established a special refugee affairs office within the Consulate, but the problem was so big nearly everyone within the Embassy became involved in one way or another. With the Vietnamese invasion of Cambodia on Christmas Day 1978, an exodus of Khmer refugees added to the burden.

As director of the binational center I had no official responsibility for dealing with the situation, but having worked at JUSPAO Saigon from 1970-1972 and again as USIA East Asia policy officer in Washington from 1973-1975, I was intensely interested in the plight of the refugees. One of the largest of the refugee camps was on the outskirts of Songkla on the coast of the South China Sea, and I made it a point to visit the camp each time I went to our AUA branch in that city. It was not a pleasant spectacle. Large families fresh off their boats were crowded into makeshift shelters, entirely dependent on Thai beneficence for their very existence until they could be resettled elsewhere. The United States was contributing to their upkeep, but the main responsibility for their care fell to the Thais. How they handled it made me more appreciative of Thai generosity to their neighbors in distress. I visited a similar camp of Laotian refugees in the northeast on the Thai side of the Mekong River near Udorn. Many of these people had been in

---

[115]. For discussions of the Vietnam exodus see Barry Wain, *The Refused - The Agony of the Indochina Refugees*, New York, Simon & Schuster, 1981; and Marjorie Nieuhaus, "Vietnam 1978: The Elusive Peace," in *Asian Survey*, (Berkeley, University of California Press), Vol. XIX, No 1, January 1979, pp 85-94.

the camp several years awaiting resettlement. Some wound up in the United States, Australia, or Europe. The more difficult cases simply remained and eventually returned to Laos.

I became more personally involved when a refugee named Chanh Tran appeared in my office at the AUA asking for assistance. He identified himself as a former employee of USIS Cantho (in the Vietnamese delta) but had no papers to prove it. The refugee organization had him, his wife and two children slated for resettlement in Australia; but he was holding out for the United States. Tran said he recognized me from my several visits to Cantho. If I could verify that he was a former US Government employee he would get his wish. Needing stronger proof, I cabled his former boss, then in Bogota, who quickly confirmed that Tran had indeed been a valued USIS staff member. "Charlie" Chanh Tran is now a prosperous businessman in Los Angeles, has become a good friend and has taken every opportunity to express his appreciation for my assistance.

Later, following my retirement, I was able to use my connections to rescue my former Vietnamese tutor from a refugee camp on the Thai Cambodian border where she had been interned after walking across Cambodia under difficult and humiliating circumstances. She was eventually admitted to the United States as a refugee and now lives and works in Los Angeles.

Retirement Looms

When appointed director of the AUA I was 58 years old and expected to continue working until my 65th birthday. But in February 1979 nine members of the United States Supreme Court, most of them over 60, unanimously overturned a Court of Appeals decision that had declared unconstitutional the Department of State's requirement that Foreign Service Officers retire at age 60. Congress had imposed the 60-year retirement age, they said, and it must stand until Congress ruled otherwise. Later Congress did just that, but it was too late to save me from retirement. I would turn 60 on December 1, 1979, and had no choice but to retire at the end of that month.

I set two goals for myself, one to continue working even if on an entirely volunteer basis, and the other to somehow maintain my Asian connection. I began to write letters to friends and acquaintances from my years in the Foreign Service. One of them went to Professor Robert A. Scalapino, director of the Institute of East Asian Studies at the

University of California at Berkeley, whom I had first met in 1975 while preparing to take over my position as Regional Programs Officer in Tokyo. He wrote back: "I'll be in Bangkok on July 4. Let's talk then."

The Scalapinos (his wife Dee had accompanied him) were guests of U.S. Ambassador Morton Abramowitz. We met at the Embassy residence, and at the end of our conversation Professor Scalapino invited me to join his Institute. It is from there that I write these memoirs many years and another career later.

My impending retirement had no effect on my daily workload. The AUA and its multiple activities continued to occupy me most of my waking hours, but as the countdown continued much of the urgency was taken out of things which had previously seemed frightfully important.

Then in December the AUA gave us a farewell party that even surpassed the one that had welcomed us to that delightful place. I wrote to our family and friends: "We have mixed feelings as we come to the end of an always interesting, frequently exciting 29 years with the Foreign Service. Thailand has been much too brief—only 16 months. We have been painfully aware of the continuing tragedy in Cambodia next door. Nevertheless, we have enjoyed getting to know the warm and friendly Thais, exploring the ancient ruins of Sukhothai and Ayuthaya where Thai culture began, relaxing on the marvelous beaches of Pattaya and Phukhet and, most of all, working at the American University Association Language Center, It has been an experience we will treasure for years to come."

Larry Daks, my successor, arrived right after Christmas. As a parting gesture I left him a 16-page memorandum, "On Being Director of AUA," outlining the joys—and the problems—he would encounter as head of America's finest binational institution. Mort Smith was right. I loved the job. My only regret was not being able to continue on for another five years.

We departed Bangkok with heavy hearts on January 1, 1980. Before mid-year we had settled in Berkeley, California, where I immediately began another career working with the University of California's Institute of East Asian Studies.

Thai Royal Princess Maha Chakri Sirindhorn presents an award for cultural achievement to the author who accepts it on behalf of the American University Association Language Center (AUA) in Bangkok.

AUA Chairman Phra Bisal Sukhumvit facing camera, enjoys a reception for the Center's English teachers at the author's residence. At left is AUA Linguist Dr. Marvin Brown. Mrs. Kendall is in the background.

AUA Linguist Dr. Marvin Brown and wife Kwan.

AUA English Teaching Specialist Julia Burks, right, with Mrs. Kendall.

Farewell to the AUA. Farewell to the Foreign Service. Kendall is retiring. (USIS Bangkok Artist Payul N. Krachang)

After retiring from the Foreign Service, the author (front row, right) applied his USIS skills to organizing more than 50 international conferences for U.C. Berkeley's Institute of East Asian Studies in conjunction with its director, Professor Robert A. Scalapino, front row third from the left. Shortly after this meeting the U.S. and Mongolia established diplomatic relations.

XIII Berkeley - A Second Career

Yes Virginia, there is a life after the Foreign Service.

The actual act of retiring gave me an eerie feeling. It meant I was no longer obligated to anyone except my family and myself, but at the same time I had ceased being a member of the organization that had been my "home" for 29 years. I even had to turn in my diplomatic passport. Nevertheless, with my guaranteed annuity I could look forward to a comfortable retirement in an intellectual environment at the University of California at Berkeley. This would give me the Asia connection I was anxious to retain and enable us to live near our three daughters in the San Francisco Bay Area.

Return to China

Before returning to the United States I wanted to visit China where I had served for two years in the Fourteenth Air Force during World War II. A visit to the post-war People's Republic of China, I felt, would be useful to me in my new association with the Institute of East Asian Studies (IEAS). In anticipation of the return visit I had been studying Chinese with a tutor for six months. Now, retired and with no official responsibilities, Margaret and I went to Taiwan where I took an intensive language course and practiced it with numerous waiters and store clerks to bring my proficiency up to a conversational level. Three months later, in late March, we joined a tour group (the only way we could enter China at the time) in Hong Kong and visited Guangzhou, Guilin, Hangzhou, Shanghai and Beijing. I found vast changes from the war-torn country I had known in my youth; but while we saw few signs of wealth, neither did we see any abject poverty as had been so common before. People in the countryside and in the cities seemed to be well fed and adequately dressed even though there was a dreadful monotony in their Mao-style clothing, and the strong hand of social control was readily visible. Everywhere we went we encountered friendliness toward our American group. I found that my Chinese worked, and Margaret forgave me for all the time I had spent practicing it in Taipei.

Institute of East Asian Studies

On April 15, 1980, we returned to the United States for good, a nomadic career in the Foreign Service behind us. We rented an apartment while we searched for permanent housing. Eventually we found just what we wanted in a small tree-shaded condominium in North Berkeley, eight blocks from the university campus.

As soon as we were settled I checked in with Robert A. Scalapino (he liked to be called Bob). His official title was Robson Research Professor of Government and Director, Institute of East Asian Studies (IEAS). A man of my age (actually six weeks older), he was a prolific writer with over thirty books and hundreds of published articles on East Asian topics to his credit. He was widely acknowledged as America's leading Asianist and was regularly invited to Washington for consultation on Asian affairs by the White House and the Department of State. His former students taught in prestigious universities and occupied positions of responsibility throughout Asia and the United States. His appointments calendar frequently included high-level visitors from the Asian academic and political world seeking his counsel.

Scalapino received me warmly saying he and his staff would welcome whatever expertise I could bring from USIS. Explaining the origins of his institute, he said Berkeley's antecedents for teaching and research in the East Asian field stretched back into the 19th century[116]. By the mid 1970s the growing popularity of East Asian studies at the university led to the establishment of the Institute on October 1, 1978, as an Organized Research Unit with Scalapino as its founding director and responsibility for coordinating activities by the centers for Chinese, Japanese and Korean studies. The Institute also included an East Asiatic library of nearly half a million volumes in their original Asian languages—Chinese, Japanese, Korean, Manchu, Mongolian and Sanskrit—that attracted research scholars specializing in Asia.

At the time I arrived on the scene Scalapino had a small staff that handled publication of research monographs, international conferences, colloquia, seminars and visiting scholars plus a Group in Asian Studies that coordinated programs for students majoring in the broad field of Asian studies. Some sixty distinguished Berkeley professors who taught

---

[116] The university, founded in 1868, is the oldest in the University of California's nine-campus system.

a variety of East Asian subjects were affiliated with the Institute. In 1981, Douglas Pike, my former Foreign Service colleague, joined IEAS bringing with him fifty file cabinets filled with of materials on the Vietnam War that served as a nucleus for an Indochina Studies Program and Archive.

At any given time IEAS played host to a dozen or more visiting scholars from Asia as well as postdoctoral fellows and Asianists from other American universities. My service in Japan, China, Vietnam and Thailand plus travel for USIS all over Asia gave me a common bond with the visitors; and I often encountered old acquaintances among them.

Apart from research monographs the Institute also published *Asian Survey*, issued monthly by the University of California Press and edited by Bob Scalapino and Leo Rose, a South Asia specialist. The journal carried scholarly articles on political, economic and security topics by authors from throughout Asia and the United States. I knew it well from having used it in my work with the AUA library in Bangkok where it was very popular among Thai scholars..

At first I worked as an unpaid volunteer preparing a brochure describing the institute and its functions and shepherding research manuscripts through the editorial, publication and distribution process. It was only a short time before Bob invited me to become a salaried member of his staff.

A Book on Vietnam

Nguyen Long brought me my first task as a co-author. Long had obtained a PhD in political science under Scalapino and returned to Vietnam to teach at Van Hanh University in Saigon. After the communists took over in 1975 he remained on the job thinking he could work with them. He lasted only three weeks before they threw him out. It took him four years to finally escape Vietnam by using counterfeit documents to pass himself and his family off as Chinese. At that time the Vietnamese communists were trying to rid the country of its Chinese population. When Long and his family wound up in Indonesia as boat people he notified Scalapino who arranged for them to come to the United States. On their arrival Bob gave Long a stipend and told him to write a book about his experiences while they were still fresh in his mind. Long wrote in what he described as *nuoc mam*[117] English. I became aware of all this when I encountered Scalapino struggling with the rewriting task. With my own Vietnamese experience still fresh in my mind I volunteered to take over the job. Bob said, "Gladly, just keep me advised."

Six months and several drafts later Long and I, with the help of a retired university press editor, produced a finished manuscript. In it Long described in intimate detail the multiple security measures used by the communists to control the population, their effect on people's lives, and his escape to freedom. IEAS published the work under the title *After Saigon Fell: Daily Life under the Vietnamese Communists*, by Nguyen Long with Harry Kendall, Berkeley 1981. The book drew excellent reviews, sold out two editions and was translated into Korean. In the process of writing the book Long and I became fast friends[118].

Subsequently I collaborated with a Mongolian scholar on a manuscript about Soviet KGB outrages in his country during the Stalin era. This work was published under the title *Poisoned Arrows: The Stalin-Choibalsan Mongolian Massacres, 1921-1941*, by Shagdariin Sandag and Harry H. Kendall. Boulder, Westview Press, 2000, I also assisted a Cambodian woman with a book on her struggle for survival as a child in the Khmer Rouge killing fields and her adjustment to student life at Mills College in Oakland. While that book has yet to see the printed page, just writing it proved to be the catharsis she needed to become a normal, productive individual living a happy life as wife and mother to three young sons.

Conference Coordinator

Shortly after I began work at the Institute we employed Joanne Sandstrom, a former high school English teacher from Los Angeles, as my editorial assistant. (She and her husband and their two sons had just completed a sailing trip around the world.) Joanne proved to be a quick

---

117. Fish sauce used liberally by Vietnamese on many of their dishes.

118. Long first tried to earn a living by teaching in San Francisco's bilingual schools but found the income inadequate to support his family. He turned to business in Los Angeles and has prospered from entrepreneurial activities in landscape gardening and in real estate.

study and was soon ready to take on more responsibilities. About the time I was beginning to feel superfluous Scalapino informed me of his plan to enlarge the Institute's program of international conferences and asked me to serve as coordinator for them. This was right up my alley.

My years with USIS served me well, both as a program organizer during my various assignments and as "head hunter" for the regional programs office in Tokyo. But there was a difference. At the Institute we were engaged in academic dialogue rather than trying to bring audiences around to our way of thinking.

Bob Scalapino was a strong believer in the value of international conferences. He looked upon them as a means for bringing together specialists to discuss major issues in contemporary U.S.-Asian bilateral and multilateral relations, and for promoting scholarly research and publishing materials of consequence for the academic and government communities. In effect, the Institute of East Asian Studies published the proceedings of many of our conferences in its series on Research Papers and Policy Studies. Under Scalapino's leadership his institute achieved the reputation of being at the forefront of research on East Asian affairs.

The Institute's conferences were cooperative ventures that alternated between the United States and Asia. For each of them the host organization bore the responsibility for in-country costs while the guests paid their own travel expenses. As a state-financed educational institution our budget was inadequate to cover expense of these meetings, so we sought outside funding from private foundations. Of these, the Asia Foundation in San Francisco was our most frequent collaborator, though we also received financial assistance from The Rockefeller Brothers Fund, The Ford Foundation, the Pew Trust, Scaife Foundation and several others. Scalapino was a past master at fund raising. Foundation directors responded positively to his requests because they felt assured of productive and worthwhile results. In addition, his reputation enabled him to attract leading scholars who considered it a signal honor to be invited to take part in his conferences.

During the decade 1981-1991, Bob and I assembled teams of top ranking Asia scholars, government officials and business representatives for some 50 conferences in the United States and abroad. Our themes dwelt primarily on political, economic, security and strategic relations— both multilateral and bilateral—in the Asia Pacific region. My role included issuing invitations in Bob's name, making all the necessary travel and meeting arrangements and overseeing publication of the conference proceedings that were edited jointly by the co-sponsors. Scalapino, of course, led the U.S. delegations to all of the meetings and co-chaired them with his Asian counterparts. Together with various teams of scholars, he and I traveled to most of the capitals and major cities of Asia: Moscow, Islamabad, New Delhi, Tokyo, Shanghai, Seoul, Ulaan Bataar, Manila, Bangkok, Kuala Lumpur, Singapore, Jakarta and even to Western Samoa. At times, when an invited participant was unable to attend, I often wound up making the presentation in his name. More than 30 books grew out of these conferences.

Extracurricular activities provided a lighter side to the meetings, but during these recesses the participants strengthened their interpersonal ties and went back refreshed for further analyses of the issues at hand. A list of Asian participants would contain names of prominent scholars from virtually every country in Asia, many of whom had been or would become government ministers and even prime ministers.

Even more important than the outcome of the conference discussions was the interpersonal networking that led to many long-term relationships. I profited immensely from my association with a large number of outstanding individuals, both Asian and American, who took part in the meetings. It was a pleasure working with Bob. Besides being highly respected by his peers, he was always ready with guidance when most needed and warmly appreciative of my efforts.

Scalapino Retires

In June 1990 Bob Scalapino retired as director of IEAS and from U.C. Berkeley with more than 40 years teaching behind him. The institute he had founded and directed for twelve years honored him with a three day conference named after his most successful book, *East Asia: The Road Ahead*. Sixteen of his former graduate students from the United States, Japan, China and Indonesia demonstrated the skills he had taught them with reports on their current research. Although officially retired, Scalapino continues as active as ever, writing, speaking, and taking part in an unending series of international conferences in Asia and the United States.

Professor Frederic E. Wakeman, Jr., a distinguished historian specializing in China, succeeded Scalapino.

My Second Retirement

In July 1991 I retired for the second time. For that occasion my colleagues at IEAS organized a ceremony attended by many faculty and staff members plus my immediate family and close friends. At its conclusion, in the presence of Bob Scalapino, Fred Wakeman presented me with a handsome plaque honoring me for my "long and valuable contribution" to the Institute.

The real surprise of the occasion, however, was an album of testimonial letters from 80 of the Asian and American scholars with whom I had worked during my ten years as conference coordinator. Rereading their laudatory remarks makes me blush and wonder if they are talking about the same Harry Kendall I know. In retrospect my 29 years in the Foreign Service served me well as a prep course for helping Bob Scalapino mobilize American and Asian scholars to confront our mutual challenges in the Asia Pacific region.

As a reward for my services the Institute gave me an office, a computer and the title of "Research Associate," and I turned to writing these memoirs and other activities that keep the Asian connection alive. The lively intellectual community that inhabits Berkeley and the San Francisco Bay Area provide an unending source of opportunity in that field.

I cannot end this narrative without paying special tribute to Margaret who shared my life and work in our three decades in the Foreign Service. Though almost always enjoyable it was by no means all easy. While travel and immersing oneself in new cultures can be exciting, picking up a household and moving to another country every two or three years can also be trying, especially on growing children. Often Margaret had to bear the full brunt of seeing them through their difficulties; of soothing their tears while I spent long hours and even days, weeks or months—as in Vietnam—away from home in the conduct of official business. On many occasions she teamed up with me to give foreign audiences a woman's version of the American story, hosted dinners and receptions for people I thought it important to impress, or attended seemingly endless diplomatic functions making small talk with people she had never seen before and would probably never see again. In fact she bore out the truth in the expression that in Foreign Service couples America gets two for price of one.

Shortly after we came to Berkeley Margaret found her own niche working as a volunteer with the YWCA's English in Action program in which she helps visiting scholars from Asia improve their spoken English. She has seen many come and go, most of them leaving with a far better comprehension of American culture and English speaking ability than when they arrived. Following her example I have taken on similar classes for visiting scholars, finding that I frequently learn as much or more than I teach. Best of all though, our three daughters and their families live nearby, and they bring Margaret and me unsurpassed love and enjoyment during our golden years.

Glossary of Acronyms

AACS	Army Air Corps Communications System
ACC	American Cultural Center
AC&W	Aircraft Control & Warning
ADST	Association for Diplomatic Studies and Training
AID	Agency for International Development
AIFLD	American Institute for Free Labor Development
ARPA	Advanced Research Projects Agency
ARVN	Army of the Republic of Vietnam
ASEAN	Association of Southeast Asian Nations
ASIJ	American School in Japan
AUA	American University Alumni (Language Center)
AUAA	American University Alumni Association
BBC	British Broadcasting Company
BNC	Binational Center
CAO	Cultural Affairs Officer
CIA	Central Intelligence Agency
CIE/SCAP	Civilian Information Education/Supreme Command Allied Powers
CORDS	Civilian Operations Revolutionary Development Support
CNN	Cable News Network
CPM	Country Program Memorandum
DMZ	Demilitarized Zone
DRS	Distribution and Records System
FSN	Foreign Service National
FSO	Foreign Service Officer
FSSO	Foreign Service Staff Officer
GVN	Government of Vietnam
ICA	International Communications Agency
IEA	Information East Asia (East Asia Area Office)
IEAS	Institute of East Asian Studies (UC

	Berkeley)
IO	Information Officer
ITT	International Telephone and Telegraph Company
JACC	Japan America Cultural Center
JUSPAO	Joint United States Public Affairs Office
LSU	Louisiana State University
LTTT	Land to the Tiller
MACV	Military Assistance Command Vietnam
MR I	Military Region One (Eye Corps)
MR IV	Military Region Four (Four Corps)
NACA	National Advisory Commission for Aeronautics
NASA	National Aeronautics and Space Administration
NSC	National Security Council
NVA	North Vietnamese Army
NVN	North Vietnam
PAO	Public Affairs Officer
PPAO	Provincial Public Affairs Officer
PP&R	Policy, Plans & Research
RAVC	Regional Audiovisual Center
RPAO	Regional Public Affairs Officer
RPO	Regional Programs Officer
SMA	Separate Maintenance Allowance
TIROS	Television and Infrared Observation Satellite
TOEFL	Test of English as a Foreign Language
UPI	United Press International
USAID	United States Agency for International Development
USIA	United States Information Agency
USIS	United States Information Service
VAA	Vietnamese American Association
VC	Viet Cong
VIP	Very Important Person
VOA	Voice of America

Index

About the Author.

Harry Kendall is a retired Foreign Service Officer and a specialist in public diplomacy. In the course of his twenty-nine years with the U.S. Information Agency he interacted with audiences on every level of society in Latin America, Europe and Asia telling America's story to the world. A native of Louisiana he served in China during World War II and was educated at LSU, Yale and the University of North Carolina. He is currently a Research Associate with the Institute of East Asian Studies at the University of California in Berkeley. His previous publications include articles and collaborative works on Vietnam, Mongolia, Korea, Japan and Southeast Asia.

Printed in the United States
1283200004B/46-168